How to make a killing in the

SHARE JUNGLE

Other books by Michael Walters

How to Beat the Bear Market
How To Make A Killing In The Alternative Investment Market
How To Make A Killing In Penny Shares
How To Make A Killing In New Issues
How To Profit From Your Personal Equity Plan
How To Profit From The Coming Share Boom
My Secret Weapon - The Stop Loss System

WEALTH WARNING

Please remember that the price of stockmarket investments, and the income derived from them, can go down as well as up. If you are not sure what to do when considering investing, please get advice from a qualified financial adviser.

• BATSFORD STOCKMARKET STRATEGY SERIES •

How to make a killing in the

SHARE JUNGLE

Michael Walters

B T BATSFORD LTD   LONDON

Batsford Books Online: www.batsford.com

First published 1987
This edition (6th impression) 1998

British Library Cataloguing in Publication Data. A catalogue record for this book
is available from the British Library

ISBN 0 7134 8489 6

Published by:
B T Batsford Ltd
583 Fulham Road
London SW6 5BY
England

and
22883 Quicksilver Drive
Suite 100
Dulles, Virginia 20166
USA

Batsford Business Online: www.batsford.com

Printed by:
Whitstable Litho Printers Ltd.
Whitstable
Kent

Contents

Introduction

Safer than the 3.30 at Chepstow, more fun than the football pools, better than breaking the bank at Monte Carlo, with infinitely better odds than the National Lottery – a fortunate few make millions by playing the stockmarket every year. Some do it by luck, some by judgement, some by cheating. Anyone can play. You may not make it into the millionaire club, but even the most modest investors can multiply their money many times over. And have great fun doing it.

It could be you. It need not be complicated. Anyone with simple common sense and a little cash to spare can do it.

This book is devoted to helping you through the tricks and the traps in simple, straightforward language. It can be done. Hundreds of thousands of private investors did it in the great share boom of the eighties. Hundreds of thousands more have done it in the nineties. This time, hopefully, anyone who has read this book will know when to take their profits, when to cut, run, and hide.

The Great Crash of October 1987 wiped out many who had enjoyed a marvellous ride in the mid-eighties. There were hard lessons to be learned then – but for those prepared to listen and learn, the benefits will be reaped in the years to come.

Be under no illusion. Despite political talk about encouraging individual share ownership, life has become more difficult, more expensive, altogether less comfortable for the private investor during the past decade.

Almost month by month through the nineties, some piece of tinkering with the rules has swung the odds a little more against the individual. I have fought consistently for the small player in the pages of the *Daily Mail,* but to little avail when it comes to getting officialdom to change things.

The power of big money ultimately dictates the rules. But I have been able to help run dubious share-pushing firms out of business, to recover tidy sums for many investors, and to kill off some particularly greedy share schemes. And I have returned to tipping shares in a column which has given tangible proof that the small investor can enjoy big winners, given a measure of good luck and good judgement.

Along with letters and calls received from individual investors I believe there is a need for this book. There is too much written about investment by those who know the theory, but lack the experience of being out there in the middle of it. There is no substitute for being there, in the rough and tumble, as it happens. So this book emphasises – from the heart – how to dodge the pitfalls of private investment, and how to cope with what really happens when you try to turn a penny trading shares.

Never mind the clucking of armchair analysts who question the high-risk, high-return approach. You can play it anyway you choose, so long as you have your eyes open, cautiously and carefully, or wide-eyed and wild. Either way, this book offers the options.

Do not be fooled, though, by the financial establishment. It creates a wonderful impression of overwhelming integrity, a world where people play by the rules, where asking too many questions does not do. They know better – even when a blue-blooded bank like Barings is brought down by a rogue trader and management ignorance and incompetence which almost beggars belief. And this, mind you, watched over by the implacable authority of the Bank of England, and a bunch of regulators more interested in making rules to keep themselves employed than in actually helping small investors.. Most of what the City does is honest and sensible. But... keep asking the questions.

It is a jungle out there. The stockmarket is manipulated. It does dance to the tune played by the big money. In the old days, with brokers and jobbers dealing face to face, scuttling round the trading floor, there were abuses. But they were on a more human scale. You could not rook a man too savagely when you knew you would meet him every working day. Since Big Bang changed the rules in October 1986, the scale has changed. Trading is international, conducted by dealers who may never meet, on computer screens. The touch of a button can wipe millions off share values, or put them on.

Billions of pounds have been invested in high-tech offices and machinery. Hundreds of millions have been lost. Some of the mightiest banking and investment names in the world have gone bust, or retired hurt. Those who remain are competing to make money from a more complex, nastier world. They spend much of their time snatching quick profits from each other as momentary opportunities flash across the screens, a real-life corporate PACMan computer game. They cannot manipulate the economy, though speculators like George Soros came close as we crashed out of the ERM in the autumn of 1992. But they can certainly swing the market, or chunks of it, from day-to-day and from time-to-time. Officially, such things cannot happen. But they do. Ruthlessly. Greedily.

When a big investment house has, say, £100m of shares to sell, it can use the computer systems to cast a smoke-screen, mislead the competition, and move the market briefly one way or another. Frequently, they use computing power and cash resources to play off the futures markets against the real stockmarket to create profitable opportunities.

Never mind. They need the money, poor dears. Often their jobs are on the line. Few outsiders really understand it. Small investors have no chance of competing against such might and muscle. Do not let this deter you. When the economy allows, the big money boys are pushing prices ahead as fast as they dare. Small investors ride on their coat-tails. As the giants push big company shares higher, private shareholders enjoy the ride. When big shares rise, it pumps life into the smaller company shares where so many individual investors love to play – and where the big boys are slow to catch on.

Keep your wits about you, and you have nothing to fear. You really can make money on the stockmarket. All you have to do is to buy low, and sell high. Elementary. So obvious that it hardly bears saying. Pause, and think about it. Why is it that so few investors – large or small – succeed in doing it consistently?

Perhaps it is the thrill of the game. It is so easy to get sucked into the day-to-day excitement and to lose sight of the main objective. Everyone is busy watching prices, analysing profit moves, trying to read the chairman's mind, hanging on for that extra penny or two, and they forget to step back and see where it is all going. Before they know it, the economy is running into trouble, the market is overheated, and shares are on the slide.

Suddenly, yesterday's fat paper profit is today's real loss. What a pity we got so greedy. Better hang on, and hope it all comes back. Will it ever come back? Of course. Or some of it will.

The nightmare still sits on many an investor's shoulder. It happened in October, 1987 – a classic share slump. No one playing the market then will forget it, especially if they lived in the South of England. While prices went into free fall, a hurricane howled across the land, bringing trees tumbling down, tearing tiles off roofs, and sending chimneys crashing through ceilings. The FTSE index lost 500 points in two trading sessions. It had never before lost more than 70 points in a single day. Shares galore shed a quarter of their value before many investors realised what was happening. Small company shares became almost impossible to sell.

It was the end of the share world as many small investors knew it. Some retired, licking their wounds, hoping to play another day. Others were burnt so badly that they will never return. A few – the quicker or the more cautious – blessed their foresight in selling ahead of the slump.

The Crash of October 1987 looks easy to understand, with hindsight. It had all got too much, many prices had gone beyond reasonable bounds, millions of small investors were coming to gamble for the first time, and the great push onwards and upwards simply could not be sustained. The market hit the kind of buying frenzy which tends to occur near the top of all great booms. As usual, the boom gave way to a slump.

How easy it is to write such a glib, predictable line. If only we had all been so smart at the time. Yet it is remarkable just how predictable it should have been to anyone who follows stockmarket history. The lesson to be learnt is clear. Sure as night follows day, stockmarket slump follows stockmarket boom. Then it rolls on around – the slump is followed by a boom. And so on.

There is nothing clever in this book – no snake-oil formula guaranteed to make a fortune. Simply the basic application of a little common sense, plus a collection of old lessons which are worth learning anew after the experience of the eighties. And a determination to tell it like it is, not the way they pretend. The old lessons do work, believe me. As a financial journalist for over 36 years, and an investor for much of that time, I have slogged through the slump of the seventies, and the Great Crash of 1987. I lost money in both. Each time, I started with a little capital and made a respectable sum – not a fortune, but enough to feel good. First time around, I lost it all. Second time, starting from practically nothing, I made roughly the same amount, though it was worth less because of inflation. I also spent a fair bit while I had it, kept some, and lost about half. Third time around I am going nicely. This time, I plan to do better. What I make, I will keep – or most of it.

Talking to other investors, tipsters, and men who have built substantial businesses, they have had similar experiences. We all made silly mistakes. We look back with amazement at how daft we were. And hope to learn from it.

None of us has come up with anything too profound. We laugh in disbelief at our stupidity. There are no great insights which will make us a fortune in the future. No matter how big the businesses my pals have built, how much they made and lost, it so often comes back to common sense, and basic principles. Keep your head, stick to what you know, and what ought to be right.

This book hammers at the common sense lessons, and reinforces them with others learnt the hard way. It is written from experience. I know what it means, how it feels, to make money and lose it on the stockmarket. Winning is marvellous for a while, lifts your day. You become blasé and cocky. Losing hits you in the pit of the stomach, makes you feel sick and depressed – then passes. There is always (unless you have been really daft) another chance.

When the market is booming, most shares go up. People start saying slightly scornfully; "Any fool could make money in this market." It is not true. Only the arrogant and ignorant say it. Making real money in shares is never that easy. But in a rising market, the odds do swing significantly your way. It IS easier, the risks ARE more modest. The chance of a costly failure is much smaller.

Whatever anyone tries to tell you, playing the stockmarket is a form of gambling. If you object, do not take the risk. But when you bet on the stockmarket, the bet should stay alive for much longer than a trip to the betting shop. And you have ample opportunity to retrieve some of your stake money if things are not going your way.

Unless you are playing more sophisticated games, you only lose all of your money when the company you back goes bust. There was a spate of company collapses in the late eighties and the early nineties, but there have been relatively few in the mid-nineties. Public companies rarely go bust once the market is into its stride.

Anyone who reads this book should be able to tell when trouble is looming, and sell long before a collapse. Common sense is crucial.

Playing the stockmarket is not difficult. All you need is a little money – the kind you can afford to lose – and a level head. As the millions who have made profits from the spate of privatisations will know, buying and selling shares can be simple if you want it to be.If you are sensible, there is nothing to fear. A careful investor, observing simple, basic rules, can do as well as any massive City house, perhaps better.

The sophisticates have no monopoly of skills – nor do they lack their share of stockmarket stupidity. I remember the top analyst at a big-name house who insisted that Brent Walker shares had assets of £10, and were worth at least half that. Through 1995, the price was 2p or 3p. The same firm repeatedly backed Maxwell Communication Corporation as I wrote piece after piece explaining what an illusion it was. And a person with a most impressive title tried to calm my fears about one controversial retailer – his company was advising it, of course – unaware of a major item raising eyebrows in the published accounts. And so on.

Everyone gets it wrong sometimes, of course. Through the eighties I was converted from a critic to a supporter of Polly Peck. To this day, I do not understand how I overlooked the tricky exchange translation in the accounts. But I did. Though I tipped the shares successfully many times, I will always regret not telling readers to cut their losses when the price began to fall apart.

When any share soars, small investors enjoying the ride will always outnumber the big City institutions. The City names will have more money at stake. When a company goes bust, there will usually be lashings of big City money locked in. But the private investors will each be taking a comparatively small hit. You know the cliché. The bigger they come, the harder they fall.

Private investors have the inestimable advantage of agility. The big boys get caught. When things go wrong, they have too many shares to sell, and no one to buy them. The small investor may take a loss, but the chances of being able to get out at a reasonable price are much greater when you have only a few shares to sell, instead of hundreds of thousands. Share investment can be enormously complicated, laden with computer-driven gobbledygook. Or it can be as simple as backing a name you like, and watching what happens. You do not need to be clever. Sometimes luck can be enough. No one can beat a lucky investor. Share portfolios picked with a pin do sometimes beat the experts.

But it pays to learn what you can about the basics. That helps swing the odds in your favour. There are simple traps to avoid, elementary ideas for spotting possible winners. The more you learn, the luckier you get, the more you improve your chances. And the more you learn, the more fun you will have. Investment is a game. The elation of spotting a winner and seeing it come right can yield enormous satisfaction, even if the cash profit is modest.

The stockmarket can be fun, and it should be. Get it right, and it can transform your life. You really can make enough profit to make a difference to the way you live. Some shares do leap ten-fold, a few rise a hundred-fold. If you have just £1,000 in one of them, it can change your life. You do not even need a runaway winner. Double your money once, then do it again. Do it a third time, and your £1,000 becomes £8,000. When the market is booming, lots of shares double, and do so in six months or a year. Many investors pick them, and make worthwhile profits. They do hit a few losers along the way, of course, but you would be astonished how many smaller investors quietly score tidy winnings on the stockmarket – when times are good. The biggest problem is resisting the temptation to keep playing when the game is over. You must know when to sell, when to turn paper profits into hard cash.

Keeping the profits is crucial. Too few investors actually take the profits they make. Paper profits are no good. The only ones which count are those in your bank account. Learning how and when to take profits is not difficult. The stop-loss system I have advocated for nearly 30 years is a simple, almost foolproof way of achieving it. This book explains, at length, how it works. The problem is mustering the self-discipline to do it. Bitter experience from the Crash of 1987 has hammered the discipline home to me. Perhaps this book will help you to learn.

Be sure, there is fun to be had and money to be made in the stockmarket. The nineties may not yield the super-fast profits we saw in the mid-eighties, when many shares trebled or quadrupled in a year, and doubling your money in 12 months was almost commonplace. But the chances are out there.

How can I be sure? There are no guarantees. I know, though, from talking to small investors, and reading their letters, that earlier editions of this and my other books have helped them. One Monday morning in February, 1992, I tipped one tiny shell company at 4p. Three days later, it was 7p, suspended while a new venture was pumped in. Of course, I was lucky with my timing. Of course, that was an exception. But some *Daily Mail* readers did invest. In May 1995, I wrote a piece recommending Queens Moat Houses, which had returned to the stockmarket after a reconstruction. As I wrote, the price was 6¼p. By the time it appeared in print, the price was 9¼p. The next day, it touched 21p, before falling sharply over the following days. At any stage, it was possible to buy or sell millions of shares at a time, at the quoted price. Double your money in a day. Unfair examples? Two flukes? Perhaps.

In November, 1993, I recommended what became Utility Cable at the equivalent of 6p. In June 1994, I told readers to sell on my stop-loss system at 30p. Just before that, the shares touched 40p briefly. In October 1992, I tipped EFM Dragon warrants at 3½p. I said sell at 7p in April 1993. In September 1993, I recommended McCarthy & Stone Preference at the equivalent to 29p. A year later, they topped 90p. In March 1995, I recommended Unipalm at 118p. In September, on a bid approach, I recommended selling half at over 500p. By November they were over 850p, though my stop-loss for the remaining half was at 440p. And there was Memory Corporation, which doubled in a few months. In the early summer of 1998, Greenwich Resources doubled in two weeks after my tip. And so on.

If this sounds boastful, I am sorry. My *Daily Mail* column has had some losers since I resumed tipping in October 1992. But, with one or two special exceptions, none of the losses have been greater than 20% if readers sold as instructed through my stop loss list. Winners or losers, the results have been there, in print, for millions to see.

Believe me, the responsibility involved in tipping a share for such a massive potential audience is considerable. I take it very seriously. The results help illustrate whether or not the contents of this book make sense to anyone wanting to try for themselves.

Finally, the answer to everyone who wants to know why, if I am so smart, I have not done it myself. I have, sort of, but because I have little capital, I have not made my fortune yet. In the introduction to *How To Make A Killing in Penny Shares*, I explain how I multiplied some of my money thirty-fold in one small company in the eighties. In fact, that was up more than forty-fold at the peak, before it fell sharply over the next couple of years. I took some profits near the top, the rest on the way down. By the summer of 1998, I am sitting with shares in another company where my original investment is up seven times inside three years, with another up just over 18 times in less than five. One is a small company which most would consider highly speculative, the other is much more substantial. Sadly, I did not have enough cash to put more than a small amount in each, and though I bought more on the way up, it has not yet made enough for me to take off for sunnier climes – yet. So here's hoping – for me and for you.   Good luck.

Michael Walters
August 1998

CHAPTER ONE

Riding The Boom, Ducking The Slump

Buy cheap, sell dear. That is the way to make money. Keep that in mind, and you will not go far wrong. It sounds so simple as to be almost silly. Of course that is what you do. But if it is so obvious, why is it that everyone does not do it? We all ought to be able to make a fortune.

The simple notion of buying cheap and selling dear is at the heart of this book. The whole idea is to try to help make it clear just what is cheap on the stockmarket, and what is dear. The best place to start is with the big picture – the economy. Nothing clever. There are times when it is best to stay out of the market, and times when the odds are very much in your favour. And the state of the economy has much to do with deciding which is which.

Broadly speaking, shares are cheapest when everyone feels gloomiest. We all tend to feel gloomier when the economy is depressed. As it picks up, and more money starts to circulate, confidence rises, people begin to spend, and profits rise. We all feel better.

Share prices rise, too. By then, you may have missed the very best prices. Shares will be well off the bottom. But the unsophisticated investor should wait until the worst is over. It is far safer then to venture into the share jungle. Those who go in when it is gloomiest get the richest pickings, but they take much the biggest risk. When the mood is good, the chances of picking a dud are much less. The brave buyer goes in at the bottom. But who knows when that may be? Happily, I called it more or less correctly in the autumn of 1992 when I published *How To Profit From The Coming Share Boom*, built around an earlier version of this book. The opportunity seemed clear to me then, but I did try to impress upon everyone who bought that book that they were taking a relatively high-risk strategy.

The economy is the key to market mood. It is very easy to get confused about the economy. So many economists with so many opinions, so many solutions, so many mistakes. You know the jokes – lock 20 economists in a room, and you will get 50 opinions. Or the Yeltsin variation? Boris Yeltsin says one of his plans to take Russia forward means firing 750,000 soldiers from the Soviet army, and replacing them with 47 economists. "Why 47 economists?" asks one of his comrades. "Everyone knows economists are so highly paid that it will cost as much to keep them as 750,000 soldiers". "Ah," says Yeltsin, "just think how much more damage 47 economists can do."

Economics can be frightening. But forget the jargon. As a prospective investor, all you really need to know is whether the economy is getting better, or getting worse. You do not need to be too smart to work that out. Your own instincts will tell you, and the headlines will make it clear. Sharply rising interest rates, higher unemployment, falling profits – they all add up to a weaker economy. And vice versa. Obviously it is most profitable if you can buy when the economy is down, and sell when it is roaring ahead. Nothing lasts forever. Sure as can be, good times will be followed by bad. No matter how grim it seems at the bottom, there will be better times.

If you can be smart enough to sell out and cling on to your cash at the top, when everything seems to be too good to be true, you will have it ready to invest when all seems too bad to bear, just right to reap the rewards of a return to prosperity. No matter what, cash is always worth much more in bad times than good.

Through history, good and bad times follow each other with unerring predictability. Whatever we might like to think, we never manage to order our affairs well enough to achieve perfectly-balanced sustainable prosperity, though in the late nineties there is a popular minority dream that we might be set for an unprecedented run of steady growth and low inflation. Let us hope so. Best not to count on it. Sadly, somehow there is always something to throw us off.

It is not just that way in economic affairs. Stockmarket commentators like Bob Beckman track all manner of cycles in nature. Beckman's books like *The Downwave* and *Into the Upwave* have examples galore. Even natural forces, like the eruption of the mighty Mount Pinatubo volcano in the Phillipines, can impact on world economies and the stockmarket. The idea is that the volcanic ash in the air clouds the sun, shifts climate patterns, and brings devastation to crops in key areas, forcing prices higher. Some of it rings true in the late-nineties. In America, they started panicking early about the possible impact of El Nino, the warm water current which could bring substantial upheaval to weather patterns. By 1998, almost everyone must know that El Nino has caused all sorts of climactic changes, some of them with major economic consequences. La Nina, with cold spells to follow, may come next, though so far we have been spared the economic upsets in this country.

You do not have to agree with the interpretation commentators like Beckman put on things to appreciate that we are locked into cycles galore. In stockmarket terms, every schoolboy knows about the South Sea Bubble of 1720. That was not the first speculative boom and slump. Nor the last. More recently, we have had the Great Crash of 1929, the Secondary Banking Collapse of 1974, and another Great Crash in October 1987 – followed by booms, every one of them. In between, there has been a series of lesser rises and falls.

All of the more recent share crashes were linked to periods of economic decline. Effectively, the stockmarket anticipated economic troubles. For those who were ready to step back, it was possible to see that the economy was getting overheated in the twenties, seventies, and eighties, and was due for a setback. Anyone who managed to do that, and was wary of the market as a result, did very well.

It is not the purpose of this book to try to convert everyone into an economic genius. It is not necessary. You can do very well in the stockmarket without it. Go back to our basic proposition – when the economy is labouring, near the bottom of a recession, shares are low and listless. As the economy begins to recover, so shares brighten up and move higher. When economic recovery is complete, share prices are likely to be romping across the high ground. So long as you sell before the economy and share prices start falling away again – and there is a crucial chunk of this book explaining when to sell – your chances of doing well have been vastly increased.

It is as well, though, to outline some of the economic fundamentals, the kind of things which indicate most clearly which way the economy is really moving.

Interest Rates

In the nineties, interest rates are the main lever the Government has left itself to influence the economy. Interest rates govern the price of money, the most basic commodity used by industry. On their own, they can provide a crude but effective guide to whether or not it is time to invest. When interest rates are high, put your cash into whatever yields the highest return for the longest fixed period. Keep clear of investments which do not give a fixed return – like Ordinary shares in companies. As interest rates get ever lower, shift out of fixed return investments (whose capital values will be rising), and into those which give a return which will rise in line with profits – like shares.

A Simple Rule

At its crudest, it is almost possible to advance an iron law of profits for the patient investor. If you can shut your eyes to all else, you will do well by putting your cash into fixed-interest securities, like Government securities, when interest rates are 14% or above. Sit with them until interest rates fall – as they will eventually – and when rates drop below 10%, switch into shares.

That is a crude, over-simplified system which requires the minimum of action. The turning points may only occur at five or ten-year intervals, perhaps more quickly, perhaps more slowly. There will be false dawns and temptations along the way. You will almost certainly switch too early, and miss the very best returns. Yet if you have the patience to follow the system, you will outperform the average investor – though it does require a great deal of patience, and self-restraint almost to the point of paralysis. It might not be that clear-cut more than a couple of times in your investing lifetime.

High interest rates clog everything up, make business difficult all round. They raise the cost of borrowing, and make it more expensive to buy plant and machinery, and to provide the capital to buy the raw materials and pay the labour needed to meet the orders which will eventually yield profit. Superficially attractive to investors on fixed returns, they actually hurt them, too, since they almost always occur in periods of high inflation.

High interest rates also raise the cost of long-term credit, like mortgages, and short-term credit, like bank overdrafts and credit cards. That leaves people with less to spend, so orders fall, industry suffers, and the whole economy slows down. The number of jobs declines, so there are fewer people with money to spend, and so on. The whole downward spiral gathers pace, and we all end up poorer as a result of high interest rates.

Real Interest

While the Government often chooses to ignore it, concentrating for political advantage on the simple headline rate of interest, there is a crucial difference between nominal interest rates and real interest rates. Between October 1990, when we entered the European Monetary System with a cut in bank base rates from 15% to 14%, and October 1991, nominal interest rates came down three percentage points to 10%. Over that same period, in fact, real interest rates soared from 3.1% to 6.8%. The real cost of borrowing more than doubled.

How come? In the real world, it is impossible to ignore the cost of inflation. Nominal interest rates do not tell the true story. If you can borrow at 5% a year (though we never bother with the fine print, quoted interest rates almost always cover the cost of money for a year) when the rate of inflation is 5%, you are effectively paying nothing for the use of the money you have borrowed for a year. In order to find the REAL cost of cash, you must deduct the rate of inflation from the nominal rate of interest. So if nominal interest rates were 14% in October 1990, when inflation was 10.9%, the real rate of interest was a mere 3.1% – not so bad. A year later, while nominal interest rates were down to 10.5%, inflation had tumbled to 3.7%. So the real cost of cash was 6.8% – historically very expensive. No wonder industry was still screaming with pain in the winter of 1991-1992, no matter how longingly the Government hailed the end of the recession. The true cost of borrowing was crippling. It might have looked as if falling interest rates guaranteed a stockmarket recovery on the back of an industrial boom. But anyone who counted the true cost of money could see that it was not so simple.

It took until we were shunted out of the European Exchange Rate Mechanism in October 1992 until the chains came off, and interest rates began to fall, getting business really moving again. Even then, the debate continued, with the Bank of England pushing hard to keep interest rates up, to restrain the supply of money, and to suppress inflation. As inflation fell, even the lower nominal interest rates still bore pretty hard on industry through 1995. Through 1997, the position changed. The advent of a Labour Government saw control of interest rates passed to the Bank of England, where they took an ultra-cautious view of the economy. The Bank engineered a rapid series of rises, fearful that otherwise inflation might return in 1999. That, though, risked depressing industry too far. Especially since it pushed the pound up against other key currencies.

Inflation

The rate of inflation is clearly closely linked to interest rates as another key economic indicator. Inflation has become public enemy number one for most politicians. In the 1960s, investors were happy to see it jog along at 2% or 3%. It meant that profits appeared to move steadily ahead on paper. Come the seventies, and inflation over 25%, and everyone was horrified. It had to be driven out of the system.

In the nineties, the Tories declared war on inflation. The Labour Government has made a great show of continuing that campaign. Panic measures in the wake of the October 1987 Crash, however, pumped more money into the system, and sent inflation soaring. The fight against inflation helped deepen the recession of the early nineties as the Government cut back the supply of money and pushed interest rates up.

At base, inflation arises from too much money chasing too few goods. Prices are pushed higher as people become ready to pay more to get what is available. Less money in circulation chokes inflation, and more expensive money makes for less money.

The impact of inflation on the economy is broadly similar to high interest rates – it pushes up the real cost of money, and the real cost of assets. While nominal profits are higher, they are worth less because money buys less and less. Crucially, inflation can be a killer for older investors on fixed incomes. It erodes the real worth of their income.

For investors, though the high profits which are reported in times of rapid inflation may appear good, they are an illusion. Profits are more valuable when inflation is lower, and big investors will be more confident about buying shares when inflation is under control. No one, though, wants to be caught in fixed interest investments when inflation is rising. Their capital value is eaten away. So when inflation is rising, the best defence is to be invested in shares of a company whose profits and asset value are advancing with inflation. That is the ultimate protection. The trick is to get out before inflation gets so high that it damages the economy, plunges everything into recession, and shares fall as worries mount over possible falling profits ahead.

In crude terms, you want to buy shares when inflation is low, and sit with them as it begins to rise. You should be looking to sell, to switch your profits into fixed-interest investments as inflation peaks, and starts to fall. Be careful, though, on the way up. It will not do to switch into quoted fixed-interest investments like Government Securities and company loan stocks too early as interest rates rise, because their capital value will be falling. At such a stage in the cycle, you need to go into cash, and to put that cash in National Savings, a building society, or a bank, where the capital will be secure.

Exchange Rates

Interest rates and inflation are crucially caught up with what happens to the pound and other foreign exchange rates. After a long spell when the pound was, in theory, left to float free and find its own level, in the autumn of 1990 we entered the European Monetary System. Everything became more complicated. In fact, under Chancellor Nigel Lawson we had earlier tried to link the value of sterling to the German Mark for several years. When we entered the European Monetary System, we subscribed to the Exchange Rate Mechanism. That links the exchange rates of all of the EMS members. All currencies were supposed to be confined to movements within bands against each other. When a currency looked like breaking out, the EMS central banks were committed to moving into the foreign exchange markets to buy or sell currencies to try to defend the rate. Ultimately, though, EMS members were expected to follow broad economic policies to ensure that their currencies conformed. The pound went in with a pledge to stay within a broad band against the German Mark. The Mark was the strongest in the system, and German aversion to inflation after the horrific experiences of the 1920s had encouraged the Bundesbank in following economic policies which had proved remarkably effective in securing a low inflation economy.

The idea was that if we linked our currency with the Mark, we would be forced to follow policies which eventually brought our performance close to German levels – the convergence idea. But unification began to push up German inflation. That prompted the Germans to adopt a tough anti-inflation policy, with relatively high interest rates at a time when the UK and many others in Europe really needed lower interest rates to combat recession. Thanks to membership of the Exchange Rate Mechanism, the UK was inhibited from cutting interest rates to boost the domestic economy for fear of provoking a sterling crisis. In the end, high interest rates stifled our economy so much that the currency crisis struck, and even sky-high interest rates could not hold the pound up. The pound was devalued, and we crashed out of the ERM, free to pursue a more sensible domestic economic policy. Hopefully, the nonsense about rejoining the ERM is dead for ever – though you never know. Instead, we now have the worry about Economic & Monetary Union. Sometime in the next Millennium.

The Euro

EMU and the Euro, the common European currency, pose all sorts of new problems. The basic argument of the anti-Euro group, which significantly includes many top businessmen, is that a common currency will effectively surrender control of our economy. What happens will be dictated effectively by a combination of Germany and France, with Germany ultimately emerging as the real power behind the European Central Bank That will set a common interest rate across Europe, with some suggestion that it will eventually want to dictate a common tax policy. This would ignore differences in national economic cycles. There will always be times when a high interest rate suits one economy, and a low rate another. Private investors cannot worry unduly about this in the late nineties. But keep a wary eye on political progress. It could upset the stock market eventually.

Devaluation

Devaluing the pound in the autumn of 1992 helped the economy by effectively reducing the price of exports from Britain, making our goods cheaper around the world. That, and perhaps our reluctance to accept Common Market rules imposing extra costs on industry, meant the mid-nineties saw an export-led economic recovery. At the same time, a cheaper pound meant it cost us more to import. In theory, that should reduce the attractions of buying goods from abroad, and divert extra home demand into UK goods. That is more questionable, and in the mid-nineties, the economy was moving in fits and starts, badly lacking confidence in many areas. By 1998, it had all turned around. The big worry was not devaluation, but an increase in the value of sterling. That meant that while imports were cheaper, our exports cost more for others to buy. Some of our costs of production were lower, but since we depend crucially on exporting our services, we were becoming less competitive in world markets. By mid-1998, a succession of companies was reporting profit setbacks from the strength of sterling—definitely something for the small investor to worry about.

Money Supply

Leaving the ERM left the Government with interest rates as the main weapon to determine the direction of the economy and to fight inflation. There is, however, the opportunity to tinker by altering tax rates, public spending, and the supply of money. An increased supply of money is frowned upon as inflationary, but the Government weakened in its resolve with the approach of an election. As more money was pumped into the flat economy, fears of a return to faster inflation took hold once again. Though it was still attracting relatively little attention in 1998, this was a factor in the Bank of England decision to raise interest rates. Amid all of this there are always worries about rising unemployment versus soaring wage costs, whether our balance of payments (the level of imports compared with exports) will slump, how the price of oil will influence us (inflationary if it goes up, but helpful in some ways because we are a significant oil producer), and so on. The complications are countless, and the interpretations of them infinite. Tens of thousands of people make a very good living writing and debating them.

Reading The Trend

In the end, no one knows the real answers. No-one gets it right all of the time. The private investor, thank goodness, does not have to know or worry too much about it. All that really matters is getting a feel for the overall trend. It is pointless trying to be too clever about the economy. Whatever happens, you will not understand it as well as the hosts of analysts employed in the City and around the world with nothing to do but dissect what is going on and to report on it. They are feeding information non-stop to the various investment houses. Whatever happens anywhere, someone will have a view on it, and will have analysed it before you become aware of what is going on. In most cases, it probably does not help them much. Some never see the wood for the trees. All that matters to the individual investor is the broad trend. You can pick up on that by reading newspaper headlines, watching the TV news, being alive to what is going on around you. If homes are being repossessed, thousands are losing their jobs, and companies are closing, the broad trend is clear enough. Just think for yourself – basic common sense.

Contrary Thinking

In a way, the most important element is to understand the need for contrary thinking. This notion has become so popular as almost to be hackneyed, and worn to death. But do not neglect it. Those who trumpet the value of contrary thinking do not always give real thought to what it involves. At base, contrary thinking is simply thinking for yourself. Observe the majority opinion, and question it. There will be times when the only sensible thing to do is to go with the masses. They will be right, and their momentum will carry everything forward, especially in the stockmarket. But there will be a time when it is right to step aside.

This is crucial in relating the economy to the stockmarket. Successful investing is about thinking ahead. When times are good, the stockmarket is the place for your money. But when times are getting too good, be wary. Some of the most successful investors in the world prosper by sticking to a well-worn old phrase – 'The trend is your friend'. It is well-worn because it works. The movement of the herd determines what happens to stockmarkets. When buyers outnumber sellers, prices go up. When sellers are most numerous, prices fall. Successful investment involves riding on those tides.

A trend is a trend until it stops being a trend. That may sound daft, trite nonsense. But think about it. Go with the masses while they are carrying everything their way. Then jump off when they stop. The trick is to spot when the change is going to come, and move just that little bit earlier. The small investor may not need to be quite so sharp. It may be enough to spot when the change has started, and to move in the early stages, before the trend starts running sharply in the other direction. You do not need to be an economic genius. All you need to do is to look at the general picture. If almost everyone seems convinced everything is wonderful, wealth and prosperity are here to stay, think seriously about selling. Trouble is ahead, sure as can be. If you miss the actual turn, and find the general mood is beginning to grow more cautious while you are still hopeful, never mind – sell. You may have missed the top, but it is far safer to be out before the crunch comes. And when the majority seem to be worrying away, it may be time to buy.

Thinking About Buying

When the economic scene gets so black, so grim, that people fear good times may never return – THINK about buying. As sure as can be, you are getting near the bottom. Take note, though. While I have no hesitation in talking about selling just as you think times are most wonderful, I have not suggested a definite 'Buy' when you think you have hit the bottom. Taking profits is never wrong, no matter how much extra profit you may miss. Buying at the bottom is more dangerous, because you are risking precious limited resources, and none of us can ever be certain when we have reached the bottom. Fears of a setback are always with us when the economy is in reasonable shape. Until it is clear that interest rates are rising sharply or the economy is heading down, though, shares should be a sensible bet. Even if the economy should go into reverse, it may be that any setback will not last long.

In the late nineties, many more people in the Western world have moved into buying shares. They will be tempted to see any significant setback as a buying opportunity. And they will be well aware that the authorities will be eager to start cutting interest rates to stimulate the economy should things get sticky. So investors may try to look ahead, choose to ride out any setback, hoping it is temporary, and may well muster enough buying muscle to make any decline short-lived.

A Labour Government has rarely been too bad for the share market. The shrewd investor will watch events closely, and be ready to sell quickly if profits start to dwindle, and the market loses confidence, no matter what. Never mind the economy if it looks as if the market mood will cost you money – guard your profits and your cash at all costs. Do not be misled. Even if the economy looks bright and breezy, set fair for a while, the stockmarket is a jungle. It is dangerous. You are at risk from the moment you venture in. Any share could fall sharply at any time for a totally unpredictable reason. So, once again, only use money you can afford to lose. I keep saying it. I mean it.

The most crucial advice in this book comes near the end. Read my advice on when to sell. Read it before you buy. Then read it again. And please, please, *take notice of it.*

CHAPTER TWO

Should You Be In
The Stockmarket?

You can make your fortune in the stockmarket. Be sure of it. Many
people do. You do not hear much about it. They keep it quiet, sometimes
even from friends and family. Every so often it hits the press. You read
about an old lady who shopped at Oxfam, and left hundreds of thousands
of pounds when she died. In her will, the cat got the lot. A disgruntled
relative tells the world that she had a few shares, always liked to play the
stockmarket. No one dreamt she did so well.

That says a lot. It illustrates the fascination of the share game. One
retired relation of mine cost his family a small fortune because he refused
to consider tax planning. He wanted to keep his cash in shares. He
enjoyed following the prices in the newspaper, chatting to his broker.
Good luck to him.

Often it is not so much about making money as having a hobby, the
most consuming hobby of all. The pounds you make are points on the
scoreboard. Whether you want simply to play the game, or dream of
making your fortune, it helps to know a little about the rules, the sort of
things which make prices go up, and which might make them fall. In
truth, there are no clearly defined rules. New elements intrude constantly.
There is always something you never thought of. We are not really talking
about rules, but a set of clues. If that makes you want to despair, too bad.
Anyone who pretends to give you more clearly defined guidelines is
fooling themselves. But that does not mean it is not worth trying to learn

more about how it works. This book is dedicated to the positive thinkers, those who want to go out and try it.

Successful share dealing can change your life. You might make a real killing. Thousands succeed, often from very modest beginnings. One of the nicest things to happen to me is when I meet someone or get a letter from someone who started with the help of one of my investment books, or after something I wrote in the *Daily Mail.* I come across them every so often, and I am delighted. Sometimes they have done very much better using my advice than I have ever managed myself!

One fund manager friend once let slip that he had put £100,000 or more into one of my favourites. Oh, and he hoped it would do well for the sake of his friends, who had put a similar amount in. Some readers ring to tell me they have made tens of thousands. Others have started with a few hundred pounds, and worked it up to a few thousand. Whether they have made big money, or small, they have all had fun. Terrific. Do not let me kid you. Most people will not make a great deal of money playing the share game. Some will get sucked in, and end up losing a lot of money. I hope that does not happen to anyone who reads this book. Heed what it says, and it will not.

Be under no illusions, though. The essence of successful investment is sensible assessment of the odds. Forget pious nonsense about responsible investment, so popular around the City and in the columns of financial journalists who tell others what to do, but never risk a penny of their own. Gamble as madly as you like, so long as you realise that you ARE gambling. Be realistic. The greater the gamble, the longer the odds, the more likely you are to lose. It is dangerous out there. There is no such thing as a safe share. All are risky. Some people should not be allowed near the stockmarket. There are no rules to keep them away, nothing to prevent a fool and their money being soon parted. Just try to make sure you are not one of the fools.

Before you start planning that penthouse in town, the villa in Spain, and the new car you will buy with your share winnings, pause a moment. Then pause again. Share dealing is a risky business. No matter how careful you may try to be, you can lose money at it - all of your money. Companies do go bust, famous names among them. Investors who enjoyed astonishing gains in Polly Peck have been left with shares that could prove worthless (though Asil Nadir is still promising that he will make money back for all investors). Brent Walker became a debt-laden shell before being broken up, Queens Moat Houses almost vanished beneath a mountain of debt, Laura Ashley limps along, a shadow of the company which was swamped by demand when it first came to the stockmarket. Even Trafalgar House, owning names like Cunard and the Ritz, brought investors massive share losses in the mid-nineties. Lesser lights galore went out in the recession which followed the October 1987 stockmarket slump.

And the astonishing Maxwell affair (astonishing mainly because so many apparently respectable City houses trusted and traded with a man branded a liar by a Department of Trade report) demonstrates that even giant companies can be dominated by crooks. When companies go bust, the shares become worthless. You lose every penny you have in them. There is no one to complain to, no one to blame but yourself. If you put all of your savings in a dud, you lose all of your savings.

Bad? There is worse. Many people borrow to buy shares. They put their home up as security against the loan. When it all goes wrong, they lose not just their savings, but their home as well. You would think no one could be so stupid. They can. And if the market should enjoy a marvellous run, and you find you are making enormous profits, you, too, might be tempted one day. Do not laugh. You will be sucked in almost without realising it, greedy to make that much more. You would be astonished how a sudden rush of success can change the most sober-minded people into over-confident raving egotists. The warning is no joke, no cheap sensationalism. It happens. I know. I have seen the letters, spoken to people who have done it. Once I worked with a financial journalist who got sucked into share gambling. First he sold his house, then his flat. Then he switched to a less attractive but higher paying job to keep up. He changed that, and then dropped out of sight. You would be amazed how greed can tempt people to go over the top. Then it wipes them out.

You could have bought shares in Grand Metropolitan, the brewing and leisure giant now merged into Diageo, for 24p in 1974, and sold them for well over 900p in 1992. Wonderful. But what if you had paid 85p in 1974 before they fell to 24p? You would have suffered a swift, savage loss. It was brilliant if your timing was right, deadly if it was wrong.

You could have bought Brent Walker at under 100p, and seen it top 600p in 1989. In 1997, it lingered at 2p, fully-valued. The figures differ, but there are similar tales of advertising agents Saatchi & Saatchi, and WPP before financial reconstruction. Building products group Spring Ram soared and slumped. Parkfield, Roger Felber's video and engineering group, went from wonder stock to bust inside 18 months. Polly Peck crashed to earth in 1990. John Gunn, once the City's favourite son, bombed out at British & Commonwealth. And so on, and so on.

Compile your own list. In the early nineties, it was not difficult to find crashes galore, large and small. Each one brought shattering losses to investors, people like you and I, not just faceless City giants. These days, there are fewer total collapses, but even among new issues, there have been some very nasty surprises. It is not easy. It may not be fun. The stockmarket can be a savage place. Each crash wrecks marriages, ruins careers, shortens lives. Legend has them diving out of windows on Wall Street during the crash of 1929. Maybe that never actually happened. But the crash blighted the lives of hundreds of thousands of Americans through the 1930s. In Japan in the autumn of 1997, at least one loser jumped, and another died at his desk from stress. In England, the Great Crash of 1987 saw a trainee accountant run up losses of over £1 million in just two days, playing the option market. Thousands of traders were forced to sell their homes to meet market debts. Many who were more fortunate, or perhaps more prudent, had to sell cars. Or, more painfully, were forced to take their children out of private school. Tales of little personal tragedies, not big news, were everywhere. Never forget. Crashes could come again. One might be just around the corner, when you least expect it.

Playing the market is risky. Never forget it. The risks may be too great for you. Prices can turn without warning. The stockmarket may be too rough for you.

If you do want to play, it is simple to cut the risks down to size. Before you take the plunge, you must go through the boring basics. Everyone ought to do it. Stripped down, they mean that you can only afford to play if you can afford to pay. NEVER USE MONEY YOU CANNOT AFFORD TO LOSE.

Insurance

Be sure about that. Do not fool yourself. Most people I know say they cannot afford to lose a penny. If that really is so, shares are not for you. In truth, though, most people with a steady job can squirrel away £1,000 or so, and use that to play, if they really want to. But, whatever you do, be sure you really want to, and really can afford to lose it. Do not cut corners to play the market.

First, if you are married, your home should be financially secure. You should be able to cover the mortgage payments comfortably each month, or pay the rent. Do take out proper insurance. A mortgage guarantee policy is essential, covering the cost of your mortgage if you should die or be unable to work through illness or disablement. Consider, too, whether you require a policy to cover your mortgage payments if you should be made redundant. Check the fine print carefully. Too many policies have terrible loopholes, letting the insurers off the hook just when you need them. You should have general life insurance, for perhaps three or four times your annual salary, ideally for more. Term insurance may suit you better than an expensive endowment. Plus a pension scheme, one run by your employer, or a personal pension plan with a reputable, long-established name. By that, I mean you should only go to a company which has been established for more than 25 years. That is a sweeping generalisation, unfair to perfectly solid newer companies. Too bad. You are not in the business of being fair. You want to be sure, above all. No matter what red tape the Government introduces to protect people, it will be far from foolproof. Bitter experience tells me that most of us are no match for a good salesman or woman. They can make you believe almost anything they want to, and will be furious at my advice. to stick to long-established companies TAKE NO NOTICE OF THEM. It is your money they want, your cash and your future which will be at risk if you buy something unsuitable from someone who wants to earn a commission from convincing you.

Me? I invite nothing but complaints by offering such advice. But maybe I have learnt something. I first bought insurance more than 30 years ago. And got that wrong. A few years later, doing a showbiz interview, rock singer Screaming Lord Sutch asked me to sit in while someone tried to sell him insurance. The salesman opened a thick file of cuttings apparently praising his company. Everyone, from the *Financial Times* onwards, seemed to love it.

It sounded odd. I made some investigations around the City. Sutch, happy to say, took my advice, and never bought the insurance. The salesman was trying to sell him a Dover Plan, from the notorious company put together by Bernie Cornfeld, the American whose tag line became "Do you sincerely want to be rich?". It later fell apart. I refused to allow the company to advertise in the newspaper group which employed me then, and returned the gifts they sent me. Many others were happy to go along with it.(Some family finance writers are absolute suckers, easily swayed by a flattering line of chat, or an expenses-paid trip to far-away places to see the latest product. Others actually write brochures for insurance companies, apparently blind to the massive conflict of interest between taking cash from one company and giving independent advice to readers). The real point, though, is that you must be careful about insurance. Add up the annual premiums, and you are making a massive investment. You want your company to last for ever, to be there 30 years from now.

A long-established, slightly stuffy house is best. Say someone like Standard Life, Legal & General or the Pru (despite the attacks on it for mis-selling pensions). They may not top the performance charts short or medium term. But they will be there, giving value, when you need them.

Savings

Then you need some savings put by for the legendary rainy day. It always comes, eventually. Go to somewhere boring and easily accessible. The National Savings Investment Bank gives good, rock-solid returns. Please note – these are different from National Savings Certificates, which tie up your money for five years in exchange for a higher return. For many people, five years is too long a commitment. Your building society is also worthy of your consideration.

Sadly, it would be nice to urge you to go to the local society which may offer a fraction of a percentage point more in interest than the nationals. Be careful. Societies do not go bust. They are always rescued by the Building Societies Association, which leans on a big brother society to take them over. But when the smaller ones hit trouble, it can take months before you can get your money out. So big might just be best.

TESSAs

With the rainy-day money safe, you ought to look at TESSAs, while they last. New ones will be abolished in 1999, though any taken out earlier will be allowed to run on to maturity. Tessas are Tax Exempt Special Savings Accounts. They allow you to save up to £9,000 free of tax, so long as you leave the money in the account for five years. You do not put it all in at once. The maximum deposit is £3,000 in year one, with up to £1,800 in years two, three, and four, leaving only £600 for year five. The rates of deposit can vary.

Interest can either be rolled up or taken out. Some accounts attract bonuses, and so on. Details vary considerably. Rates usually fall or rise in line with general rates, but there are some fixed rate offers. Watch for penalty clauses on withdrawal or transfer. If you take your money out inside five years, you lose the tax relief. For anyone intending to play the share market, a Tessa might be too restrictive. For long-term savers, they are fine.

Individual Savings Accounts.

Announced late in 1997 for introduction in 1999, individual savings accounts are intended by the Labour Government to encourage low-income earners to save. They will allow savers to put up to £5,000 a year in, with up to £1,000 of it in cash or National Savings products, and up to £1,000 in life assurance. At the time of writing, the details are not clear. Watch the family finance pages, or consult some sensible financial intermediary like Hargreaves Lansdown in Bristol.

Unit Trusts

After some form of cash-related saving, the next step might be to tiptoe into the share market through a unit trust or an investment trust. Unit trusts employ managers to buy shares with the cash from investors who buy units in the trusts. The value of the units moves in line with the price of the shares the trust holds.

The idea is that a professional manager is better equipped than the individual to pick good shares, and can handle the troublesome paperwork – especially useful when it comes to investing overseas. You pay for the privilege, of course. The trusts usually take a margin of 6% between the price at which you buy and the price at which you can sell back to the managers. They also take an annual fee of 1% or more. The size of the trust rises and falls as investors buy or sell units. Each unit gives you a stake in the fund corresponding to the proportion of your investment. Most trusts have between 40 and 120 shares, so you effectively claim a tiny stake in each of 40 to 120 companies.

Because it spreads your investment, it spreads the risk of getting something badly wrong and losing a high proportion of your cash. It also, of course, reduces the beneficial impact when the trust buys one outstandingly good investment.

Unit trusts are strictly regulated, and are solid investments. None have gone bust, even when control of the odd one has fallen into the hands of a villain. Bad managers, however, can produce poor performance, and you might find your units decline in value quite sharply. In exceptionally difficult times, there could be quite long delays in being able to sell your units, though generally trusts can quickly be converted back into cash.

Respectable management groups also have some poorly performing funds. Most jog along with performance just below the overall average for the sort of shares they invest in. There are more than 1,400 trusts, some of a general nature, others going for capital growth or income, and others opting for particular industries or geographical areas. They are an ideal way of investing overseas, if you want such exposure, though I would not advise anyone to consider any significant investment outside the UK or the US, unless that is part of a plan to spread a substantial portfolio.

Once again, stick to the established, big name management houses. M & G, Save & Prosper, Legal & General, Fidelity, Perpetual and Mercury may not always top the performance lists, but are good and reliable. If you see a fund shrinking in size, sell it. The best performers, and those easiest to manage, are the ones which motor on steadily, or attract a flow of new money. If any fund performs badly for a year or two, do switch into something else. Managers will try to tell you that trusts are for the long term. But there is no merit in sitting for long periods with a poor performer. Or if you think the whole share market may be going into long-term decline.

Some management groups offer cash funds. Often you can switch out of a trust specialising in equities and into the cash fund at a reduced dealing cost. That makes sense when you are worried about a market setback. Thoroughly investigate before you buy that your management group offers such a facility. As with any investment, CHECK THE WAY OUT AS YOU GO IN.

The authorities will not thank me for it, but I would be cautious about investing in any trust which is not firmly based in this country. Jersey and Isle of Man funds may be perfectly sound, but the Isle of Man in particular has a chequered financial past. Better stick to the mainland.

When you want to buy, ask for a discount. Some unit trust houses will give you one. Some brokers will offer commission rebates. Watch the press for advertisements.

Tracker Funds

The Tracker funds are unit trusts which seek to mimic the main indices, the main measures of stockmarket movement. The most prominent of these is the FTSE 100 index, known widely as the 'Footsie'. This records the movement of the top 100 shares, and is the one most widely quoted when news programmes talk about a rise or fall in the UK stockmarket. Tracker funds try to invest in the same top 100 shares in the correct proportions, so that when the market moves up, they move up. And vice versa. Because there is no element of active management, they have cheaper running costs. They also rank as a cautious, conservative investment which should rise over time, following the general upward trend of share markets. Several companies offer them. Try to check performance charts and costs before you buy one. It is amazing how the performance of these (in theory) identical funds varies. On the whole, though, they make a good choice for investors wanting a low-risk exposure to share investment.

Investment Trusts

Investment trusts are an attractive alternative to unit trusts. They have a fixed share capital, and employ managers to invest that capital in a wide range of shares. The price of the investment trust shares responds to supply and demand for them in the stockmarket. Obviously, the better the manager does, the more valuable the fund becomes, and the greater the demand for the shares. That is the theory. In practice, for long periods most investment trust shares sell at less than the value of the shares they hold – a discount. That discount can be attractive. It generally ranges between 35% and 10%.

It means that sometimes – at the extreme – you can buy an investment trust share for 65p, and have 100p of money working for you. Sometimes a bidder will buy a block of shares at a discount, and try to bid for the rest with a view to selling the underlying shares, and unlocking the whole of the asset value by liquidating the trust. When it happens, that yields a useful gain to the trust shareholder. In the early nineties, investment trust holders were helped by a strong promotional campaign which made people much more aware of investment trusts. That reduced discounts, and gave useful gains to existing shareholders. The same campaign, though, is pushing up management charges, which have in the past been well below those for unit trusts.

Like unit trusts, different investment trusts have different objectives, some going for growth or income, particular industries, or areas of the world. Unlike unit trusts, they can invest in unquoted companies. When they get them right, they do very well. In the early nineties, however, that brought several disappointments – though there has been a useful recovery as the economy has picked up.

Investment trusts are also allowed to borrow money, unlike unit trusts. That means they can make more money for their investors when they get things right and make investments which give a return greater than the cost of borrowing. If they used borrowed money to buy poor performers, of course, that drags overall performance down.

Investment trusts can also have different classes of capital. Several attribute the dividends on all of the portfolio to a separate class of income share, while allotting most of the growth to capital shares. There are many variations. You need expert help to distinguish between them, but they can be attractive, especially for those seeking a high return.

Trust Warning

Sadly, it is now necessary to insert a hefty warning about certain unit and investment trusts. The problem has been around for a while, but only in the mid-nineties has it become sufficiently disturbing to warrant a special warning section. What troubles me is the proliferation of specialised funds, those concentrating on particular industries or countries. For sophisticated investors, these can be useful vehicles for putting part of your cash in areas which really need closer attention than a casual investor can manage. Unfortunately, the rise of the marketing man and the ever greedier competition to sell products has meant that such funds are multiplying apace, and are promoted aggressively. Each tends to have a moment in the sun, and then fades with fashion. Too often, they produce poor performance, largely because they are sold when interest in their particular area is at a peak – which often means when prices are at, or moving towards a peak. Get into these specialist trusts, and you need as much skill in sorting likely winners from losers as you do in picking shares. And this is not an area where many of the family finance journalists who write about them are too well equipped. They are happy to be taken on an all-expenses paid jaunt to the latest emerging country, write glowing articles about the opportunities, and to move on.

That will not do. Avoid these specialist funds, especially if you are planning to move into penny shares. You will find dangers enough there, without having some of your safety-first cash in the Emerging Thailand Ding-Dong Fund. That warning has been in earlier editions of this book, and struck home with a vengeance in 1997 when economic ills spread across the whole of Asia. Once-trendy funds, some of which had performed very well for a while, slumped. Unit trust investors lost a great deal of money.

Open Ended Investment Companies

Adding to the confusion, we are beginning to see the debut of Open Ended Investment Companies in the late nineties. These are simply a variation on the unit trust. They trade on a single price for buying and selling, and wrap up the costs and fees in a different fashion. They are being created in the hope that we can sell them to our Common Market cousins, who apparently do not understand our system.

All of the major established fund management groups are likely to be issuing them. If you are interested, apply the same judgements that you would for unit trusts.

Personal Equity Plans

Many unit and investment trusts offer special facilities for combining with Personal Equity Plans. These were introduced from January 1987 to encourage individual investors into the stockmarket, but will be killed by the Labour Government in 1999. They allow you to put up to £6,000 a year into a general PEP, and an additional £3,000 into a PEP investing in a single company. Provided you keep the cash in for a year, capital gains and dividends are free of tax. All PEPs must have a manager. This foolish complication puts fees into City pockets, and in many cases wipes out the tax savings on the PEP. Some managers do the investment for you, others allow you to choose your own shares. Investment has to be in UK shares, and general PEPs can take up to £3,000 of unit trusts or investment trusts. The advantages of buying into a new PEP are marginal ahead of abolition in 1999.

How Many Shares?

It is a pity that getting to share investment should involve ploughing through a mass of preparation. Heed it. Once you have followed the rules about safe financial planning, and earnt your Good Cash-Keeping Seal of Approval, you can get down to the real stockmarket nitty-gritty. Do make sure the basics are right first. They may not matter for 30 or 40 years. But if anything should go wrong, and you are forced to fall back on the basics, you will be grateful that you put them in place properly. Believe me, insurance and savings difficulties will crop up at some time, just when you least need the worry. There is nothing to say you need be so serious about playing the stockmarket. Savings and insurance are life-support systems. Shares are a diversion, an entertainment.

Remember, you are only using money you can afford to lose. And you can be as brave or as barmy as you choose. You can spend as little as £25 – say £10 for a share, and £15 dealing costs. But that would be daft. I have one share in several companies. I buy them to ensure that I receive all of the documents, and can get access to the meetings. Thankfully, the *Daily Mail* pays my dealing costs. They are not serious investments. I even get the odd dividend cheque for nought pounds and nought pence.

Sometimes readers write to ask how they should split £200 between shares. Good luck to them. I never put them off. But it does not really make much sense. If you want to make money, you ought to start with at least £1,000. If that really is too much to risk, perhaps you ought not to play. Obviously, if you can manage more, so much the better. Having, say, £2,500 to split between two shares is a better bet. If you want to try with £200, do not let me stop you. At that end of the market, you might well feel it best to go for low-priced, high-risk shares. That way, if you do get it right, you will get a decent return.

The Fun Of It

You can certainly treat share dealing as a game, a wild gamble. Once you start, you will enjoy the sheer fun of it (unless your first venture is a disaster). Scratch any giant industrialist, and you will find he sees making cash as part of the game, just keeping score. After, say, the first million, you do not need the money to live. You know the theme. You can only eat so many dinners each day, drive one car at a time, live in so many houses, and keep so many ladies happy five times a night.

The cash becomes squiggles on a bank statement. Does it really matter to Peter Wood, the man who invented Direct Line insurance, whether he earns £24m, £13m, or just £357,000 basic? Did Lord Hanson worry about his pay when it was £1.36m ? In the early nineties, Sir Ralph Halpern's £1m plus wage packets probably meant almost as much to him as a passport to the lists of the nation's top wage-earners as they did in hard cash terms. Never mind the humbug about press intrusion. As status symbols go, cash goes a long way. Apart from the greedy privatised industry fat cats, whose pay has an extra political sting, many of the big earners are probably quite pleased that their pay catches the eye. If you are not an Olympic gold athlete, attracting comment over your bulging pay packet is probably as good a public substitute for a gold medal as anything. There is more than mere money in it for the private share punter, too. The money is a bonus, but getting it right is just as good. The warm glow when your favourite share soars is really special, like playing Monopoly with real money. You can get the same satisfaction whether you have £50, £5,000, or £50,000 in play.

Do not be put off by any notion that you should have at least £5,000 in each share. That might be economic sense, but that is the money man talking. If you want to play for peanuts, and enjoy the game as a game, go ahead – and good luck. That way, at least, you avoid the sickening feeling that slams into your stomach when your biggest investment turns turtle. It happens, and believe me, it hurts.

Can You Cope?

Above all, try to be honest about what you want from playing the stockmarket. And about whether you can cope emotionally, not just financially. It can be a drug, an obsession. It can take control of you, and monopolise your life. Your job and your marriage could suffer. You might end up gambling away all you can lay your hands on, elated when it goes well, dreadfully depressed when it turns down. I have seen it happen. Do not let the bug get you. Be sure you can control what you are doing. Decide how much you can afford to play with, and stick to it. If you lose it, let it go. Perhaps the lesson is there to be learnt – you do not have what it takes to cope with the share game. You might be surprised how serious the dangers can be. Do not shrug them off. Think carefully.

Hare Or Tortoise?

Then you need to decide whether you are a hare, or a tortoise. Whether you are ready to take a gamble, and the risks which go with it, or would prefer to go for steady, quality shares, the kind of things which many will tell you should let you sleep at nights. Are you eager for a quick profit? Or can you sit patiently waiting for gains to filter through?

There is no particular virtue in one approach or the other, though many people applaud the plodder. Already, perhaps, you may have guessed that my own patience is limited. For me, the greatest investment cop-out is to concentrate on long-term performance. John Maynard Keynes, the great economist, remarked that, in the longer term, we are all dead. It is hard for me to suppress the feeling that if you are not in a share which is moving today, you have missed out. There is time enough for a slower mover tomorrow, when you have banked some profit and can afford more of a waiting game – though there are undoubtedly times when it is right to be out of the market altogether. But staying out should be a positive decision – dynamic, if you like, not dozy. The share game is not for sleeping.

Growth Or Income?

You need to decide, too, whether you are after capital growth or income. The two are not mutually exclusive. This book is biased towards the seeker after capital growth, where the real fun and action is. If you want income, perhaps an insurance-linked guaranteed growth bond, or Government securities might suit you better than shares. If you want income with some capital growth, look at a high income investment trust or unit trust. Patience, though, is vital, especially to a share beginner. Choosing a steady share allows you time to learn what is going on. No one will learn much from one which doubles or halves in a fortnight. That will be down to beginner's luck, good or bad. Months spent watching prices will give you a feel about an individual share, and how it behaves in different market moods. That can pay off later.

The amount of time and effort you put into watching investments will help determine how you invest. Ideally, the cautious investor will want to watch long and hard, perhaps opting for make-believe investments, tracking them on paper before actually buying. The careful investor also spreads the risk, splitting cash between shares so that one loser does not drag the whole portfolio down too far.

Taking A Gamble

Others will hope to spot special situations, and plunge the lot on them. Spreading your risk may be safer, but it waters down the benefits of a big winner. Finding just one big one is difficult enough. When you are convinced you have it, you may want to leap in, all or nothing. That strategy attracts little support among City investment advisers. Every time, they opt for the slow, steady route. That way, the adviser is proof against accusations of irresponsibility. In appearing to guard your back, he is also guarding his own – one of the first principles of City conduct. It is your money – make your own rules. But think about it first.

In practice, many first-time investors are looking for an out-and-out punt. The last thing they want is some boring name from the glorious past of British industry, paying a predictable dividend that barely keeps pace with inflation. Many such shares have come under terrible pressure in the nineties. And they would never suit the kind of players who want to treat the Stock Exchange as a glorified casino. There is nothing against either approach. Put all of your cash on the red if you wish. Just understand what you are doing. If you lose the lot, there is no one to blame but yourself.

Someone Else Knows More

If you win, hallelujah! Just do not get carried away by it. Never believe that you have found the winning formula. That is a way to disaster. One winner and you will be entering the most testing time of your new-found career as an investor. You will know just enough to think you can do it – but not remotely sufficient to understand that you will never know quite as much as you really need to know.

Be sure. Someone, somewhere always knows more than you do. The Guinness scandal gave a glimpse of what the big boys were up to as a matter of routine. That came to light as a result of an American insider trading scandal which revealed ace market player Ivan Boesky as merely the spider at the centre of a web of privileged information, a cheat buying knowledge illegally. We have our own mini-Boeskys, make no mistake. They understand the market better than you, they can get more information than you, and they know far better how to use it. They will gobble you up if ever you cross their path.

Everyone Has An Angle

Cynical? Perhaps. Cynicism is an essential tool for every investor. There is very little certainty about investment – but you can be absolutely sure that everyone you deal with has an angle. Brokers want to earn commission from doing your trades, to feed on what you know. Bankers want to earn from you, lend you money. Tip sheets want you to subscribe to them, and some may have other reasons for recommending the shares they do. Company directors want you to believe in them so that you will help promote their shares. Investment authors want you to buy their books. And so on.

Look for the angle. It might suit you very well, might do you good if everyone is pulling in the same direction to get the share price higher. Often the angles will be too well concealed for you to spot them. But they will be there. Always ask yourself what is in it for you – and for the other fellow? That is a crucial investment rule.

CHAPTER THREE

Where To Start

There is very little you need to know if you want to invest in the stockmarket: the name of a share to buy, the name of a bank, stockbroker, building society or share shop to buy it for you, and how to write the cheque to pay for the shares themselves, and for the dealing fees which come along with them. Some of the brokers I know would be happy to take used fivers in a carrier bag. The virgin investor can score by luck alone. One newspaper proved it by opening the back pages of the *Financial Times* and throwing darts. This 'Bull's Eye Portfolio' beat one picked by City experts, supposedly skilled in the art of share selection. Goodness knows what happened to the shares picked by the newspaper's own tipsters.

In fairness, we have had some great years and some embarrassing moments on the *Daily Mail* with the convention that we should pick 'Shares Of The Year' or some such nonsense. All of the papers seem to do it, regardless of whether the people who do the picking can distinguish a share from an expense sheet. If you should ever read such things, take them with a pinch of salt. Pointing blindfold at a share list might be better. Of course, you are just as likely – rather more likely – to come an absolute cropper by relying on luck alone. Or perhaps by kidding yourself that you do have a little understanding. That can be lethal. We all get it wrong sometimes. It takes real application to search out a whole portfolio of obscure non-starters. Yet some apparently sensible people manage it, usually with the prompting of some share pushing telephone adviser, a new friend who assures them he can put them on to a winner. And then churns them in and out of a succession of duds. I shudder when I get the letters. Happily, I have helped put an end to a few of the villains, though they keep creeping back.

These days, too, there are many people with a tidy little portfolio made up of privatisation issues. Most have done reasonably well. Share trading looks simple and relatively low-risk to such folk. Do not be fooled. When the Government wants to rig the market in your favour, it can. Privatisations are the exceptions. Most investments do not work nearly so well. Much of the time, the market is slanted heavily against the small player, and leaning more that way each day.

Do not let it put you off. Just be alive to the reality. Once that is understood, you only really need to know as much about the City and share investment as you feel you want to. You are never likely to master it all. After 36 years of financial journalism, I am still learning. Every so often, I make terrible misjudgements. And I keep stumbling across things I never knew, and things that I will never understand. It does me good, I tell myself. If ever I should think I have mastered it all, next stop the funny farm – or the workhouse. If you want to play your hunches, back the tips you get at your local, or from your favourite newspaper, good luck. It might work. Nothing in my book says you cannot or should not take a gamble, so long as you can afford it, and realise that is what you are doing. The more you know about what you are doing, though, the more comfortable you should be. And it will be more fun. Certainly a working knowledge of the stockmarket will swing the investment odds in your favour. You know the old line – the more you work, the luckier you get.

Try to be realistic about it. Your knowledge and experience will be limited, but you may be able to see things others miss – or you may simply get lucky. It is easy to be intimidated by the City. The air of

mystery and tradition, money and power, spiced with a dash of the old
school tie and the gentleman's club can appear distinctly off-putting. The
atmosphere lingers on despite the overseas invasion which followed the
change in Stock Exchange rules in the Big Bang of October 1986. The
rise of the meritocracy and the computer-literate number-crunchers has
not killed off all of the old ways. The odd top hat still surfaces, and one
or two magnificently sombre wood-panelled offices survive to house
the senior partners – though these days they may be old rooms
transported to nasty new buildings. A man in a pink frock-coat still
guards the doors of the Bank of England.

The splendid tradition may cling on, gently emphasising the divisions
between them and us. They, it appears, are steeped in generations of
money matters, born with an inherent understanding of such things. The
rest of us may try, but can never attain quite the same eminence. That
image is less evident these days. Instead we have the legend of the razor
sharp traders, glued to screens which give them instant information so
that they can use superior skills to make – or lose – millions in an instant.
Or there are the 'rocket scientists', people who can operate computer
programmes of such complexity that no mere mortal could keep pace.
And they work alongside a bunch of the wannabe Leesons, lads who live
on their wits to trade vast fortunes of company cash, and try to keep one
step ahead of disaster. Whatever the type, they all appear far too lethal for
the average investor to approach.

Do not fall for it. There are brilliant minds in the City. And there are
street-smart traders who could fool you in a flash. But sometimes they
make the most remarkable mistakes. From time to time, I stop and
wonder at the audacity which allows me to attack the most eminent
money men or industrialists in print. I may have access to other highly-
experienced people to help reinforce my ideas, but what do I know when
set against such worthies? Then I remind myself of what has gone before,
of the massive mistakes we have all seen in so many great enterprises – or,

perhaps, of the folly which kept us so long and foolishly in the transparently absurd Exchange Rate Mechanism, and then cost the nation billions of pounds as we were turfed out of it in September 1992. The Government and those clever chaps in the Treausury got it so absurdly wrong, when any fool could see it made little sense. We are still waiting for the apology.

Undue deference does not pay. The big names in the City and business are not always right. Listen to what they say, but make up your own mind. There are fewer fifth generation fools in the City than there used to be, but some survive. And there are a few crooks and chancers. Alongside them are hundreds of thousands of ordinary people doing ordinary jobs, as liable as all of us to get a little muddled now and then.

In a way, the most intimidating aspect now is the techno-flash reliance on computers and figures. Those so-called 'rocket scientists' who devise computer programmes to determine the value of this, that and the other are way beyond my comprehension.

It does not matter. Sometimes it becomes clear for all to see that what they are doing does not amount to a row of beans. They may make a fortune for themselves and their companies. But every so often, it goes badly wrong, gets out of control, and Barings Bank comes crashing down. In the real world, there are so many variables that sometimes it is impossible to reduce them to arithmetical formulae. Reality sometimes swipes them from behind. The figures may look right, but the answer is all wrong. More than once I have heard about an elaborate programme which guarantees a sure-fire profit. It always works – until it smashes into that freak, one in a million chance. Then everyone is wiped out.

Then there are the people who shade the truth, all the way from little white lies to grim black crookery and thievery. Events at the Lloyd's insurance market and recent court cases may have made it appear that the City is full of con-men, simply concerned with robbing everyone blind. It is not so. Most of the City is tolerably honest. But business is business.

Be Sure It Makes Sense

What really matters to you is whether the things you are concerned with make sense to you. Nothing else counts. IF YOU DO NOT UNDERSTAND IT, DO NOT DO IT.

Money men have an angle. They want to sell you something. They may be leading you up the garden path, they may be lost themselves, or they may be guiding you to investment heaven. But if you cannot follow every step of the way, forget it. Never hesitate to ask them to slow down, go back, and start again. The instant you get lost, stop them – and make them explain it all over again.

NEVER, NEVER, NEVER, LET ANYONE BLIND YOU WITH FIGURES. NEVER BE AFRAID TO APPEAR AN ABSOLUTE IDIOT. If you do not understand, keep asking until you do. If you cannot get to grips with it, you have found your answer. It is not for you.

Trust yourself. You will be the loser if you get it wrong. If you allow yourself to be blinded by jargon that you do not understand, but did not query for fear of looking foolish, who is the real fool? It will be you, and it will be your money that has gone.

Do not hesitate. Of course, there will be things that you will genuinely be unable to understand. Nothing wrong with that. Leave them to the experts. Be sure, though. There will sometimes be things you will not quite be able to grasp – because that is exactly what is meant to happen. Respectable City houses spend a great deal of time and trouble on the way their documents are worded. Often they have drafts galore, considered carefully by committees, changed again and again. Sentences are rarely sloppily worded by mistake, rarely obscure without a reason. If there is something which does not quite seem right to you, you may well have spotted the flaw which the wording was intended to conceal, to gloss over. Do not feel stupid if you do not understand. You may be slow on the uptake. Or you may be quite the opposite. You may have spotted the catch.

55

Above all, the investment game should be simple common sense. STICK TO WHAT YOU UNDERSTAND. Ask the questions which seem sensible to you – and make sure you get answers you feel comfortable with. Otherwise, walk away.

The Language Of The Market

Any sensible investor will recognise, of course, that you need to be able to understand the basics before you can ask the right questions. If some of the vocabulary seems off-putting, do not worry. You will grow used to it. If some of the arithmetic appears a problem, never mind. You rarely need do the sums yourself. You can almost always find the answer somewhere, or get someone to provide it. Most of the answers are readily available – in newspapers, investment magazines, and on the electronic information services which your stockbroker or banker should have at their fingertips.

If calculating a price/earnings ratio sounds tricky, look it up, or ask someone. It is in the share price table carried by many leading newspapers. What matters about the price/earnings ratio – as in all City sums – is what it tells you, not whether you can work it out yourself.

What Is A Share?

To start at the very beginning of the investment jargon game, you need to know what is a share. Easy. Exactly what it says. A share is a piece of paper which represents a part of a business. Say four people get together, and each puts £25 into a business. That company will have £100 capital invested in it. Each of the four investors will have a one quarter share of the business. They can slice the shares up any way they wish – each of the four can have one £25 share, or 25 shares of £1, or 50 shares of 50p. And so it goes. All public companies work roughly that way, but bigger. They have millions of shares, each one entitling the holder to one equal part of the company. The more shares you have, the bigger your stake in the company.

People frequently use 'stocks' and 'shares' interchangeably. Strictly speaking, stocks are securities which earn a fixed rate of interest, whereas dividends on shares can rise and fall. Some shares are actually called stock units. There is no practical difference. Stocks or shares, the description does not really matter.

Nominal Value

British Telecom is one of our biggest public companies. It has shares with a nominal value of just 25p each. Nominal, or par value does not matter much. It is simply the face value a company chooses to put on the shares – an accounting convention. In UK companies, nominal value is usually between 1p and £1. All UK companies, by law, must have a nominal value, though American companies often have shares with no par value.

A company can just as easily issue capital of £100,000 in 100,000 shares with a par value of £1 each as it can 10,000,000 shares with 1p par value. The par or nominal value means nothing in itself. A share with a 1p nominal value is not necessarily worth 1p, just as a share with £1 nominal value may not be worth £1. Shares are worth what someone will pay for them – the market price – and nothing else.

Do not be put off good shares because they have a par value of say, 5p, and a price of 120p. Conversely, do not think you have found a bargain by paying 5p for a share with a nominal value of £1. In practice, the main significance of par or nominal value lies in calculating what dividend you actually get.

Dividends

Dividends are the equivalent to the rate of interest you get on your share. They are usually described as so many pence per share, or expressed as a percentage of the nominal or par value of the shares. A 10% dividend means you are paid 10p a share on shares with a nominal value of £1. If your shares have a nominal value of 10p, then the 10% dividend is worth 1p a share. It is just an arithmetical device, nothing more. Most shares are called Ordinary shares (or equities), and produce dividends that are decided by the board of directors. Broadly speaking, these rise or fall as profits rise or fall, though there is no set rule. Dividends are normally paid twice a year, usually as an interim dividend (normally the smaller payment), and as a final dividend (often larger, and sent after the profits for the full year are known). There is often quite a long delay – sometimes months – between dividends being announced and the actual cheques being sent to shareholders.

Fixed-Interest Capital

Companies have several forms of capital other than Ordinary shares. Most are paid a fixed rate of dividend, or interest. As compensation, they usually have first claim on profits, so their dividend can be viewed as safer than Ordinary dividends. If a company goes bust, normally the fixed-interest capital will have a greater claim on the assets than the Ordinary shares, so fixed interest holders stand a better chance of getting something back. Fixed-interest capital is normally most attractive to those seeking higher income, and might be ignored for capital gains purposes in normal circumstances, though I touch later on capital growth opportunities. The most widely traded forms of fixed-interest capital are preference stocks, loan stocks, and convertible loan stocks.

Contract Notes And Share Certificates

As soon as your broker or banker tells you they have bought, you are the legal owner of your shares. The City's motto is "My word is my bond".

Although that bond may sometimes look a little grubby, the system honours it. The contract note is what you get from your broker or banker giving the details of what has been bought or sold, the price, commission and other charges. It is legal proof of ownership, so you need to keep it safe. You will have to refer to it when compiling your capital gains table for your tax return. A few weeks later, you may be sent a share certificate by the registrars acting for the company whose shares you have bought. Ask your broker or banker to chase it up if you do not recieve your certificate within two months.

Nominee Accounts

Sadly, the Stock Exchange continues to be shoved about by the big investors, and to reshape systems for their convenience. Inevitable, really. As part of this, they are moving towards abolishing share certificates. The Exchange wasted hundreds of millions of pounds on a computer system called Taurus to try to do this. Many reckon it cost one Exchange chief executive his job. Then the Bank of England took over with something called Crest. This is being made to work, and now covers virtually all share deals. It means that, mostly, investors will only get share certificates if they ask for them. You may have to pay extra for the privilege. Most share certificates are being phased out, to be replaced by entries on a computer system.

This is part of a modernisation scheme which has speeded up the way the stockmarket settles bills. The old account system of two-week periods in which no one paid, but settled bills ten days after the end of the account, has gone. Now deals are supposed to be settled up five days after buying or selling – known as T plus five. In fact, many brokers and clients prefer to deal on ten day settlement – T plus ten. That allows everyone a little more time to sort things out. There are variations on this. You may be able to deal for payment 25 days later – T plus 25 – if you agree to pay extra, though sometimes you might not have to pay more. This rush to settle means that brokers increasingly worry that investors will not be able to send them share certificates and cheques in time to settle. So they are nudging investors into nominee accounts. These are accounts operated by the brokers, holding the shares in the name of the account – the nominee account. Usually, companies send dividends and such to these nominee accounts, not to the individual holders of the shares. Because the nominee accounts lump all of the holders of a particular share into one account at each broker, that often means the nominee account will send only one copy of company documents to that account, though the account may represent hundreds of investors.

This absurdity means that the broker has to make an extra effort to get copies of documents for each individual client whose shares are registered in the nominee name. Some brokers do, others do not. Many charge for doing it. So if your shares are registered in a nominee account – at your broker's request – you may have to pay extra to your broker if you want to see the report and accounts the company sends out each year. And you might well find it difficult and expensive to get permission to attend the company's meeting. You may also find it well-nigh impossible to gain the right to vote at them.

It is an appalling system which runs directly counter to all political pretence at wanting a nation of responsible shareholders exercising their rights, exerting a restraining influence on greedy company bosses, and so on. It could easily be remedied by a small change in the law allowing all nominee accounts to pass through the names of individual investors so that they retain all of the rights they have if they were registered as private individual shareholders. If you plan to be an active investor, insist on shares being registered in your own name, even if it costs a little more.

Nominee accounts also have another, more unsettling problem. Though most brokers will have structured their systems to ensure that nominee accounts are covered by the Investors Compensation Scheme (more of that later), that might not always apply. So if something goes wrong in the nominee account, you could find it hard to prove title to all of your shares. And, at the very least, you are likely to face months of uncertainty while the muddle is sorted out.

Nominee accounts, then, are an impudent imposition upon small investors. I have emphasised the drawbacks. In truth, if you choose a sensible broker, you should have few real worries about the security of your shares. Many brokers now carry insurance against mishaps which far exceeds the miserly cover under the Investors Compensation Scheme. If you deal in a Personal Equity Plan, you are likely to be forced to use a nominee account, whatever.

The Company Calendar

Each company has a calendar, dates on which it makes big set-piece announcements through the year. The most important cover the interim profit statement, and the preliminary results for the full year. You cannot count on either of these crucial statements being sent to you as a shareholder. Though most companies post a copy of their interim statement to shareholders, it goes out several days after the contents have been announced to the Stock Exchange. In theory, all investors should be treated equally. Companies are not allowed to give advance knowledge of the contents of any significant announcements to anyone. Impeccable as the theory may be, the practice is very different. Some investors are more equal than others, and have gained in influence since Big Bang in 1986. Company announcements are sent first to a Stock Exchange department. There they are checked, processed, and flashed around the City on sophisticated and costly electronic communications systems. All of the big investment houses, the brokers and such, have them. So the City gets any company news the instant it is released, and can buy and sell long before the small shareholder gets a whiff of what is happening. Individual investors have to wait, and wait. The Oracle system available on Teletext TV screens speeds access up a little, but it is a poor substitute for the City screens. There is also Market-Eye, another relatively costly TV screen service which brings news and prices. The expensive 0898 telephone systems are way behind. The whole unsatisfactory system is becoming even more confused. In the name of greater competition, the Government has ruled that company announcements should now also be sent to news systems which compete with the Stock Exchange. In some cases, this gives a different set of subscribers the first bite at sensitive information.

Hopefully, it will all settle down after a while. The Stock Exchange is working on various systems, and there is an increasing number of sources available to those with personal computers. By the time this book is published, there should be some reasonably efficient access systems available on the Internet, the global computer network. To get to that, of course, you need to spend £600 to £1,000 on computer hardware, subscribe to an access provider (£10 or more a month), and pay for telephone time (generally local calls now, but check before you sign up to the Net). Then you will need to study how to work it all. Almost all company news items are sent to the newspapers, though increasingly bad news is not always fully circulated, or is sent late in the day when papers might miss it. Whatever happens, there is no guarantee that news of your company will appear. The *Daily Mail*, for example, comments only on what it considers the most interesting items. The *Financial Times* publishes almost everything, sometimes two or three days late. For the private investor, it is hit or miss. Only in the unusual event of a company posting news overnight, and delaying any announcement until the start of share dealings on the following morning is there anything like equal access to information.

Interim Reports

When you get your interim report, it will carry an estimate of profits for the first half of the trading year, plus the amount of any interim dividend. There may also be a short comment on progress. As with any normal company profits announcement, most of the news will have been forecast by stockbrokers who follow the company, so the City knows what to expect. Only a real surprise will move the share price much. Quite often, prices fall on good news. It will have been anticipated by the City backroom boys who bought ahead of the figures. Unless there is something extra special, they will have taken their profits well before any news reaches you. In practice, many companies also quietly tip off their City friends. It is considered bad form to surprise your big shareholders. Tiny Rowland did it early in 1992, and attracted a terrible fuss when Lonrho cut the dividend, even though over half the City had hated him for two decades. If a company finance director sees City expectations are out of line, someone will quietly ring the company's brokers. Or maybe there will be a cosy dinner or lunch. A nod and a wink will ensure that the real position is conveyed. I was horrified to spot a blatant example of this one year at ultra-respectable Tate & Lyle, the sugar giant, with brokers gently downgrading profit forecasts just a fortnight after the annual meeting. The company had let some brokers know of a few problems, without a word to the mass of shareholders at the annual meeting – the ideal time to do it.

Brokers often submit their own profit forecasts to companies – just as a matter of courtesy and to see that they have not made any silly mistakes, you understand. Companies can then nudge the forecasts into position. Do the brokers and their privileged clients buy or sell as a result of this sort of information? You bet they do.

Quite how this nod-and-a-wink fiddle squares with treating all investors equally is beyond me. Some companies do not do it, and more are beginning to think hard about it. But most play this not-quite-insider game. You are a small shareholder? You didn't realise the brokers were changing their forecasts? No one told you? Too bad, old chap. The authorities are beginning to sit up and take notice of this abuse, and generated quite a little storm in the summer of 1998. Normal City form suggests that there could be changes to the system in theory. In reality, the news will still somehow reach the right people when it suits them.

Preliminary Profits

The most important announcement is that of preliminary profits for the year. It is not usually sent to investors, because it is normally followed a few weeks later by the report and accounts. They are called 'preliminary' profits – or 'prelims' – because they may technically not be fully certified by the auditors, though there is unlikely to be any further change.

The full report and accounts can be anything from a slim 20-page black and white job to a glossy affair with 60 pages or more, full of colour photographs. There may be a statement of company philosophy, and perhaps a few special offers of cut-price company products. Glossiness does not necessarily denote investment merit. In fact, it may mean quite the opposite.

The Annual Meeting

The accounts must carry at least three weeks' notice of the time and place of the annual meeting. All Ordinary shareholders (if they are not screwed up in nominee accounts) are entitled to attend, ask questions, and vote on half a dozen routine proposals. You can vote even if you do not go along. Companies must send out proxy cards, allowing you to post your vote if you wish. In most companies, there is one vote for each share. The votes will normally cover the election or re-election of a few directors (some stand for re-election every few years), and will probably seek permission to issue new shares without consulting shareholders. There will be a motion approving payment of the dividend, and allowing the board to decide the pay of the auditors – daft, since the auditors in theory report to the shareholders, not the board. The chairman may well say something about current trading. Sometimes that will be circulated to shareholders, and to the press. But if you skip the meeting, you may miss whatever has been said. Usually, it will not be of great consequence. Just sometimes, though, there is high drama. Many companies post their final dividend cheques a few days after the annual meeting. Remember, as a shareholder the theory is that you own a piece of the company, and the directors are employed to manage it on behalf of the shareholders. If you do not like the way things are being done, you are entitled to write to the chairman and tell him so. Sensible letters deserve sensible replies. Usually they get them. If they do not, there is little you can do, except sell your shares – or, in extreme cases, tell the *Daily Mail*. In practice, individual shareholders are something of a nuisance, to be tolerated. But most companies have the sense to go through the motions. And some really do care.

CHAPTER FOUR

Why Shares Rise And Fall

Share prices rise because there are more buyers than sellers. They fall when there are more sellers than buyers. That is the standard, half-mocking City reply to the classic question about what makes shares move. The chap giving the answer might have no more idea of what is really going on than the questioner. His answer is correct, but it tells you very little. He does not want to reveal what he knows – or what he does not know. So in grand City style, he bundles it up in a bit of a joke.

Quite often, though, you can unearth no better explanation. Share prices frequently appear to move for no reason, pure chance. In reality, that is not so. There is always a reason. It may not be terribly significant. But you do not know it. If you are in the shares, or about to buy them, it makes you money – or costs you.

So the joke might not be so funny. Do not get caught like the City smarties. ADMIT YOUR IGNORANCE to yourself. No good pretending you know something you do not, then risking your money on it.

Perhaps much of the price move was due largely to chance of a sort. The people who actually shift share prices are the market-makers – the City's share wholesalers – though from autumn 1997 something called SETS has been jerking prices of the top shares around. We will get to explaining that later. Before Big Bang, the market-makers used to be called jobbers, and worked rather differently. Now there are as many as 15 market-makers in some shares, all undertaking to set prices and buy or sell quantities of that share. The prices they will trade at appear on screens throughout the City, with an indication of the number of shares for which the listed prices hold good. For larger deals, they are entitled to change prices, though for the SETS stocks, these rules have been set aside. Each one watches the competition, and moves prices in accordance with what his rivals are doing. In most shares, there are two or three leading market-makers, who set the trends which most others follow. So they play follow-my-leader.

It could be that the leading market-maker in one share decided he was not generating enough business. So he knocked the price down to see if he could attract buyers. Other market-makers might follow him down. To keep his price advantage, the first one might cut again.

The price has fallen. From the outside, it looks as if something must have happened. Not so. It may even be that no shares have changed hands. The story will rarely be quite as simple as that, but it could be – especially in the shares of smaller companies, where there are only two or three market-makers, and one is dominant. Sometimes the price could change for reasons which appear to make even less sense. Perhaps the market-maker had a bad morning – he could not finish *The Times* crossword, the train was late again, and he tripped leaving the lift. In a foul mood, he sees the pound looking weak, so he lowers the price of all of the shares on his book, just in case something happens. After lunch, he feels better, and the pound is steadier. Since no one has come in to buy and give him business at his lower prices, he leaves them where they are. His bad mood could have wiped millions of pounds off the share value of the companies concerned, for no real reason. Too bad. It may seem grossly unfair to the small investor, hanging on every move in price. The company may be trading better and better, but the shares are drifting down. The two things are not necessarily linked. It is no good complaining. NO ONE EVER SAID THE CITY HAD TO BE FAIR.

The title of this book was chosen quite carefully. It IS a jungle for small investors. All too often they get gobbled up because they think there are clear rules which everyone plays by. You only need to find the real system, the one the biggest names or the most famous tipsters use, and you can be sure of making money. Forget it. Self-interest is the only rule which is honoured consistently.

Self-Interest Rules, OK?

Self-interest explains the kind of general move which often costs private investors dearly when the market is dull. Trying to generate some interest in trading, market-makers frequently lower prices when business is quiet, and the mood depressed. They also reduce the number of shares they are ready to trade at their listed prices. It makes sense. Most market-makers will actually be holding some shares. They make their money from the difference between the price at which they buy, and the price for which they sell. Any shares they actually hold tie up money, often borrowed money. If they can shift shares quickly by making a small cut in prices, they will, especially if the market is falling. The quicker they trade shares on, the less interest they pay on their borrowings, and the less danger of being caught out by a big fall if the market is hit by bad news. At other uncertain times, they cut prices in the hope of avoiding having to buy more shares – unless they see the chance of selling quickly at a profit. So in dull periods, the instinct is to lower prices and trade in fewer shares. If depression hangs around for some time, prices can be marked down gently but regularly. In smaller company shares, that can mean savage falls over, say, three months, without any change in the underlying fortunes of the company. Or many shares actually being sold.

The reverse tends to happen, of course, in good times. Market-makers are quick to raise prices when demand is good, so they can take a bigger margin between what they buy for and the price they sell at. Few shareholders complain about the laws of the jungle then.

On top of all of this, of course, there are all kinds of games between tough traders competing in a business where large amounts of money change hands. Stockbrokers are always trying to guess how many shares the market-makers actually hold. If, for example, it appears that market-makers are short of stock (do not hold much) they could be caught out by a rush of buying. Because market-makers are usually obliged to deal in the size and price they quote on their screens, they could be forced to sell shares they do not have. If that happens, they will try to raise prices sharply, to encourage people to sell to them quickly, and fill the hole. Otherwise, they might find prices are forced still higher against them, and eventually have to pay much more to buy the shares they have promised to deliver.

There are many variations on this theme. Sometimes market-makers will set prices sharply lower, especially if there has been a buying rush in a particular share. Shaking the tree is what many market folk call it. The market-makers might actually have sold more shares than they own, and the rise in prices might be costing them a fortune as they buy in shares they have already committed to sell at lower prices. You might think that they would push prices up quickly, to get extra shares to supply the buyers, and anyone holding those shares might see a quick profit. On the contrary. Sometimes, the market-makers hammer the price, hoping to panic the gamblers and force them to sell cheaply. So an excess of buying can actually have the effect of pushing the price down, in the short term at least.

There are many such variations, where logic appears to be turned on its head. And that is without touching on what many feel often become wholesale attempts at manipulation by some houses, often linked to positions in the futures market or the options market. No way to run a stockmarket, wiping millions off the value of public companies because of nasty little games among the professionals? Crazy and irresponsible? Perhaps. Obviously the system is imperfect. It always has been. It is getting worse. The individual investor cannot hope to keep pace with all that goes on. If you are going to play, resign yourself to the inevitable. There is always the chance that you will get caught out by some price move which appears to make no sense. The unexpected is always lurking in the background, ready to catch you out.

What Ought To Make Prices Move

Do not become discouraged. There are certain fairly clearly defined basic factors which do influence prices. You can get by without knowing them all, but it is wise to have some idea. You need to learn how to use that to your advantage. So it makes sense to be aware of the sort of rules the other investors think they are using. No rule is absolutely reliable, and it may not always have the impact you expect. As we have seen with the example of shaking the tree, if you give it a little thought, you can turn many of the rules on their head – a sort of game of bluff, and double-bluff for want of a better description.

In the end, though, it is simple. You want to buy shares in a company which is doing well, and will do better. Rising profits generate increased dividends which attract investors who seek higher income. Along the way, that brings capital gains.

It is difficult to know where to start if you are trying to assess how well a company may be placed. Each year, every company must send out an annual report and accounts. It is of limited value, because it is largely historical, a fuzzy snapshot of what the company looked like on the final day of the last trading year. Share prices are all about what is going to happen next. But studying the past gives you a firm base, a starting point, and can yield valuable clues to the future. Even if you are not a shareholder, most companies will send you a copy of their most recent accounts, if you write to the company secretary at the registered office, ring their investor relations office, or even visit their web site on the

Internet. It is a good idea to visit their web site, even if you do not want a copy of the report and accounts.

The report and accounts is split into several main sections; the chairman's statement; the directors' report; the profit and loss account; the balance sheet; the statement of the source and application of funds (or the cash flow statement); the auditors' report; the notes.

The Chairman's Statement

The chairman's statement may be accompanied by a separate report from the managing director, or chief executive (usually simply different titles for the chap who actually runs the company). Some companies publish reports from managers of individual sectors of the business. These may provide an idea of how things look in the current year, and perhaps a useful feel of what the company actually does. Note the names of the operating companies (there is usually a full list near the back of the report). Often the names bear little relationship to the name on your share certificate. Great Universal Stores, for example, owns Burberrys, Times Furnishing, and mail order giants like Marshall Ward. Did you realise that Hanson used to own Imperial Tobacco, Ever Ready Batteries, and London Brick? Posh-sounding Grand Metropolitan owns Burger King. Now Grand Metropolitan and Guinness are merged into daft-sounding Diageo. Zeneca used to be part of ICI (the plant protection and pharmaceuticals part). If you identify the actual operating companies, you may see them around, and be better able to judge the complete picture of what is going on in the company as a whole.

The Directors' Report

The directors' report deals briefly with what the company does, outlines changes in structure – e.g. sales or purchases of major parts of the business – and lists how many shares the directors own (have a beneficial interest in), and how many they look after as trustees (non-beneficial). It may show what options they have to buy shares, though these are often detailed in the notes now. It should also show any changes since the previous accounts, and may detail moves between the end of the year and publication of the report. In addition, it should list anyone holding more than 3% of the shares.

Obviously it is worth checking to see what the directors have been doing with their shares, and whether they control the company. A holding of 50% or more obviously gives them complete control, but over 30% can usually be regarded as effective control. A stake of this size diminishes the chances of a hostile takeover bid, unless some outsider also has 29.9% – which means a bid could be in the offing. If there are several outsiders with more than 3%, or someone is building up a share stake, there is more chance of a bid.

The Profit And Loss Account

People often confuse the profit and loss account and the balance sheet. The p and l deals with how the company has traded through the year, and whether it has made any money. The balance sheet shows what the company owns and had available to use to make that money.

All of the p and l figures show a comparison with the previous trading period, which gives a crude indication of how the fortunes of the company have been moving. Obviously, a rising trend is encouraging, but it is important to check the notes to see that there have been no exceptional factors to influence any change. Most items have a number next to them, indicating which note gives further details. The p and l account shows how the profit or loss for the last trading year was made up. The top line is usually turnover, revenue or sales (effectively the same thing). Then comes the cost of sales – a hefty figure that covers all the normal costs of running a business. If it rises by a smaller proportion than sales, then there is a bigger increase in the next line, the trading (or gross) profit. What comes next varies. It may be the share of profits or losses from related companies – businesses the main company does not own completely. Part of their profit will have to be knocked off the main company's total, because this belongs to the other shareholders in that business. If the partly-owned companies made losses, there will be a credit to the main company, representing the share of losses to be borne by outside shareholders. These items are often called minority interests. There may also be an item for other expenses. That may include staff costs and depreciation. The depreciation represents a figure knocked off each year for wear and tear on premises, machinery, fittings and such. In theory, it is set aside to cover the cost of replacing these items when they are worn out.

Then there will be a line showing interest charges or credits. And perhaps the contribution to the employee profit-sharing scheme, if such exists. Below that, you have pre-tax profit, the figure most widely quoted by the press.

It is not the most important figure. Net profit, struck after paying tax and meeting any dividends on preference capital (if there is any) fills that role. Because of capital allowances, past losses, profits in low tax areas, and so on, the tax charge might well be below the figure you might normally expect. There is always some debate over whether analysts should apply a theoretical full tax charge so that they can compare like with like when looking at different companies. Nowadays, however, general practice is to take whatever the company says, leaving perhaps a query in the back of your mind. Net profits show what is available to pay dividends, and the next line in the accounts often gives the actual cost of paying whatever dividend the directors recommend. In practice, dividends do not always cost what accounts say, but that need not bother you. What is left after paying dividends is available to be transferred to reserves, where it can be used to expand the business. The bigger the reserves, the better, so long as shareholders get a decent dividend. Some companies then show earnings per share, one of the most widely-used figures in the investment world. This is calculated by dividing the profits after tax and preference dividends (sometimes known as net profits attributable to Ordinary shareholders) by the number of Ordinary shares in issue. Be careful. Issued capital will be listed in the notes, but do distinguish between authorised capital (how many shares the company could issue) and issued capital (how many shares it has actually issued). Take an example of how to calculate earnings per share (widely abbreviated to eps). Assume that after tax and preference dividends, the company has net profits of £500,000, and it has one million shares in issue. That company has earnings per share of 50p. Divide earnings per share into the share price, and you arrive at the price/earnings ratio. Say the shares sell at 450p, the price/earnings ratio would be 9 (450p divided by 50p).

The price/earnings ratio – often simply called the p/e ratio – is the most widely-used of all investment measurements. Sometimes it is expressed in different ways – people talk about a share selling at so many times earnings, or so many years' earnings. It is the same old p/e ratio. Effectively, it shows you how many years it would take the company to earn net profits equal to the stockmarket value of the company.

You will not find the p/e ratio in the annual report. It would be misleading to put it there, because it depends on the share price, which is liable to change at any moment. As the shares rise, the p/e rises. As they fall, so the p/e ratio falls.

The Balance Sheet

The next major section of the report and accounts is the balance sheet. This displays what the company owned and owed on the last day of the trading year (companies can choose their own dates for trading years).

The assets are listed first. There are fixed assets: land, buildings, plant and machinery, and so on.

Next come current assets: investments, stocks, cash, and debtors (the money owed to the company). The bigger the assets, the better. Check the date on which the fixed assets were last valued. Though the slump of the late eighties and early nineties caused problems, it could be that the true value of property is understated if there has not been a revaluation in recent years. Look at plant, machinery and stock values still more sceptically. Outdated plant and machinery may not be saleable at the balance sheet value, and if a company gets caught with a lot of stock that has declined in value, that is a problem. A higher stock position could well be bad news, rather than good. Perhaps the company is struggling to sell what it makes. That situation will nearly always be accompanied by a rise in the overdraft.

There will also be a figure for creditors, covering money the company has to pay out within a year. This could include overdrafts, and possibly tax bills. Subtract creditors from current assets, and you get net current assets – or net current liabilities if short-term debts exceed the quickly realisable assets. Next the balance sheet adds fixed assets and net current assets (or takes away net current liabilities). Then it subtracts other liabilities – the money the company owes but does not have to repay for a year or more. These generally include large loans that run for a fixed number of years before repayment. Take one from the other, and you have the net asset value of the business, the price you would, in theory, get if you shut up and sold out. The greater the excess of assets over liabilities, the richer the company, especially if assets are strong in cash or saleable property. Be careful, though. Strong asset value might not always indicate a healthy company. If a high proportion of the value is in fixed assets which might not easily be sold, the business could run out of cash – especially if there are large fixed loans which must be repaid in the near future.

Beneath this is a section showing how it is all financed, through capital and reserves. There will be the amount of paid-up share capital, covering the preference shares and Ordinary shares in issue, at their nominal value. Then there are reserves, the sums left over through the years from profits after tax and dividends. Put them together, and they are known as shareholders' funds.

Increasingly, investors are coming to appreciate the importance of not allowing debt to grow too high, and so they watch the proportion of debt to shareholders' funds. That is called gearing. The higher the gearing, or the proportion of borrowing, the more investors worry. It means the company will have to earmark much more revenue to pay out interest, leaving less for dividends and for growth. And there is the worry of how that debt is eventually going to be paid back.

If a company hits trouble, gearing assumes particular importance. Loans are usually extended under elaborate agreements with the lenders, dictating that the loans must be repaid if certain ratios are hit. Though such details are not made public, they can be vital. They have triggered regular crises at Eurotunnel, for example, year after year as revenue has failed to meet undertakings given to the bankers, or other targets agreed in confidence have been missed. The lenders will always have a claim on company assets before anything is repaid to investors. At Eurotunnel, there has been quite a stand-off. The banks do not want to take over the assets and run the tunnel, but the company has struggled to generate revenue enough to pay the interest on debts.

Source And Application Of Funds

All accounts carry a page dealing with the source and application of funds. This shows where the cash has come from through the year, and where it went. Coming in, there will be profits, depreciation, asset sales, and new borrowings or share issues. Going out, there will be the cost of dividends, tax, and buying companies. Obviously, it is better to see more cash coming in than going out. Using this with the balance sheet notes can often give you a clearer idea of what is actually happening. You really want to see as much cash as possible generated from trading.

The Auditors' Report

Somewhere in the company's accounts will be a modest, but vital, section – the auditors' report. This used to be a few brief lines, certifying that the financial statements gave a true and fair view of the state of affairs, and conformed to the Companies Act. Now it is much more complicated, and has more to do with auditors covering their backs than anything else. They are worried about legal action from investors or bankers if anything goes wrong, and the investors or bankers try to claim that the auditors should have spotted it. Read what the statement says. You will appreciate it is a wonderful essay in passing the buck back to the directors. Common sense might cause you to wonder why anyone should pay the auditors for such an exercise, but that is the way it works these days. A glance will normally suffice to tell you whether there is anything that the auditors consider should concern you. If it ends up saying the accounts express a true and fair view, that is probably as good as you are going to get. If it differs, watch out.

Strictly speaking, the auditors are accountants employed by the shareholders to verify that the directors are running the business in accordance with the Companies Act, and that the figures in the report and accounts are what they say they seem. There is considerable debate over just what this means, and in recent years, auditors have been encouraged to blow the whistle if they stumble across fraud. In reality, auditors interpret their responsibilities in limited fashion, and can be persuaded to accept all sorts of practices which normal people would consider outrageous. Never imagine that a clean audit report guarantees that all is well.

There are frequent moves to tighten up on audits. They may produce results. But it would be foolish to expect too much. It would certainly be wrong to suggest that a determined board could not persuade auditors to agree to practices which some might consider unusual, and wrong to suggest that they could not be fooled completely by a determined crook. Think of what Robert Maxwell got away with. So do not place too much faith in a clean audit report. Most companies which go bust have one in their last accounts. In the rare cases when auditors signal something is wrong, they do it in a stilted code. The accounts are normally presented on a going-concern basis, which means things are fine. If there is any qualification to that phrase, it can be serious.

The auditors may, for example, say that continued operation as a going concern is dependent on further finance, or on the continuation of existing support from bankers. That means the company has run out of money, and could go bust if anyone asks for their loans back. If the auditors are unable to form an opinion as to whether the accounts give a true and fair view, sell at once. They are telling you something is badly wrong.

Almost any qualification is serious, but one or two can be shrugged aside. Sometimes companies do not conform to some recommended accounting rule, and the auditors are obliged to draw attention to it. They may agree that it does not matter. If so, they will say that the accounts give a true and fair view, subject to the variation. One further point: check who the auditors are, and where they are based. Big names are by no means infallible, and there may be a potential conflict of interest if another part of the same accounting firm is supplying business advice services to the company whose accounts they are auditing. But smaller accounting firms may be more vulnerable to pressure from companies if they do not have other big name audit duties. Directors do lean on auditors, and auditors do sometimes bend. Watch out, too, if some regional branch of a big name accountant is doing the audit on a major company. Local politics may play a part in that one.

Corporate Governance

These days, there will usually be a separate section in the report dealing with corporate governance. It will almost certainly promise that the company conforms to the recommendations of the Cadbury Committee, the Greenbury Committe, or the Hampel Committee. Stock Exchange rules now require the company to say if it does not conform to whatever is the latest version of these talking shops. If it says it does not, terrific. You have found a company run by an individual with the nerve to stand up against the establishment, and do things his way. The results could be very good, or very bad. Certainly they should be more interesting than the average. The Cadbury Committee issued a whole series of ideas of how companies should be run – splitting the function of chairman and chief executive, having independent non-executive directors, and so on. It has given the big investors a little stick with which to beat company managers from time to time, and provided managers with an excuse to suggest they are doing things properly if they conform to the Cadbury code.

Sensible investors will view this stuff with something approaching contempt. It is largely red tape involving extra expense of time and money. Whenever there is a company scandal of some sort, you can be sure the previous set of accounts will have proclaimed that they were doing everything in accordance with the Cadbury code. It creates jobs for the boys, and generates fees for accountants and so on. For the serious investor, it is a mildly irritating irrelevance.

The Greenbury Committee

This is the son of Cadbury, and covers the recommendations on executive pay of a committee headed by Marks & Spencer chairman Sir Richard Greenbury. It might have helped curb the wildest excesses, but on the whole, it means less even than Cadbury. Pay little heed to whatever the company report says about conforming to Greenbury. Perhaps the directors are overpaid. But if they are doing a good job for shareholders, that is all that really matters. And Greenbury has done little to stop the pernicious practice of paying enormous golden handshakes to departing directors when they are kicked out. The rewards of failure can still be massive. The Hampel committee is the 1998 version of this stuff, combining bits of both.

Notes

Many of the really interesting items in company accounts can be unearthed from the Notes. These add a certain amount of the detail to the big figures up front. Before you get into them, read the statement of accounting policies carefully. Later in the book, dealing with creative accounting, I cover some of the tricks to watch for. One useful preliminary check, though, is to get the accounts for the year before. Compare the two statements, and look for changes. Do not imagine that a word here or there does not matter. It does. If you spot the smallest alteration, make every effort to see what it could mean. Nine times out of ten, it WILL be of consequence. These days, it will often mean that the board has found some way of presenting the figures in a slightly more flattering – or less damaging – light.Scanning the fine print of the Notes is well worthwhile. In the initial stages, you may well feel you have had more than enough from ploughing through the main parts of the report and accounts. Fair enough. As time goes by, you will appreciate what nuggets there are in the Notes.

Depreciation

This is a regular source of interest. It can be vital. Take two transport companies. Company one may write down the cost of lorries over four years, or 25% a year, setting aside a quarter of their cost against profits. Company two may write lorries off over five years, or 20% a year. Of course, company one may be able to run the lorries for five years. If their value has been written down to nil after four years, no depreciation will need to be set aside against profits in year five. Profits benefit significantly. Company two will have shown higher profits in years one to four, but will still be writing the lorries off in year five. So company two should have lower profits in that year. In the real world, things are not that simple. But you can see the scope for flexibility. One regular source of such accounting speculation has been the way security companies use depreciation. At one stage, I began to focus on one of our quoted security companies. It was not clear from the accounts just how the company treated security installations in the accounts. Competitors told me it was common practice among their companies to bundle the cost of labour and other items in with the cost of the equipment when it was installed, to count that as an addition to the value of the installation (to capitalise it), and to treat it as an extra asset in the balance sheet. Some companies would then write off that cost over ten years, providing depreciation equal to 10% of the capitalised cost each year. My company, it appeared from the accounts, wrote some installations off over 14 or 15 years, thus knocking only perhaps 7% off profits each year as depreciation, not the more widely used 10%. That meant profits appeared higher.

But it also meant that when business was slack, and clients were going bust and abandoning security contracts, income from the installations stopped. No one wants a second-hand alarm system. So while the equipment (and labour) had gone into the balance sheet as an asset, it had become effectively worth nothing when the contract was abandoned. And profits would have to bear the cost of depreciation for the remainder of the 14 or 15 years, though no income was coming in

In reality, the whole question of accounting for alarm installations is vastly more complicated. It was easy to see how the fine print in the security company accounts which worried me might prompt the sceptical investor to proceed with caution.

Do not despair if it all sounds desperately complicated. As you become more familiar with the game, you will find it easier to unravel. What should be clear, however, is that there are all sorts of questions lurking in the fine print, if you can root them out. Depreciation is certainly worth watching. Obviously, in times of high inflation, some assets are losing value more quickly than before, while others are gaining it. Property and land might be rising in nominal value. But they attract modest depreciation charges anyway. The cost of replacement plant and machinery could suddenly be rising much faster than before, and depreciation rates may be lagging. Higher depreciation levels could eat into profits, and the company might not have enough cash to replace machinery when it wears out.

Check whether capital spending is above or below depreciation each year. If the annual level of capital spending is higher than depreciation, then depreciation might be expected to fall in future, allowing more revenue through to profits. But if a business is not investing for the future, can it be expected to maintain profits? There is an easy short cut to higher profits by cutting on important maintenance. What happens, for example, if a hotel chain puts off redecorating for a year or two? Profits rise at first, then perhaps fall as visitors shy away from their tatty premises. Watch especially carefully if you are in a company where research and development is important. This might be vital to a company's future. Not quite the same as depreciation, cutting it clearly offers scope for boosting short-term profits, possibly at the cost to medium-term growth.

Extraordinary And Exceptional Items

These days, hopefully, extraordinary and exceptional items are not the worry they used to be. Once tucked away in the fine print, now they should be up there in the profit and loss account, plain for all to see. They cover the one-off or unusual items which might distort the normal pattern of company profits. Make a mental note when you assess the quality of profits. Obviously, the more predictable and routinely repeatable profits are, the better they are. These higher quality profits should command a higher share price.

Sometimes it is possible to predict a big profits change because of the absence next time around of an extraordinary or exceptional item. The accounting regulators have tried to make it all much clearer. So they have, at the cost of disturbing what was sometimes a smooth pattern of profits growth. It means you do have to think a little more carefully about the nature of any profits record. But you should have been doing that anyway. The new rules make it more complicated, in that you do have to make allowances for more things. It is easier to get tangled up – but easier, too, to untangle knots you may not have realised existed before. In any event, never think you can really be sure. Anyone who wants to fool investors will probably have found a new way of hiding the truth before the regulators realise it.

Scrip Issues

Once you have worked your way through the report and accounts, and struck up a nodding acquaintance with the contents, you are well on the way towards mastering an elementary crib on the coarse art of investment analysis. There are, however, a few more items which crop up fairly frequently, and repay attention. Scrip issues are generally the most welcome. The scrip issue comes under several different names – a capitalisation issue, a share bonus, or a free scrip issue. It is sometimes called a free scrip issue because it gives out shares without asking anyone to pay for them. Strictly speaking, it is just a sophisticated piece of book-keeping. A company with a fistful of reserves transforms them into share capital, and gives them out as extra shares to the people who already own them – the shareholders.

In reality, nothing tangible is given away. All that happens is that the nominal capital increases, and everyone has more shares. The company itself is not, in theory, worth a penny more. So the share price should simply be adjusted to reflect the change in capital. If there has been a one for one bonus, giving every shareholder twice as many shares as they had before, the price should halve. Nothing gained, nothing lost.

Psychologically, though, the impact is valuable. Shareholders love it. Time and again at annual meetings, it is the one thing shareholders agree on: "Please, Mr Chairman, could we have a scrip issue?" Good luck to them. They know a good thing. News of a scrip issue usually sends shares up. They may rise again just before the new shares are sent out, then again after they have been issued. It is an important sign of corporate confidence. Take shares trading at 400p. On news of a one for one scrip issue, they might edge up to 405p. Ahead of the actual issue, they might touch 420p. After the issue, the price is halved to take account of the new shares. Then the price might rise to 215p as the lower price attracts more buyers. That means it is equivalent to 430p before it all began. Wonderful what a little paper shuffling can do. Everyone likes to feel they are getting more for their money. It seems better to buy 500 shares at 200p each than 250 at 400p, or even 100 at £10 a time. When shares get too high, the market frowns. Anything over 500p looks heavy, and heavy is not so much fun. Many investors buy only 'penny' stocks – shares selling for under £1 (a mere penny gets you nothing much these days). A scrip issue suits them. It may cut the price down to their size.

Share Splits

Sometimes companies achieve a similar effect by splitting their capital. Shares with a nominal value of £1 might be divided into two shares of

50p, or ten of 10p. Again the reality is largely cosmetic. But it leaves the shares looking more inviting to some, and that helps.

Consolidations

In the nineties, there has been a flurry of share consolidations. These are the reverse of splits. They happen mainly in companies which have hit trouble, and require a capital reconstruction. Sometimes there is a split, a reshuffle, then a consolidation. What it means is that the directors decide the price has become too low to be taken seriously. So they might consolidate ten shares into one, reducing the number of shares in issue, and multiplying the share price ten-fold. So it might go from, say, 2p to 20p. Or even from 2p to 100p if there is a 50-to-one consolidation.

Sometimes consolidations are good news, encouraging big investors to take the company more seriously. Too often, though, among tiddlers which are still recovering, it simply creates more room for the price to fall. So watch carefully. If a share is trading at 1p to 1½p, it takes big selling to push it down the next step to ¾p to 1¼p. But if there has been a 50-to-one consolidation, the price will not go up to show a spread of 50p to 75p, the equivalent to the previous middle price of 62½p. It might be 60p to 65p. Then sellers can come in and push it down to, say, 50p to 55p. Or 45p to 50p. Before you know it, your higher-priced share is actually worth less than it was in the old penny form. Be especially careful if tempted to trade as a consolidation is going on. There have been half a dozen scandalous examples where muddled or unscrupulous brokers have dealt for clients at completely the wrong price, and investors have found themselves paying 10 or 20 times more than they should have done for such shares.

Rights Issues

A rights issue is different. You have to pay for the extra shares in a rights issue. The company sells new shares to existing shareholders. It is a means of raising cash, and giving all shareholders an equal chance to join in, if they wish. The company chooses how many shares are issued, and in what proportion, depending on how much cash is being raised. It might be one for one, one for two, four for seven, or even a heavyweight three for two, where you are being asked to buy a higher proportion of shares than you already have.

In the late eighties and early nineties, rights issues proved a distinctly mixed blessing. Most were rescue efforts, pulling in desperately-needed cash to save companies from collapse. Weighed down by bank borrowings, companies turned to shareholders to give them relatively cheap new money to pay off expensive loans whose interest payments they could not keep up. In many cases, shareholders had cause to be thankful for such dubious mercies. At least the company could manage a rights call. The weakest simply went to the wall because no one would back an issue, not wanting to throw good money after bad. Not that everyone has to agree. Some shareholders are unwilling, or unable, to put up extra money. So most companies have their rights issue underwritten. For a small commission, big investors agree to subscribe for all of the new shares which other investors do not want. Normally, rights issues are priced at around 20% below the market level. If the quote should fall below the rights issue price while the issue is still open, more shareholders will turn it down, and the underwriters have to step in and take more of the shares.

A few companies do it differently. They opt to sell the new shares way below the market, at half price or less. This is called a deep discount rights issue. The shares appear cheap, and the company saves the expense of underwriting. Financially, it makes no other great difference, except that the company may end up issuing more shares on which it has to pay dividends in the future. In good times, it is a gesture of corporate confidence. In trickier times, it has been known to backfire as the shares slump towards the deeply discounted level, and it all goes wrong. When the market is reasonably calm, most rights issues are sweetened by forecasts of higher profits and dividends. That helps offset the depressing impact of more shares being thrown on to the market. If a rights issue flops, it can dog the shares for months, even years. Every time the price perks up, it will be hit by selling from underwriters seeking to get out.

Sometimes rights issues are best left alone, particularly if they look like a rescue act by the old management which got the company into trouble in the first place. New management might well be worth backing, however. Whatever, you lose little by refusing. If you do, you still have the same number of shares as before, but since there will be more in issue, you just have a proportionately smaller interest and, therefore, a slightly smaller slice of a larger cake.

If the terms of the rights issue are judged correctly, others will be willing to buy your right to the new shares. Calculating the premium on this entitlement can be complicated. Ask your broker or banker. It may be possible to sell some of your rights issue entitlement – the nil-paid shares – without laying out a penny, and use the cash that is raised to take up a smaller number of the rights shares. That way, you get something for nothing – or it feels like it.

Any broker will be able to tell you what these nil-paid rights are worth. The *Financial Times* and other papers have a section quoting such prices under 'Rights Offers'.

In reasonable markets, rights issues are generally positive moves. What you really want most is new shares from a smallish company under new management. It is a standard ploy for ambitious company promoters to buy into sleepy companies, then raise new capital by a heavy rights issue. That way they give themselves the opportunity to buy extra shares on the cheap. In the mid-nineties, it was happening more than ever. More details of how to make the best of this come later in this book.

Bigger companies do benefit from rights issues, too. The reputation and skill of the directors is what counts. The share price may take a while to settle comfortably after rights issues, but sometimes simply using the new money to pay off expensive loans can have a dramatic impact on profits. Or the money can be used to buy exciting new ventures. Be careful, though, of companies which have too many rights issues without obvious signs of growth. They may be running the business badly, and effectively passing the rights money back to shareholders in the form of dividends. All the while, they will be enlarging the number of shares in issue, creating more potential sellers, and muffling the impact of any good news on the share price.

Pre-Emption Rights

Pre-emption rights became a ticklish subject in the mid-nineties. Previously, it was held that existing shareholders should have the first call on any new shares the company wanted to issue – the right of pre-emption. Gradually, companies have begun whittling away at this, suggesting they should be able to issue new shares to anyone as they wish, without always offering them to current investors. There will be much huffing and puffing, but it is likely that small investors will lose out, as usual. The big boys will increasingly get the first crack at any shares which are going.

Clawback

Part of this has seen simple rights issues replaced increasingly by a close cousin, the open offer and clawback. This way, companies sell new shares to a big investment house, or a group of investors, at a set price. The buying group agrees to allow shareholders to apply for (or clawback) some of the shares at the issue price, often in the same sort of proportion as would have ruled in a rights issue. This method can mean that the new shares are placed closer to the market price than with a rights issue. It also has accounting advantages, allowing companies to treat goodwill in a way which does not reduce profits. Do not worry about that. Clawback does tend to undermine the rights of small shareholders. If there are new shares, existing investors ought to get first chance of buying them, putting extra cash into their company without the expense of paying stamp duty and commission through a broker. And if there is a small profit to be had from the nil-paid rights, it ought to go to existing shareholders. The swing to clawback and open offers is yet one more small change which puts profits into the pockets of the big boys at the expense of small shareholders. The good news for the company with a clawback is that it can be sure of getting the cash quickly, and can use it at short notice if a buying opportunity crops up suddenly. It also ensures instant City support for the scheme, and locks influential investors in more firmly behind the management. Nonetheless, it leaves a nasty taste for those who believe shareholders – large or small – own the business, and should get whatever advantages are going from the company they own.

CHAPTER FIVE

How Does The Market Work?

Once you have a rough idea of what you are looking for, where do you find it? Nothing, of course, ever comes as simple as it might first seem. Buying shares on the Stock Exchange is not what it used to be. The Stock Exchange does not really exist any more, and many of the stockbrokers in business to buy and sell shares do not want to know about small-time individual investors. The great grey tower block sitting in Throgmorton Street, slap in the centre of the City, near the Bank of England and Mansion House, is no longer where the action is. It might be called the Stock Exchange Tower, but now it houses only market officials and the offices of assorted stockbrokers.

The trading floor has gone. The six-sided boxes which used to flash on TV screens so often have disappeared. Share trading now takes place on the telephone, and over computer lines. You can glimpse the new dealing rooms, each owned by a different house, in the background whenever some City pundit comes on TV to tell you how the economy is going or whether the market has crashed. Funny, that. They never seem to think it worth bothering when shares have had a brilliant day, and rocketed to a new record. You see vast halls, crammed with rows of desks, each desk bearing two or three screens, maybe more. The dealers, men and women, spend much of the day on one of three or four phones at their fingertips, while every so often a Tannoy system booms out an announcement or instruction.

Once upon a time, I used to be taken through a steel works, an engineering plant, or an automated bakery. I would feel sorry for the people who had to work there, day in, day out. Now I shudder every time I see the City's battery chickens cooped up at their desks, eyes fixed on the screens, ears a buzz with noise. Dreadful, even though many of them make a tidy fortune for enduring it.

The old system was blown apart by Big Bang. In October 1986, 200 years of Stock Exchange history changed. It needed changes to ensure that London kept pace with international 24-hour trading. In the name of greater competition, Sir Gordon Borrie at the Office of Fair Trading forced the market to abandon the old idea of having brokers to take orders to buy and sell from the public, and another class, the jobbers, to hold the shares, set prices, and deal with the brokers.

For private investors, the old system was superior. It was open to abuse, but escaped many of the conflicts of interest in the new system. Now jobbers and brokers can be combined into market-makers. Integrated investment houses are the City equivalent to one stop shopping. You can dream up a bid, employ the bankers to carry it through for you, and have their broking house make the market in your shares, then buy and sell the same shares for outside investors. In theory, a 'Chinese Wall' stops one department telling the other what is going on. If the bank is working on a bid, it is not allowed to tell the broking boys to pile into shares of the bid target. That would be illegal use of insider information. There are all sorts of measures to guard against it. Judge for yourself how well they work, and how many small, subtle, but enormously lucrative, advantages can be gained by doing the lot in-house. Believe me, you cannot begin to comprehend the fiddles, large and small, which go on – all within the rules, of course.

SETS

SETS stands for Stock Exchange Electronic Trading System. Introduced in the autumn of 1997, it is intended to use computers to match buying and selling orders automatically. In the initial stage, it covers shares in the top 100 companies, but there are plans to extend it to the next 250. The theory is that this will cut dealing costs, make life more efficient, keep us abreast of overseas trading systems, and so on. Inevitably, it has not worked out that way so far. Indeed, at one stage it looked as if trading might be restricted to just one hour on New Year's Eve 1997 because the authorities feared that too many rogue prices would be put through the system if the market stayed open longer. While the machinery works, the operation of SETS has proved fraught with problems. In the early stages, it has accounted for less than 40pc of the trades in leading stocks, with many brokers preferring to deal through a parallel system which effectively runs on the established market-maker lines. SETS has proved vulnerable to a variety of problems, and has thrown up some wildly erratic prices. Small investors should be wary. In the first and last 30 minutes of the day, there are many more odd prices than at other times – so many, indeed, that the Exchange is opening half an hour later in the morning in the hope of making it better.

Now there is a risk that you could find your order put into the computer, and being filled at a poor price. Be sure to specify what price you expect your broker to trade at. Obviously, you need to give your broker some flexibility, but do not give him much. If in doubt, ask him to confirm any deal and price with you before he executes it. Hopefully by the time you read this, the worst difficulties will have been ironed out. Hopefully, all will be well before the SETS system is extended to the top 250 shares. But do be careful. This is yet another of those tricky areas where the boys in the know, on the ball, might sometimes be able to take advantage of the small investor.

Insider Trading

Insider trading – the use of privileged information – has existed as long as the stockmarket. Not so long ago – 25 or 30 years – everyone understood that a decent stockbroker was the one who got good information in good time. That was why you used him. A nod and a wink, part of the old pal's act, ensured that the music went round and round, and everyone did quite nicely, thank you.

Share dealing was more exclusive then, of course. Now maybe 17 million people own shares, thanks to privatisation issues and the late nineties fashion for building societies and the odd insurance company to convert to public companies. There was a great explosion of private investor interest in the eighties. Thousands of eager new investors rushed to buy and sell for themselves. Many did very well, too, until the Crash of October 1987. That wiped some investors out for ever. But many have tiptoed back through the nineties, and have been joined by a new generation of investors. They have enjoyed a long, rather nervous bull market from 1992 on through the late nineties. This boom might be the most exciting and enduring yet, with more players than ever. Growing Government recognition of looming problems over pensions have helped focus many minds on the need to make adequate provision for old age, and on the notion that it is best to do it for yourself.

In spite of the ups and downs of the market, the message that shares offer the most rewarding home for your savings over the longer term has become engraved on the heart of many a saver. Backed by talk about the new economic paradigm – the idea that we have entered a long period when economic management has become sophisticated enough to keep inflation in check and economic growth coming through steadily – interest in share investment is greater than ever. Sadly, though, everyone is now being encouraged to consider equity investment. Should they try it, they will find that the odds on success will not be equal for all. Be under no illusion. Insider trading does help swing the odds in the favour of a privileged few share traders. It takes place every day. It may be illegal, but it is impossible to stop, and extremely difficult to prove. The insider uses confidential information to buy or sell shares before the rest of the market knows what is going on. Every so often, someone is taken to court, and charged. Much more often, suspect cases are quietly dropped because the chances of winning a conviction are slim.

Most of those convicted are unsophisticated people playing for peanuts in a relatively naive way – amateur investors. The Lords of the game get away. The only big fish to get caught in this country was Geoffrey Collier, a top trader at merchant bank Morgan Grenfell. He got off with a relatively light sentence. They have been tougher in America, sending ace arbitrageur Ivan Boesky to jail, along with banker Dennis Levine, and junk bond king Michael Milken. These highly-publicised cases have been supported by a number of more modest convictions. But closer examination reveals that many of those convicted have later been released. And the games go on.

In the City, there are syndicates of professionals making millions by swapping confidential information. The Stock Exchange monitors every unusual price rise. They happen almost every day. The Stock Exchange has a good idea of the identity of many of those involved. It has a super-sophisticated computer system which can track every deal, and will surely catch the unsophisticated private punter. Proving what the real cheats are up to is a very different matter.

Agents and Principals

Big Bang did not make it any easier. Never mind the ethics of bundling sophisticated merchant banking together with private client broking. Think about it on a more mundane level. The broking firm which you may approach to buy shares for you as your agent could actually turn out to be a principal as well. Remember those terms – agent and principal – because they might crop up when you trade. Watch out for them.

The agent does what you tell him, and goes away and deals elsewhere for you. If he is a principal, he will buy or sell for you, but his firm may hold some of the shares you are trading in. His firm may actually sell you shares it is holding, or may actually buy your shares to hold for itself. The broker should tell you this, and it should not influence your price. Sometimes it could get you a better deal.

Just imagine, though, that your broker's firm has bought a large block of shares in a particular company. It got them for a good price because it bought so many. Every share it sells on may yield not just the normal commission, but a profit of 1p or 2p a share. The biggest and most respected names in the City regularly make hundreds of thousands – millions, even – in a day that way. Sometimes, individual salesmen/brokers are offered a piece of that profit if they hit selling targets. If you happen to ring, what are the chances that you might be steered towards the share in question? Make up your own mind. That example – it happens – reflects a far greater conflict of interest than insider trading. Stretch it a shade further. Just suppose the broking house is also advising a particular company. If that company wants to make a share issue – a clawback, perhaps, as mentioned earlier – it will be important to keep the share price up ahead of the deal, to ensure the company gets the best terms. Who is to say how many casual clients will be encouraged to buy in the days ahead of the deal? Later, when the broker has agreed to find buyers for the new shares, and the market is turning sticky, will the private clients be encouraged to take a few shares? Doing them a favour, letting them in on a good thing? Or stuffing them into something you cannot shift? Insider trading? Maybe. Maybe not.

Anyone who plays the market must accept insider trading and conflicts of interest as facts of life. Few buy or sell shares without thinking they know better than the person at the other end of the deal. For every buyer, someone is selling. It is the capitalist system in the raw. If it upsets you, keep out.

Investor Protection

After much debate, the Government and the City have come up with new regulations designed to provide more investor protection than ever. You had not noticed? What with Barlow Clowes, Roger Levitt, Guinness, mis-selling of life insurance, and bent investment brokers hitting the press? Oh dear what a pity. Every investor has certainly been paying extra to finance this orgy of red tape. The authorities have been trying – very trying – most of us in the business would say. Forests have been cleared to provide the paper to print the rules to be sent to thousands of people who cannot understand them, even if they wanted to. Hundreds of millions of pounds have been spent, trying to devise regulations to protect investors. They have achieved something – but far less than the effort and expense might suggest.

The simple fact is that it is impossible to protect fools from being parted from their money. Or to guard against every clever crook, or the combination of cunning and incompetence which allowed Nick Leeson to bust the bank of Barings. On a more mundane level, it is impossible to supervise a smooth salesperson all of the time. Sadly, all too many of us are a poor match for someone with a good, persistent line of patter. The Financial Services Act covers all sorts of things financial. The share investor, though, needs to know about the Personal Investment Authority (0171 538 8860). That is the top dog, sort of, among the investment regulators. It has taken over most members of FIMBRA, and if you have problems, the PIA is your best starting point. The Securities and Investments Board (0171 638 1240) might be some help. It has a central register telling you if people belong to what they claim to on 0171 929 3652, and whether they are allowed to take your money.

Perhaps SIB should not be your first call. Stockbrokers are covered by the Securities and Futures Authority, which runs a complaints bureau and an arbitration scheme for sums under £25,000. You can find that on 0171 378 9000.

If all of that seems a trifle vague, too bad. The regulators drive me mad when I try to deal with them. Sadly, I cannot guarantee that any of the addresses or numbers are correct, or that you will find the right place to complain to with your first or second try. They seem to spend most of their time moving into ever-bigger offices, and changing their names and responsibilities. I find myself getting shunted from one to another with irritating frequency. Keep at it, though, if you have a problem. You should get help in the end. And if you ring with a query, do explain to them just what it is someone is trying to sell you, or trying to get you to do. In some curious way, they cannot always be as helpful as they would wish. But they do find it useful to know what is going on. Even they recognise that the practice often differs from the theory they lay down.

If the worst comes to the worst, you might have to fall back on the Investors' Compensation Scheme. This covers you if your broker goes bust, or breaks the rules and loses you money. It could give you back the first £30,000 of any loss, and up to 90% of the next £20,000. There are ombudsmen scattered around as a last resort.

Any sensible investor will be wary of committing more than £30,000 to any one firm, unless that firm offers extra protection over and above the Compensation Scheme limit. Even more clearly, the sensible investor avoids getting into a jam in the first place. Use your common sense, watch out for the angles, and you should be fine. Precious few of the sorry tales I come across involve people who have been quite as careful as they should have been. Usually – not always – the victims have contributed to their own downfall with an element of greed or sheer stupidity. Follow the rules in this book, and you should avoid that. Never imagine that any of the regulators will help you. They might, but all too often, private investors fall foul of the red tape which allows the regulators to shunt them aside and ignore the problem. Do understand that. Investors appear to be treated as a nuisance, not people who need help, by the regulators who are supposed to protect them.

Where to Buy

Alerted yet undaunted by this alarmist stuff, where do you actually turn to get on with the business of share buying? There are four main channels; a member of the Stock Exchange; a bank or building society; a telephone execution-only service; or an independent dealer in securities belonging to FIMBRA or the PIA.

Stockbrokers

Despite my grim warnings, stockbrokers – members of the Stock Exchange – are still much your best bet. Their conduct is covered by the rules of the Stock Exchange, and very strictly covered. If they should go bust (or get 'hammered' in Stock Exchange terms), or you can prove that they have cost you money by breaking the rules, you will qualify for the Investors' Compensation Scheme. Or you could win an award from the SFA arbitration scheme.

Many brokers are convinced that they should return to the old Stock Exchange system of unlimited compensation. Some have been trying to restore such a plan. Quite right. Others have their own schemes. Some offer over £5m cover for each investor. Quilter Goodison offers unlimited cover from its parent, insurance giant Commercial Union. Others have followed them. Check when you talk to them

The motto of the Stock Exchange is "My Word Is My Bond", and it still means something. Most stockbrokers are honourable, and will handle your orders carefully and correctly. Their investment advice requires greater caution. Most give honest, well-meaning advice. But the small investor cannot reasonably expect to take up too much of the time, or attention, of the most skilled and experienced brokers.

Different services are developing. Some brokers offer a no-frills, discount execution-only dealing service. They simply do what you tell them, buying or selling on your instructions, charging a commission, and giving no advice. Others operate a more expensive discretionary account, where they will manage your money in accordance with guidelines agreed in advance, and may buy and sell without consulting you. They should send regular portfolio valuations and such, and allow you access to research ideas. This may be too costly for the small investor. In the middle, there are firms offering an advisory management service, making recommendations and dealing after your approval, perhaps with some cheap dealing in certain circumstances, and extra charges for additional facilities they may offer.

As a rule, you will find it cheaper to deal with one of the brokers outside London. Lower overheads allow them to charge less, and they often have more time for individual investors. Many provincial brokers make a real effort to cultivate the small player, seeking to build a relationship which they hope will pay off over time. They need the business more than the London broker, and make that extra effort. There is the added advantage that it may be possible to call into the office to see them. Face to face discussions are much better than dealing on the phone all of the time.

So do not spurn the local man. He may not be quite in touch with the City gossip, but he may compensate with a sounder knowledge of local companies, and smaller situations. For the private investor, that can be invaluable, especially in the early stages of a bull market. Spotting promising smaller companies before London wakes up can be enormously rewarding. And some have floated some small companies with remarkable success.

One note of caution. Make sure that the local broker (or, indeed, any broker) is what he says he is. Check that the firm does belong to the Stock Exchange. DO NOT TAKE IT ON TRUST. It should be a mere formality, of course. But sometimes small share shops, or local dealers of some sort spring up. They create the impression of being proper brokers, and rely on no one bothering to check. They can do the most diabolical things. So beware.

There is one other distinction to keep in mind. We touched on it earlier. Always check whether your broker is acting as agent or principal when he trades for you. Just make sure you watch for the angle behind his advice. Many brokers these days will try to talk you out of going directly into shares. They do not want the trouble and expense of dealing in small quantities. It costs them as much to process your £1,000 deal as it does to handle one worth £50,000 – though they will certainly be charging the big trader less than the full rate of commission. Such brokers will nudge you towards a unit trust. They may have one of their own. Forget it. If you are reading this book, you want to do it yourself.

Many big London brokers will turn up their noses at anything under £100,000. Fair enough. They are not the sort of people you want anyway. They will not spare you the time and trouble you deserve. Do not get indignant at being turned away. For a successful investment relationship to work, both sides need to be interested.

Actually finding a suitable broker is not easy. Ideally, you want someone you can talk to as an equal, someone you can eventually trust and confide in, who can spare a minute or two when you need it. Personal recommendation is best, but you can only really judge by working with someone. If things do not click, go elsewhere. IT IS YOUR MONEY AT STAKE. No matter how superior they might seem, brokers are salespeople, acting on your behalf. You pay the piper, make sure you call the tune. Watch the financial press for advertisements. Then ask anyone who you think might know about the credibility of the firm of your choosing. A big name may not be enough. Some of the big boys are super, but you may well not be important enough to matter to them. You could find yourself left with some fresh-faced graduate, learning the business. He may mean well, but he may not manage too well. The *Investors Chronicle* (0171 463 3000) publishes useful surveys of

stockbrokers from time to time. The Association of Private Client
Investment Managers and Stockbrokers (APCIMS) publishes a directory
of private client brokers. Write to APCIMS at 112, Middlesex Street,
London, E1 7HY. Tel: 0171 247 7080.

Or try ProShare, a body backed by the Government and the Stock
Exchange to encourage wider share ownership. Write to ProShare (UK)
Limited, Library Chambers, 13-14 Basinghall Street, London EC3V
5BQ, or phone 0171 394 5200. In the summer of 1998, the Stock
Exchange itself decided it ought to try to help. Along with a couple of
brochures on share trading it has produced a handy list of brokers.

If you find a broking name that looks promising, tell that broker
exactly what you expect from them, and ask for an indication of what
that might cost. See how chatty they are. Ask whether you might have
access to their analysts and reports, what newsletters you might expect
free, and what others will cost. How often will you get a portfolio
valuation, and is there help in working out your gains tax return, and how
much will that cost? If you are required to leave cash on deposit with the
broker at any point, who holds it, and what interest do you get on it? Is
the bank independent, and if the broker holds your stock certificates, are
they held by an independent custodian?

The Bank

If you cannot find a suitable broker, it is worth going to your bank. No
matter what the advertisements suggest, the banks are not that well
geared up to handle individual investors. But they are getting there.
Barclays Stockbrokers have been making a special effort. NatWest claim
you can buy and sell at many of their branches. The banks have
improved enormously, and most now own stockbroking firms, or have
strong links with them. They have a recognised, clearly defined system
for handling new clients. Some branches will be more useful than others.

Charges vary. Special cheap rates for privatisations can be misleading, and some charges do look on the heavy side. The banks will be able to put you on to more sophisticated broking operations, with some access to research, if you wish. Try it and see. It is hard to give more practical advice. So far, I have seen too little about the results to judge. If nothing else, you can be sure you are dealing with an organisation of integrity. They might get things wrong, but they will not go bust or run off with your money.

The Building Society

Share dealing at building societies has been gaining ground as a result of the privatisation issues. Some societies offer a fairly full service, and actually own a stockbroker. Others have close links. Like the banks, any service is likely to be second best by comparison with direct contact with a broker. But it may suit you. At least with the banks and building societies, you are dealing with trustworthy organisations. There may be mistakes, but not dishonesty.

Telephone Services

Dealers who operate a phone-in service, concentrating on execution-only, without offering advice, are springing up. Led by Charles Schwab (formerly ShareLink), these can serve a useful purpose for small investors who know what they are doing. They offer relatively keenly priced and efficient trading. Check first that they are proper members of some regulated authority, and look carefully at the wording of any contract they send you. While it seems unfair to suggest it, be careful about newly-established operators. At least one went under because it could not cope with the demand generated by one of the privatisations. There was no dishonesty, just a muddle. Charles Schwab is generally efficient and enterprising, offering many helpful services for a fee. The Share Centre might be worth investigating for a low cost service. Hargreaves Lansdown in Bristol is generally reliable.

Investment Advisers And Bucket Shops

In the mid-nineties, there has been a resurgence of investment advisers who are not quite stockbrokers, but who appear much the same from the outside. Some are dressed up as share shops. These will take your orders, give you advice, and charge what appear to be normal rates of commission. They will be governed by FIMBRA or the PIA, and will often be staffed by former stockbrokers. In fact, they will often be passing your orders on to a stockbroker, and sharing commission with them. In many cases, they will be keen to recommend shares and get you to buy them. These bucket shops are the successors to the old licensed dealers in bucket shops securities, who used to operate what was the Over-The-Counter market, dealing in shares not listed on the London Stock Exchange. It led to a succession of duds, and proved extremely costly to thousands of small investors who got caught up in it through the likes of Harvard Securities or Ravendale.

The Over-The-Counter market has long gone, but it remains to be seen how the OFEX market which developed outside the Stock Exchange in October 1995 comes along, and how the Alternative Investment Market goes. More of them later. The bucket shops regularly buy the lists of shareholders in small companies, and write offering an investment review of that company. Ask to see the review, and you will find you are telephoned by some salesman or woman who will try to persuade you to buy shares in something else.

By the late Nineties, many of the worst offenders had given up. But some remain, and should normally be avoided. They almost always act as principals. That means they are selling you shares they own. Almost invariably, they will have bought a large block at well below the normal market price. They will then try to sell them to you at the market price, or perhaps offer you the chance of buying a little below the quoted price. Sometimes, they may have gone into the market themselves to buy a few shares, and tickle the listed price still higher before they contact you. Either way, they will be taking an enormous turn between the price they have paid, and the price you pay.

The idea will not be to do you a favour and make you a profit – it is amazing how many people still believe such nonsense – but to shunt stock through at a profit to them. There is a place for firms selling shares to small investors over the phone, and perhaps taking a profit for themselves on the way. Too few conventional stockbrokers can afford to pay such attention to small clients nowadays, so cumbersome and costly is the routine red tape. Sadly, the bucket shops almost invariably become tempted to take advantage of customers, and stuff them with dud stock at any price. From time to time, I have conducted a campaign against the worst abuses. I have been horrified to find how many otherwise intelligent people get sucked in.

Losses frequently amount to tens of thousands of pounds, with the losers often too embarrassed to complain. Be very, very careful. Some bucket shops will try to sell you shares in companies which do not have a proper Stock Exchange listing here. Usually these companies will be quoted on some regional American exchange. Usually the promoter will have bought a massive number at a fraction of a penny, and be selling them in the UK at many times the original price – I have heard of some sold at 50 times cost. Usually, it will be impossible to sell them in America, or anywhere else. Sometimes the stock will carry perfectly legal restrictions which forbid it being sold in America for a certain time – that it why it is being knocked out in this country. You will not be told that. The only buyer will be the smooth talker who sold them to you. And he will rarely be anxious to take them back. Now and then, the shares will be in companies which do not exist.

It may sound improbable. Investment advisers everywhere will assure you no such thing ever happens in any firm they have dealt with. Nonsense. Steer clear of any such advisers. The regulators rarely keep up with what is going on, and would much rather try to pass the buck to some other regulator. Perfectly respectable firms can change character overnight if some villain buys in. It happens. Salesmen will often use the same old, well-rehearsed pitch to appeal to you. If, for example, they plead that they are doing you a favour, ensuring you have a winner first time out, because they want you as a regular customer, slam down the phone. You are being fed the good old sucker line. Those operating from overseas seem particularly fond of flogging new issues. Calling from New York, Amsterdam, or Dublin, they will tell you the issue is several times over-subscribed, bound to open at a big premium. By sheer good fortune, they happen to have the last few thousand shares which they can let you have, quickly, before the issue closes. Why are they doing you such a favour? Because they want you as a regular client, so they want to be sure they form a good impression from the beginning. Heard that before? Amazing how often it still works. Never, ever, part with a single penny to anyone who rings from outside the UK. Whatever they say, you will end up regretting it.

What it Costs

Share dealing costs have been thrown into confusion since Big Bang abolished fixed commissions. Anything goes now. Inevitably, it goes higher and higher. It would be foolish to be too dogmatic about what you ought to pay. Levels of service vary so much, and costs are rising all the time. Instead of cutting charges to generate more business when there is little going on, the investment community prefers to bump them up, every time. In central London and the bigger provincial cities, too many are trapped paying silly rents for fancy properties. While rents may be plummeting all around them, they are committed to paying dearly for leases they took out in more prosperous times. So they think they have to charge bigger fees.

At the time of writing, it seems that between £15 and £20 is a fair figure for a cut-price, execution-only deal. Other firms charge a minimum of £35 a deal, maybe more. Do not be misled by cheap dealing offers for privatisation issues. They are too low to last.

Do not be tempted into believing that the cheapest may be as good as the best. It may suit you, but some are tempted into dealing with dubious firms to try to save £5 or £10 on dealing costs. It is not worth it. Any share transaction will involve quite a significant amount of your money. It is not worth jeopardising it for the sake of a few pounds. The most unexpected things happen from time to time. Even if a cut-price merchant is playing straight, but simply gets in a muddle, you will rue the day you got involved. It could take months before things are unscrambled, and you get your money or your shares. It may also be a false economy dealing cheap unless you are sure you are getting a proper price for your shares. A difference of 1p when you are selling 1,000 shares is worth £10. Will the house offering the cheapest dealing cost get you the best price? Perhaps. Perhaps not. A good broker will take time and trouble to ensure that you do get the best price on offer when you trade. Some banks, for example, deal with the market-maker they own. If he is not offering the best price, you miss out. Paying a little over the odds on commission may sometimes be the best bet in the end.

All brokers must charge a transfer stamp fee on purchases. There is none when you sell.

Dealing By Post

Serious investors should avoid the cut-price dealing offers advertised, and frequently backed, by the newspapers. I have always fought against the *Daily*

Mail becoming involved in them, though there is money in it for the paper. These are cheap, but normally require you to post your share certificates with a dealing instruction form. The broker may well be perfectly sound. But the cheap dealing is done by putting all of the trades in one particular share together, and doing them in one big lot, saving costs. For the seller, you do not know when your shares will be sold, or at what price. A delay of an hour or two could make a big difference if the market is lively. Much better to give instructions over the phone, for instant execution. That way you know where you stand. Anything else is a false and dangerous economy. Dealing through any postal service is a mistake for the serious share punter.

Know Your Client

The march of the red tape also requires every broker to get you to complete a client agreement form before trading for you. Part of the idea is that brokers should know their clients, and only put them into suitable shares. So you will be asked to say how much risk you are prepared to take, and so on, as well as supplying a fairly detailed financial background. The theory is sound enough, but with the bucket shops, I fear that it just gives them a measure of how much money they might eventually milk you for. It is also hard to suppress the feeling that the main value of the form will be to the brokers – they will be able to present it in any dispute to suggest they have behaved properly. Be especially careful if you do find yourself dealing with a bucket shop. You might find that signing to receive a newsletter has committed you to accepting a whole raft of fine print on the back of the form.

Share Listings

Not every share on the London Stock Exchange is equal in the eyes of the Exchange. Some shares have a full listing, while others are quoted on the Alternative Investment Market, the bright new hope for financing smaller growth companies.Generally speaking, shares with a full listing are the biggest, safest, and most solid companies – though in the early nineties, precious few companies looked absolutely safe. To earn a full listing, they must show a three-year trading record, and must offer at least 25% of their capital for sale on flotation. Some fully-listed companies are clapped-out shadows, clinging on to a share quote, and far more risky than any AIM stock. So the difference between a full listing and the AIM is not always too good a guide. What matters more is liquidity – whether it is easy to deal in reasonable quantities at reasonable prices. Irritatingly, AIM companies do not qualify for inclusion in Personal Equity Plans.

The Alternative Investment Market

Widely known as AIM, the Alternative Investment Market opened in June 1995 as the newest attempt by the Stock Exchange to provide a market for smaller companies without it costing the earth. Companies coming to the AIM are smaller, more speculative than those on the main market. They can even be start-ups.

The Exchange has put the onus for regulating AIM companies on the sponsors who bring them to the market. These are called nominated advisers, and the Exchange is vetting them carefully, requiring qualifying firms to have a sufficient number of people experienced in new issues. Nominated advisers are charged with seeing that companies whose flotation they back behave properly, and have the appropriate background for a share issue. Obviously that does not ensure that all AIM companies are what they should be – but few broking houses will knowingly put their name to a second-rate issue. So when you look at an AIM stock, pay close attention to the reputation of the nominated adviser.

AIM companies require a proper set of accounts, and must produce a listing document when they first come to market. This will require the same sort of historic profits information as fully listed companies. If it is a new business, it may contain an illustrative profits projection, covering two or three years ahead. This is not a forecast, but comes close to it. It is particularly valuable in allowing investors to assess companies, and not just when they first come to market. If the company is a year or two down the line, and you can get the original listing document with the illustrative projection, you have a real measure against which you can set progress. The listing documents must also carry details of the board's previous directorships going back five years, plus details of any brushes with the courts or other authorities. Be careful about this. It is valuable – but even in the first three months of AIM trading, I spotted a company where one of the prominent personalities was listed not as a director, but merely the head of one important division. That way, there was no need to list one embarrassing little episode from his past. True to form, that company hit bad trouble inside 18 months.

When it comes to dealing, there are two market-makers ready to make prices in almost every AIM share. Often there are more than two. In many cases, the nominated adviser is a stockbroker who will also provide a two-way market in the shares. Sometimes there is a nominated broker alongside the nominated adviser. That nominated broker may make a market in the shares. Many AIM shares attract a surprisingly good volume of trade, with fairly free two-way markets in 5,000 shares common to many – though the listed dealing sizes were often confined to 1,000 each way. The AIM is intended to be a cheap and easy way for companies to raise risk capital, although costs have risen quickly. It frees the directors from the need to put their homes in hock to the bank, or to give away a vast chunk of the business to intrusive venture capitalists. Sadly, the early issues have shown that the professionals are still managing to charge hefty fees in many cases.

Nonetheless, the AIM does appear to be the opportunity market. For the investor ready to take the greater risk which inevitably accompanies backing a younger, smaller company, there is the dream of getting in on some real high-flyer near the start. Carefully selected AIM issues have done remarkably well, while others have soared, only to slump as quickly. Inevitably, there will be duds and disasters on the AIM. Within four months of the opening, there were half a dozen companies trading there which made me shudder. And in the succeeding couple of years, there have been others I have hated, though the overall quality has not been too bad. Keep your eyes open on the AIM, and do not venture there until you are sure of what you are doing. Better still, get hold of my book *How To Make A Killing On The Alternative Investment Market.* I am so convinced that there is big money to be made on the AIM that I rushed into print the moment it arrived.

If you want a cautious way in, Beacon Investment Trust is the established specialist. Contact the company for details. At the very least, their investments will give you a pointer to what they think is worth buying – and their research is pretty extensive.

The Bulletin Board

The Bulletin Board, or Seats, is something you rarely hear about. It is meant to handle trade in shares which are rarely dealt in. One market-maker shows buying and selling prices on a page of the electronic screen, details of previous trades are also shown, and brokers are invited to offer to buy or sell with these figures as a guide. It does not work too well, but throws up bargains sometimes as prices drift back because of a lack of business. It might be the place to spot companies which might be used as shells. Be careful. You may buy, and be unable to sell. Only trade in bulletin board stocks if you are very sure of what you are doing. It will be best for most readers of this book to stay out of Seats stocks.

OFEX

The OFEX, or Off Exchange Market, opened in October 1995 as the Stock Exchange brought an end to trading on the rule 4.2 market. This rule 4.2 market was a facility which allowed occasional deals in all sorts of companies, ranging from giants like National Car Parking and Weetabix to complete unknowns. Many of the most interesting 4.2 stocks moved on to the AIM, while the rest shifted to OFEX.

This market is operated by the respected Stock Exchange firm of J.P.Jenkins, which has long made a speciality of providing markets in less actively traded companies. Jenkins is charging a few thousand a year for companies to list on OFEX, and requires them to submit a proper set of accounts, and meet other sensible and prudent rules. He also has a small committee which vets the suitability of companies. For various reasons, Weetabix, and brewer Shepherd Neame are among the big names which have chosen to step outside the Exchange to trade on OFEX.

John Jenkins regards OFEX generally as a nursery for companies which wish to go onto the AIM. A handful have done so, though not all will wish to make such a step. He has made a clear price record available on the TV screens which are all around the City, and his Newstrack onscreen service provides an admirable summary of the financial basics of each OFEX company, and lists all recent announcements. OFEX prices are advertised each day in the *Financial Times*, and many appear daily in the London *Evening Standard*. Make no mistake, however. Admirable as it may be, OFEX is a highly speculative market. The companies will often be smaller and riskier than those traded anywhere else, and it may be difficult to buy and sell regularly in any significant quantities. That said, there will be interesting opportunities. From the beginning, there are OFEX companies seeking to make their way up when the moment suits them. In the summer of 1998, some who followed my *Daily Mail* column were sitting with fat profits – four times their money, and three times their money – in a couple of carefully-selected OFEX stocks.

Tradepoint

Open for business in the autumn of 1995, Tradepoint is a computer-based share trading scheme matching buyers and sellers outside the Stock Exchange. Initially, at least, it is only for the big boys, it is not for private investors.

Business Expansion Schemes

Some shares traded on OFEX are in companies covered by the Business Expansion Scheme. BES companies were floated under strict rules which allowed the cost of the investment to be set off against tax, if they were held for at least five years. Sadly, many proved to be poor investments, even with the tax saving. The small companies they promoted were often hit hard by the recession. Because some of the promoters simply disappeared before the five years elapsed, or because some companies were very small, it has often been difficult for investors to find a way of getting their cash out. So some BES shares have found their way on to OFEX at very low, almost desperation prices. There are great opportunities, but readers of this book should steer clear. You need to know exactly what you are doing before you buy any old BES investments.

CHAPTER SIX

Picking Pennies Off A Plate

Oh happy days. Lights, action, movement, soundtrack of Gladys Knight singing *The Way We Were*, and the camera pans across the street. Memories are made of this.

It is 7.30 on a chill winter morning. Queues are forming outside a grey City bank. The office juniors are there, each with a thick wad of papers under their arm. Old ladies with plastic bags chat to porters from the meat market. The odd City gent, velvet collar and brolly, reads his *Financial Times* alongside men in long black coats and beards, crammed cardboard boxes beside them on the pavement. A few people are scribbling on forms, writing cheques. Secretaries join the line as police shepherd them away from the edge of the pavement, press cameras click.

By 10 o'clock, with the bank doors long open, the queue has become a scrum, with sleek City brokers directing office boys as they push through the crowd, throwing bundles across the counter into wicker baskets. At one minute past ten, the bank cries "Time", cashiers slam down the barriers across the counter, and commissionaires move to close the doors.

That was how it used to be. Another successful new issue would be on its way, heavily oversubscribed. As the eighties gave way to the nineties, the picture changed. The queues grew shorter, and when the doors closed, there would be some minor Government minister milking the TV cameras, seeking political capital from the latest privatisation issue. When times are hard, the flow of new issues dries up. There are opportunities to make money, but they are offered to selected clients only. It is left to the big money state sell-offs to provide excitement or the building society floatations. Even those brought a few disappointments – BT3 and the Scottish Power issues especially – but most were well worth backing for a quick profit. The real winners, of course, were those who bought the privatisations, and sat on them. The storm at fat cat greed in 1995 may keep catching the headlines, but the underlying gains in power and water shares have been staggering, with initial investors making up to four times their money.

The pickings may be smaller, and the opportunities rarer in the late-nineties. Nonetheless, the stagging game can be brilliant. Get it right, and it can generate substantial short-term profits without the need to tie up large sums of money for more than a week or two. And that lets you play for far bigger sums than you might be able to afford if you had to commit for months or years.

In the nineties, much of the fun has been squeezed out of stagging – the business of buying shares in a new issue, hoping to sell at a handsome profit as soon as dealings begin. In the mid-eighties, hundreds of millions of pounds, mostly borrowed money, would pour in for almost any new issue. It was routine for offers to attract ten times the amount of cash they were seeking. The odd issue would be 100 times oversubscribed. It was as close as most of us can get to money for nothing. The chance may not come again in quite such a rewarding form. But as conditions grow brighter, the number of new issues will multiply, and there will be good opportunities for quick profits.

Stagging

Outsiders may sneer, but there is nothing wrong with stagging. It provides a little extra excitement and helps make the share game such fun. From the modest punter who puts up £200 hoping to make a quick £20 or more to the syndicate which might apply for £100m of shares, it is a gambling bonanza which leaves Las Vegas standing. One burly City broker counted his stagging profits in tens of millions in 1985. Dozens of groups of fund managers, bankers, brokers, and boys about the City worked together more discreetly to make tidy fortunes. In a matter of minutes when dealings started, they would scoop more profit than the average British company could earn in a year of hard slog.

No need to moralise. No matter how much get rich quick spivvery may upset you, while the system lasts, there is little point in not taking your share. Strip away the pious nonsense about creating a share-owning democracy, and you see that a Conservative Government cynically exploited the new issue market to create privatisation profits for people in a fashion most likely to encourage them to vote Conservative. Freeing major industries from state control may have helped improve their efficiency. But in too many cases it meant short-term profits for share buyers, and higher bills from near-monopoly enterprises, bearing down on poorer people who could not afford the share game. Pretty close to robbing the poor to pay the fairly rich.

In the late nineties, the real privatisation goodies have gone, and techniques have been devised for pricing issues more greedily. But it might just mean that the less obviously desirable issues – like Railtrack – get to be priced all the more generously. That quadrupled inside two years. So do not write off the dream of new issue pickings just yet. The 1998 Thomson Travel issue might only have yielded a small profit to stags, but it offered useful perks, and did demonstrate that there is plenty of latent demand for new issues. Anything good could still go with a bang.

The Winners

The new issue system is constructed to favour the stag, to yield profits to those who support new share issues. The message really came home in the autumn of 1984 with the British Telecom flotation. All you had to do was fill in a form, write a cheque, sit back, and wait for the profits to pour in. For every pound you put up, there was a profit of 86p on the first day of dealing. A couple of months later, there was a profit of 140p for every 100p. Oh, the joys of the capitalist class.

It was not just privatisation issues which yielded fabulous profits. There was Laura Ashley, the home furnishing and fashion group.

Every share you bought at 135p could have been sold at 185p on the first day of dealing.

An exception? Not at all. In 1986 and 1987, new issues galore roared to a handsome profit in first-time dealings. Even the risk-prone British Airways lifted off to a thrilling flight.

These examples come from the mid-eighties, or earlier. The game almost ended with the October '87 Crash, except for privatisations – and a few tiddlers, if you knew where to find them. But stories of old glory are worth telling. The happy days may return. Read this chapter, note the contents, and be prepared to make the most of them if the opportunity re-appears. Something for nothing hardly sounds the way the City normally works. But the boys in the know are giving a little something to the masses in return for a much bigger take for themselves. So long as the stockmarket is in fair to average form, making money on new issues is like picking pennies off a plate. Because the system is geared to success, your friendly issuing house needs you, big punter or small, when the action starts. A good issue gives something to everyone, leaving them all feeling happy. No broker or banker worth his salt tries to squeeze the last penny out of a new issue. If a company starts stockmarket life at a discount to the sale price, a cloud could hang over it for years. Expansion plans are inhibited, goodwill is gone. If you lose by backing a new issue, the sponsors have got it wrong, not you. NEW ISSUES ARE DESIGNED TO GIVE YOU A PROFIT.

The Ideal Way Into Shares

For those new to share trading, subscribing for an offer for sale is the ideal way into the stockmarket. You pay no commission to stockbrokers, no VAT, no stamp duty, and there is no market-maker taking a middleman's turn. No hidden extras need worry you. The price you pay is the price you see on the application form. You can skip the broker, bank or investment dealer. Simply cut the coupon out of your newspaper, and post it with a cheque. Often there are special low-price dealing services advertised with the big issues, making selling as simple as lifting a telephone, or popping into your bank or building society. Easy.

Offers For Sale

In the past, most big new issues were carried out through a straightforward offer for sale. There are fewer now, and sometimes they appear only to accompany the slightly trickier and larger issues. But offers for sale are worth watching for, the simplest and easiest way to a winner – if you pick the right share. The offer will be arranged (or sponsored) by the issuing house, usually a merchant bank or stockbroker. News of it will appear on most City pages. The best general early warning system is in the *Investors Chronicle*, or specialist new issue tipping sheets. *The Mail On Sunday* also prints a useful new issue alert.

Full details of the big issues come in a prospectus, which has to be published in at least two national newspapers. Almost all prospectuses appear in the *Financial Times*. They are also available from the issuing house, and sometimes from the banks.

A prospectus can run to 120 pages – more in privatisations. The real blockbusters are not normally on offer to individual investors. In their place, there are mini-prospectuses, still 20 pages or more.

A full prospectus can be a daunting document. It is hard to believe

anyone, even broking backroom boys, reads it all. Even ploughing right
through a normal prospectus could leave you with a nasty headache, an
impressive growth of beard, and little idea of what is going on. Do not be
put off. The theory is that everyone should be encouraged to read all
about the shares before they buy. Sound advice. In practice, the bulk and
complexity of most prospectuses is enough to scare most people off. Do
not worry. A full prospectus is an optional extra for all but the really
serious investors – or those with experience enough to alight on the few
pages where they know they need to look.

A few issues publish a mini-prospectus in the press. This may be little
more than an application form bearing the company's name. It usually
gives no details of the company's business or profits. It is handy to have
the application form more freely available, but be careful. Do not consider
making a serious decision from a mini-prospectus unless you have
discovered what the company is about from somewhere else.

What You Need To Know

All you really need to know is what the City thinks of the shares. If the
boys in the market do not fancy them, they do not have a chance, no
matter what you think. It is no good being the lone genius who spots the
potential in a new issue. Success or failure will be determined by the
weight of money sent in. If that is low, the issue will flop, no matter how
brilliant the company. This is one instance where it is no use being a
contrary thinker. If you really are right, and everyone else wrong, wait to
buy the shares at a discount, after dealings begin and the issue has flopped.

Finding out what the crowd thinks can be as easy as asking your
broker, reading the City pages (you will soon learn who gets it right most
often), or watching the grey market, if there is one. None of these is
infallible, but until you get pretty smart, they will do better than you on
your own.

The Grey Market

Writing in the late-nineties, the pukka grey market is a distant memory. It only comes to life when there is real new issue excitement. But if there is a chance of making money, it is surprising what happens. So it is worth filing this little passage in the back of your mind, just in case it comes in useful sometime in the future.

The grey market operates outside the Stock Exchange, with traders offering to buy and sell new issues before official dealings begin. The better the issue, the bigger the grey market premium. Simple. When there is a grey market, the City page stockmarket reports will usually tell you about it. It is almost a form of betting, and by the early nineties, City betting house IG Index was the only grey market operator left plugging on through the recession. IG Index provides a genuine betting service. And though the IG prices are normally a good indicator, they are not always right. Well worth checking, though.

If any of the unofficial guides – brokers, press, or grey market – is uncertain about an issue, opt out. Your chances of scoring will be slim. Do not be tempted, no matter how much it appeals to you. Ask yourself how you have been so smart as to spot something good that the experts have missed. And then ask yourself if you need your head examining. If they do not go for it, it might open below the issue price, and you can back your hunch then, buying it more cheaply.

Reading The Prospectus

A glance at the prospectus will tell you who is selling how many shares for what price. There will be pages on the history and present state of the company, but little about the future. That is a shame, but the Stock Exchange imposes strict rules on profit forecasts to stop dubious promoters projecting an unrealistically rosy glow. That makes sense –

though, as we have seen, some prospectuses for companies floating on the AIM will carry illustrative profit projections.

There will be a profit record, perhaps a short-term profit forecast, and a dividend forecast. And there will be a calculation of the price-earnings ratio, and the dividend yield, two basic statistics to compare with other quoted companies in the same line of business. That gives an easy, worthwhile guide to roughly what the share price should be. Watch out. Do not get trapped into comparing the prospective – future - earnings ratio and dividend yield with the historic – past – p/e ratio and yield on other companies. It is easy to get a flattering impression of a new issue that way.

Deeper in the document will be words from the chairman on why the company is being floated. The more cash being raised for expansion, the better. Find out whether the board are simply lining their own pockets by selling lots of shares. Feel more confident if the continuing directors are keeping a sizeable stake, but not a majority of the shares. That way, they will be committed to working for themselves and other shareholders, but will lack the power to drive away any would-be bidder without consulting shareholders. Big shareholders should also give some undertaking that they will hold the shares for at least a year, maybe more. You do not want them dumping stock just after you have bought in.

Check, too, how much pay is linked to profits. That helps, in small doses. Share incentives are also good, though they should not be overgenerous. Around 5% of the capital earmarked to reward directors for good performance is reasonable, with another 5% or so for employees. Frown at anything more. It may help get profits and perhaps the share price moving over the short term, but could be an incentive to use accounting methods which inflate published profits. That can backfire.

How well I recall the long discussions with an earnest Sir Ralph Halpern when he was chairman of Burton Group. In his £1m plus pay years, he would lecture on the importance of incentives. I was cursed for attacking a scheme which would have given the Burton board millions through potentially lucrative share options. When it all went wrong, the old board was desperately keen to deny that the rush into property development had been inspired by a need to keep profits coming through to generate the performance which kept cash pouring into board pay. Yet the ill-timed dash into property lost hundreds of millions of pounds, and almost brought Burton to its knees. If it had worked, it would have boosted earnings and board pay incentives just as the shopping boom slowed. Watch the profit record. Check the notes to see there are no extraordinary or exceptional items which distort profits in one year. Iron them out, if they do, to try to establish how smooth the course of normal trading runs. Look for unusually high interest payments, or rising interest charges. That might indicate how badly the company needs new money – and the scope for growth if the new cash cuts borrowings, slashes the interest bill, and allows more profit through to new shareholders.

In smaller issues, or newer companies, be especially careful to check changes in capital. These can be difficult to unravel. Sometimes you will be dismayed to see how little the directors paid for their shares, particularly when they have recently sold a business in to form the company being floated. Every so often, I come across a venture where the promoters end up with the majority of the shares in return for a fledgling company whose value depends largely on hope, and the new money going in from outsiders. Actual profits or real assets will be thin on the ground. Or there may be some directors who paid 1p for shares being sold at 40p. No matter how tempting the prospects, walk away from anything like that.

Names To Watch

'Who's who' can be very important in determining how an issue will go. Check the sponsors – the merchant bank or broker behind the issue. Even the City's finest make mistakes, and get greedy or over-confident, and overprice an issue. In 1993 and early in 1994 there was a dreadful rash of overpriced new issues from almost all of the top names, including Rothschild, and Warburg.

Normally, sponsorship by one of the better-known, quality names can be worth a great deal. The league table changes frequently, so ask your broker about the current state of play. Sometimes someone hits a hot streak – or goes stone cold. And success tends to attract the better companies looking to float. Morgan Grenfell was the superstar in the mid-eighties, but got caught in the Guinness scandal. In the first rank of merchant banks, Warburg, Dresdner Kleinwort Benson, Rothschild, Schroder, Lazard Brothers, Robert Fleming and NatWest all have their strengths. Charterhouse have their moments, but Samuel Montagu will take a long while to recover from sponsoring the flotation of Robert Maxwell's Mirror Group Newspapers. Singer & Friedlander ranks as an also-ran, with Guinness Mahon damned by the dismal failure of their Business Expansion Scheme efforts.

Top of the broking heap is Cazenove, a firm of legendary placing power. If they push an issue, the boys will back it. They have to, if they want to stay in the club when the real goodies are passed around. Personal prejudice prompts me to sound a note of caution about the American-controlled invaders. They have enormous financial muscle, and some have great skill. On the whole, their methods still appear more aggressive than those employed by the better British houses, and their pricing tends to leave less for the individual investor. Goldman Sachs is widely admired, but was closely associated with Maxwell in the later period when he was behaving in truly disgraceful fashion.

Danger Zone

It is harder to be specific about other houses to avoid. Some small brokers are outrageous. How they survive in this supposedly tightly-regulated era merely demonstrates that, no matter how tough the rules might appear, they do not always work too well. Other small brokers are excellent. But names, owners, and personalities are apt to change so fast that it would be unwise to try to list them. Some of the most interesting ones will be newly-formed houses, led by characters who have decided to break away from the big names.

Sadly, it would be remiss not to point out that the bigger, sounder companies generally gravitate towards the bigger, sounder houses when they seek flotation. Smaller issuing houses almost invariably have to compete for the less attractive propositions.

Take special care over American companies which float in London instead of their own country. They usually plead it is cheaper and quicker here. Almost – almost – invariably they have turned out to be duds.

Form-Filling Tactics

The way you fill in the application form can be vital. Do read the instructions carefully, and do sign your cheque. More applications are rejected because of unsigned cheques than anything. If it says cross the cheque, cross it. If it asks for applications in units of 100 shares, do not ask for 150. Do not try to be clever. The system can only cope with simplified procedures. The issuing bank cannot spare the time and trouble to handle variations. It throws them out. Look carefully at the cut-off points. Try to pitch your application just above them. For example, where applications should be for units of 200 shares up to 1,000 shares, then for units of 500 up to 5,000 shares, and finally for units of 1,000 shares thereafter, it makes sense to go for 1,500 shares, or for 6,000 if you have the money. The sponsors have formed natural breaks at 1,000 and 5,000 shares. They may use them when it comes to scaling down applications. So shoot just over the top of them, if you can.

Anyone applying for up to 1,000 shares might get, say, 300. Those asking for between 1,100 and 5,000 might get 800, and people over 5,000 might get 40% of what they sought. By going for a slot just above the natural break (most people will gravitate towards those breaks), you might sneak into a higher allotment. So, in the example, anyone asking for 6,000 shares might get 2,400, whereas applications for 5,000 might get only 800. Sometimes that little extra step can attract a disproportionately large allotment. The example may overstate the advantages, but the theory is sound. Any extra edge is worth having when you are chasing a winner. And please, please, please, pay attention to the closing date and time. Application lists almost always close at one minute past ten in the morning, rarely staying open longer, and then only if the issue flops. If you miss the post, or cannot reach the receiving bank on time, too bad. No amount of pleading will get you in. Remember the great fuss about those who missed the big 1998 issue of Thomson Travel. Many missed it through no fault of their own, but the early birds did avoid that trap. If there is the chance of registering in advance, do it. That does not commit you. But miss closing time, and you have had it. Most privatisations allow you to hand forms in at a local bank up to the day before. That is a safe, sensible way of doing it.

A really successful launch might be oversubscribed 100 times, with £1.1bn chasing £10m worth of shares, so the odds are against you. Every application will be scaled down, and the issuing house chooses how this is done. The bigger the demand, the smaller the chance of getting what you ask for – but the fatter the opening premium when dealing starts. What you lose on the swings, you may gain on the roundabout.

Some companies deliberately favour small investors. This happens with some of the bigger, nationally known names when they float. They buy a little goodwill by spreading shares around. Smaller, more specialist operators may prefer fewer, larger shareholders. They cost less to service. Watch the press for clues. The more shares you ask for, the more you are likely to get – except when there is a pretty clear warning that those trying to be too greedy will get nothing at all. Some heavily subscribed privatisations have chopped jumbo applications off without a single share. The rough rule of thumb is that if oversubscription might mean scaling down heavily, issuing houses decide it is easier to give nothing at all to those who would have got only a tenth or less of what they sought. But there is no easy advance guidance. Use your common sense.

Many heavily-subscribed issues hold a ballot to decide who gets shares. The ballot may be weighted to favour bigger applications, so while a cheque for £2,000 may win no more than a lucky one for £200, the £2,000 cheque may be ten times more likely to get something than the £200 one.

Use Your Partner

Your partner – husband or wife – can be a vital investment aid. Never make one application where two will legally do. Be sensible, though. Since Keith Best MP was prosecuted for making multiple applications in the British Telecom issue, the game has changed. Check the fine print. Privatisations clearly state that it is illegal to make multiple applications. A lot of computer time and effort is devoted to tracking down multiples. The days are gone when your goldfish or your cat could make a killing in the new issue market. Do not put their names down on application forms. You are wasting your time.

Privatisations have made it clear that applications must only be for the benefit of the applicant. You should not persuade others to apply for you, in return for a share of their profits. You cannot put in on behalf of other people without telling them. You can, however, apply on behalf of your children under 18. Study the forms for details. In state sell-offs where there are sometimes advantages to be gained from prior registration, make sure you register the children in advance as well.

There is no blanket ban against multiple applications. Strictly speaking, they are frowned upon. But many issuing houses are quite happy to see them. They make an issue appear more successful. Unless it is spelt out, multiples are not illegal. The worst that can happen is that your forms will be thrown out. Some houses will turn a blind eye, especially if an issue is not doing too brilliantly.

Making multiple applications, backed by enormous bank overdrafts, used to be a cottage industry. Professional punters employed armies of pensioners to write cheques, fill forms, and address envelopes by the thousand. Cats and goldfish galore crept in. Even now, when the stags are running, City litterbins are stuffed with discarded prospectuses, each with the application form missing. Litter levels can be a clue to the likely success of an issue. So can newspaper sales counters. Sometimes punters pull up at the printing works with small vans to carry off thousands of copies of editions which bear the application forms. You must have the real thing. Photocopies are not accepted.

Bullying The Bank Manager

Bullying bank managers to get them to extend sufficiently large overdrafts is also important in successful stagging. Managers know you must put up more money than you will actually be required to pay out in a big issue, because you will be scaled down. Normally, only cheques with successful applications are cashed – though that does vary. Because applications in a winner will be scaled down, a cheque for any surplus is sent back immediately the allotments are announced. Much of the bank loan is only needed for a few days. The real stag will be selling quickly, and banking the pay-out cheque as soon as possible.

The risks for any bank are small, so long as you are being sensible. Officially, bank managers are not sure about stagging. But they can be persuaded. Ask for a stagging facility. The manager will charge you a hefty arrangement fee, so he gets his share. If you earn enough – usually over £20,000 – take out a bank gold card. They usually allow an overdraft of up to £10,000 at preferential rates, without prior consultation. Threaten to take your account elsewhere, to get a gold card from another bank, if your man is too difficult. After all, he needs your custom.

Traps For The Unwary

All of this may sound marvellous fun, a magic way of making money. But there are traps for the unwary, the reckless, and the feckless. New issues do flop sometimes. If you get it wrong, you could end up with many more shares than you really want, or can afford, in an issue which opens at a discount, below the price you paid. There is no way out, should that happen. You cannot simply cancel your cheque if the issue looks like going bad. Once you have sent your application, you are on the hook. You can be prosecuted for cancelling your cheque.

That explains why there are queues on the morning when a good issue closes. Some people have too much cash riding on it to leave anything to chance. Post your application form too far in advance, and you run the risk of a late change in the market mood. A promising issue could be left out in the cold, and your would-be winner could turn sour, after your cheque is in. Those in the last-minute queue are doing all they can to avoid getting caught out. Even they have no guarantee. There can be up to ten days between applications closing and dealings opening, though it is usually less. Always check the timing before you play.

And do not go absolutely mad. The surest-looking thing can go wrong. When you decide what to go for, work out how much you would lose if the shares were to open at a 10% discount. Then see how much you can afford to lose, and modify your application accordingly. Remember, if it is a dud, you might well get all you ask for, instead of being scaled down.

Some issues do go spectacularly wrong. The Government got caught badly in selling a tranche of BP shares around the October '87 Crash. When Manchester United Football Club came to market, the shares slumped from an issue price of 385p to 275p in a few weeks. Villain of the piece was Kevin Maxwell, who dumped over 4% of the company. Shrewd investors, though, were not caught out. They would have read the *Daily Mail*, explaining why the offer was best left alone. And the prudent punter, even without the *Daily Mail*, would have sold quickly, before the loss got too great. Always cut losses quickly.

Intermediaries' Offers

Increasingly, issuers are being allowed to float companies through a combination of a placing and an offer for sale, or an intermediaries' offer. The combination means that a chunk of the issue is placed with the big institutional investors, guaranteeing them a portion of the issue, and leaving less for private shareholders who have to compete for the leftovers in an offer for sale. It is not quite as nasty as that, because usually a big public response means that some shares are taken away from the institutions in what they call a clawback. It does mean, though, that the big boys are assured of getting in on winners, while the public must compete. That, of course, reduces the size of the public issue, makes it more likely to be oversubscribed, and should help ensure a handy premium. The intermediaries' offer is a variation on this technique. It means that the public can get some of the shares by applying for them through an intermediary. That means you must go to a stockbroker (or a bank or building society acting as a broker) and ask them to apply for you. If your application is successful, you pay commission to your broker. Great. More gravy for the boys. Wonderful how the City ensures that changes in the rules always favour the City.

The excuse for this is that it can be used for higher risk companies, say technology ventures, which the private investor may be ill-equipped to evaluate alone. If the shares have to be bought through an intermediary, the line runs, the investor will be assured of professional advice. Oh dear! Do not let it put you off. It is irritating, but if you have to pay commission to get aboard early, so be it. The system itself may discourage some investors, so that may raise the chances that you will actually get some when you apply. Keep awake, though, and study the details. Offers through intermediaries have often proved quite attractive in the nineties. Straightforward offers for sale, which allow everyone in the easy way, have tended to apply only to the less inviting issues in the mid-nineties. If you can get them, you do not want them, I have suggested, only to be accused of cynicism. Perhaps. I find it hard to distinguish between cynicism and the fruits of experience.

Offers For Sale By Tender

So far, I have dealt with tactics for a straightforward offer for sale. Most of them hold good for an offer for sale by tender, a method which has fallen out of favour in the nineties, but which could return. Tenders are less attractive. They carry an added complication because they require would-be purchasers to determine how much they will pay for the shares. The sponsors set a minimum price, and ask for offers (tenders) above it.

It is permitted, however, to make multiple applications in tender offers, so long as each application is at a different price. For example, if the minimum price was 120p, you could apply at 120p, 125p, 130p, 135p and so on – different amounts at different prices, if you wished.

Once all applications are in, the sponsors set what is called a striking price. All of the shares are sold at that price. Anyone who bids at or above the striking price gets the shares – at the striking price. If you are determined to have some, you can apply at a very high price. If everyone does that, of course, everyone gets the shares at a silly price.

Sponsors sell by tender when they are unsure what price they should set. They can judge the mood more easily, and pick what price they wish, provided they get enough bids above the minimum. In practice, they will pitch the striking price below the maximum they could have got. They will always want to leave some buyers unsatisfied in the hope of generating a good after-market, with a modest profit for the stags. Obviously a big bonanza is unlikely. When it comes to judging how much to tender, or whether to play at all, rely on the usual sources – brokers, press, or grey market. It may be best not to bother. Offers by tender are inherently less inviting than simple offers for sale.

Introductions

New issues are sometimes brought to market through an introduction. No new shares are on offer, so the issue is of no interest to the stag. Market-makers start quoting prices in shares which are already widely held, but which lack a listing. Most introductions involve a London quotation for a foreign company.

Placings

Placings are nearly as bad for the stags. The sponsor of a placing fixes the price for the shares, and can dole them out to a list of applicants. The rules governing who gets them change from time to time. No matter how it is done, it usually means useful profits for a small group, and nothing for the rest. Placings have produced most of the really big new issue winners in the mid-nineties. If you happen to deal through the issuing broker, placings can be brilliant. In some cases, your broker might be able to get you on the placing list with another issuing house.

Sadly, though, the Stock Exchange always seems to be changing the rules and making it even easier for issuing houses to sell to a narrow range of clients. Getting on the winners might become even more difficult, despite protests. One special warning is necessary. Some of the most spectacular winners in placings have been attracting considerable attention. Letters from readers suggest that some people get caught up in the excitement, and ask their brokers to buy as soon as dealings begin, thinking that they will be able to buy at the issue price or close to it, if they are quick. This is not so. The big winners open at a big premium. So if you simply tell your broker to buy when dealings start, you might find you have paid as much as twice the offer price. Do not get muddled. If you want to buy a new issue winner in the market, give your broker a limit. Make it clear how much you are prepared to pay. And do not chase prices up on the opening day.

New Issue Clubs

There have been a few efforts to help small investors get their share of new issues. These have come from new issue clubs, commercial operations which ask for a subscription, and in turn supply details of new issues and help in submitting applications. In some cases, they may be able to obtain allotments of shares in issues. If they can, that obviously improves the chances for members to get aboard some winners.

Hopefully, these services will develop. One of the early efforts, however, lacked the status to get aboard the best issues, and tended to find itself only able to offer members allocations in low quality stuff. The members became a handy dumping ground to give third rate companies a start. By the end of 1995, the position was beginning to look more encouraging. Bristol-based financial adviser Hargreaves Lansdown has been trying to improve the lot of small investors, and Charles Schwab has launched a new issue club. It offers newsletters and hopes of helping investors obtain allocations in suitable issues. These initiatives are well-intentioned, and may prove valuable. Once again, they will have to be alert to ensure that they are able to keep up a quality service. It is hard to imagine that all issuing houses will make their real winners available to these services. They will prefer to keep as much as possible for their own clients. Keep an eye on them, though, they might well be worth supporting. Small investors really do need all the help they can get in these greedy days.

OFEX Issues

In the late nineties, more and more small issues are appearing and being offered to private investors by direct mail, or through smaller broking houses. Some will be destined for the Alternative Investment Market. Most will be bound for a listing on the OFEX, where it might be impossible to buy or sell for months on end, after the first flurry. This is not necessarily bad. Broker J.M.Finn, for example, has been behind several small Ofex issues which have done remarkably well. I have recommended, or commented favourably, on a couple of them in the *Daily Mail.* At the time of writing, cancer biscuit company Energiser has multiplied fix-fold inside two years, and robot systems company Robotic Technology is up ten times. Some tiny Ofex issues have been horrifying, however. So tread with special care. Even the goodies can be hard to buy and sell at times, and you are unlikely to be able to keep track of prices or company news too easily. Some are disgraceful, barely making one announcement a year. Stay away, unless you really know what you are doing, or are ready to take a total gamble.

CHAPTER SEVEN

How To Pick A Share

It must be easy to make a killing on the stockmarket, surely? Open any sensible newspaper, and there is a page or two packed with prices, and a stockmarket report talking about all sorts of juicy gains on a good day. Some of the reasons for the rises appear trivial, others absolutely obvious. Of course, the leaders went up when interest rates went down. No wonder companies which do a lot of business in Asia dipped as the economic crisis took hold. No problem, this share picking racket.

Hindsight is wonderful. It makes geniuses of us all. Time after time, I have picked up rival papers and read a story I did not write. Obvious stuff. I curse myself for being so stupid as to have missed it. It was there for the taking. Next time, I promise myself... only to find it has happened again, a few weeks later. Looking back, you realise how much you knew all along. Opportunity was staring you in the face. But you simply did not focus on it.

And investment is tough. When you actually have to lay out your own money, it gets much more difficult. Suddenly you realise that there are 7,000 securities of one sort or another to choose from. Some days, the fallers outnumber the risers. The dozen or two movers which make the market reports are not so easy to locate when you look at the price table in the *Financial Times*. It covers more than two pages, is fearsomely difficult to read, and looks as if it makes no sense at all until you get the hang of things.

Some newspapers list the numbers of rises and falls. They can be quite a surprise. Even when the market is on a good run, there can be spells when prices drift back day after day. Sometimes, of course, the whole thing turns down, and the market can look bleak for a few months. But even in the good times, it is easy to lose a fortune by backing a bad business. Or by missing the change of mood when things go off the boil.

Whole sectors can go wrong. In the mid-eighties, gullible investors and journalists galore fell in love with advertising agencies. Saatchi & Saatchi grew so overconfident and arrogant that they flirted with taking over the Midland Bank. Martin Sorrell, their old finance director, set up a rival at WPP, and bought some of the most famous names in advertising. Both got it badly wrong. By the end of 1991, both shares were selling for pence rather than several pounds, and struggling desperately. Both had to undergo substantial financial reconstructions. Much the same thing happened to stores, once the stockmarket darlings. Sir Ralph Halpern left as Burton plunged into crisis, George Davies was fired well before Next hit the bottom, Sir Terence Conran said goodbye to Storehouse, and Gerald Ratner compounded a crash from large profits into losses by talking about "crap" in his jewellery shops. In the late Nineties everyone loved theme pubs and restaurants for a while, until Regent Inns, one of the brightest stars, admitted a spot of bother over growth rates. Not so long before, all looked wonderful winners, making fortunes for themselves and their shareholders.

Steady your nerves, though. Even as recession gripped the economy, relatively few quoted companies actually went bust. Under 40 in the worst year, though it seemed like more. The failures always catch the eye. But very few investors lose all of their money. Companies in trouble are usually rescued. And there is rarely any reason why the alert investor should be trapped in a total loser. If this book teaches you nothing else, it should show you how to avoid complete disaster. The chapter on selling shares – I keep saying it because it is crucial – is the most important in the book.

The arithmetic helps, too. If you lose half of your money, it sounds terrible, but your £1,000 has only gone down to £500. You have lost £500. Double your money, and the £1,000 becomes £2,000. You have made £1,000. In a rising market – and this book is being written as the market is hiccuping – the chances of doubling your money are much greater than halving it.

It may sound as if I am simply playing with words – halving, doubling, what matters? But the psychological impact of doubling and halving is not to be ignored. If you are going to play the stockmarket, you have to believe that you will not be daft enough to halve your money too often. And, hopefully, by the time you reach the end of this book, you will have resolved to sell and limit your loss before it grows too great. Every investor must believe that there is a fair chance of doubling their money, given a little luck. And in a fair market, that is not asking too much.

An Excuse To Fall In Love

When you trade in the stockmarket, you are looking for an excuse to fall in love, hunting an investment you can live with and grow with. Investing in British industry is the vague kind of notion which everyone thinks makes sense. Thriving companies matter to us as individuals, and as a nation. No matter how much of a gamble it may be in reality, everyone wants it to work.

It is a fine romance, finding the share partner to suit you. City pages parade the temptations before your eyes. You might want to flirt with bid candidates, or get carried away with risky option market favourites. Whatever your fancy, it makes sense to check the fundamentals first. SUCCESSFUL INVESTMENT IS ABOUT ANTICIPATION. You need to spot the attractions before the other investors, and to do that, you need to know the kind of things which appeal to other investors. Top of the list come the dividend yield and the price-earnings ratio.

The Dividend Yield

Dividend yields form the bedrock of most measured investment decisions. It is no use spotting the next takeover candidate if the bid comes in below the market price (it does happen sometimes) simply because gamblers have got carried away by the bid dream, and have lost touch with investment reality, overvaluing the company.

The dividend yield matters, especially if you are a cautious investor with income high on your list of priorities. Capital gains are super, but dividends roll on year after year, generally growing larger, no matter what the shares may be doing day by day. That counts a great deal, particularly for older investors who need a good return to bolster their income.

And a consistent and growing stream of dividend income is what the investment giants are seeking. Pension funds and insurance companies are the biggest and most important traders, and they influence share prices more than anyone. They take in money today against the promise of providing cash at some future date to pensioners and policyholders. They love an investment which will provide them with greater income in future (through rising dividends). The more secure that income, the better. In many ways, dividend yields drive the whole market. At its crudest, a share is a stake in a business which you hope will keep on producing profits so that it can pay higher dividends as time goes by. If there were no dividends, you would get no return from that share until you sold it. Rather like property companies which have grand and glorious empty buildings built on borrowed money, you might have a terrific asset, but the lack of cash flowing in to pay day-to-day bills would mean you would go bust without dividends. Just as generating an income is really what determines the capital value of a building to the property company, the stream of dividends ultimately determines the worth of a share.

Bear with me. This may sound obvious and repetitive, but it is a vital investment truth, which easily gets overlooked when markets are hot, and capital values are leaping. In the end, the value of a company to investors is the income it will generate for them. No good having a fabulous mine which will never produce gold which can be sold to yield profits to pay dividends. That mine might be given a massive value on the stockmarket long before anyone digs a serious shaft. But that can only go on for so long. Sooner or later, production and profits will be what counts. Share investment is essentially about anticipation. In the short term, anticipating what other investors will do. In the long term, about anticipating the value of the dividend flow from the profits a company produces. No matter how sophisticated the arguments you may get from others, in the very final analysis, that is what matters. Believe me.

The dividend yield is the percentage return from the annual income on a share. Working it out is not difficult. If you are paid £10 a year before tax from an investment which has cost you £100, the yield is 10%. If you buy 100 shares at £2 each, and the company pays a gross dividend total of 10p a share in the year, the dividend yield is 5%. You calculate this by taking the total dividend (10p multiplied by 100 shares equal £10), dividing it by total cost (£2 multiplied by 100 shares equals £200), and expressing it as a percentage – 5%.

The sum is more complicated in reality, because dividends are paid after the deduction of tax. You have to add back the tax before doing the sum. And in the market, they calculate the yield by using not lots of £100, but the cost of just one share, and the dividend on one share. Do not worry about this detail. You need never calculate a dividend yield for yourself. Ask your broker, or look in one of the newspaper share price tables. Most show the yield. As the share price rises, the dividend yield falls, because you are paying more for the right to the same amount of dividend. Conversely, the dividend yield rises as the share price falls, because you are buying the right to the same dividend payment more cheaply. If the dividend is increased, and the share price remains unchanged, the yield goes up. And vice versa. A higher dividend is likely to prompt a higher share price, and a reduced dividend could bring a sharply lower price.

As a crude guide, the higher the yield, the more risky the share, and the more dubious the prospects of the company. The lower the yield, the higher the market rates prospects of growth. It all goes back to what investors expect profits to do, since they ultimately determine how much money there is to pay dividends.

The market is revising its opinion all of the time, and this is reflected in changing share prices. Sometimes a good company with strong growth prospects will offer a higher yield than others in the same business because few people have realised what is going on. Those shares will be worth buying.

On the other hand, a high yield could mean that the City has spotted problems ahead. Profits may be sliding, and the company may not be able to afford such a high dividend by the end of the year. Most published yields are based on dividends paid in the previous year. They may overstate the real yield because the next dividend – the one a new buyer will actually get – could be cut. If the company is doing better, of course, the published yield may be understated, because the dividend could go up.

Pinning Your Faith On The PE

Pinning your faith on the price-earnings ratio, or the p/e, is one of the market's favourite games. Dividend yields have a certain down to earth reality. At the end of the day, you get a dividend cheque through the post, and that means real money in your pocket. The p/e means no such thing. It may just be a guess to build a dream on. P/e is about mental, not physical, jerks, and is the investment analysts' most powerful piece of juju. I explained what a p/e is in an earlier chapter. Like the dividend yield, it is one of the key tools for comparing one company with another. A high p/e means that the market is normally expecting fast profits growth. Or it may mean that a slump is expected this year, and last year's historic p/e is out on a limb, ready to be chopped off as profits plunge. Most market rules can be turned on their head. A low p/e usually means lower profits or poor growth are anticipated. Unless, that is, you know better. You may just have spotted a company with high growth potential and a low p/e. Then you may have found a bargain. Take it to your heart – after trying to make sure you, not the market, are not the one making a terrible mistake. The market does not get things wrong that often, but it does happen.

Variations On A Theme

Different strokes for different folks. The dividend yield or the p/e appropriate to one sector, one industry, may not be right for another. Sometimes the market decides it has gone wrong, and a whole sector is re-rated, up or down. Sometimes the different ratings make obvious sense. In 1986, it was hard to argue with lower p/es and higher dividend yields for oil stocks than for stores. They reflected the uncertain prospects for oil profits against the background of chaos in OPEC. Consumer spending was soaring, and profit prospects for most of the High Street looked wonderful.

After the 1987 slump, of course, that changed. Oil shares did not win higher ratings, but the swift players began to dump stores, starting a slide which continued well into the nineties as profits collapsed. In the early nineties, supermarkets suddenly switched from the great dependable growth favourites – 'everyone has to eat' – to rather more dubious assets. There were fears that as inflation slowed, there would be less room for the companies to raise prices, and less profit margin to be made. And there were worries that one of them would start a serious price-cutting war – something more than the unending barrage of routine cut-price claims – and would force everyone to follow, slashing margins. A year or two later, by the mid-nineties, the market had regained its nerve as it became clear the leaders were not really vulnerable on price. The focus then shifted to which was making the most progress, with all of the shares gaining ground, but Tesco doing best as it appeared to enter a phase of more aggressive and effective management initiatives. And in the mid to late nineties, the stockmarket rockets were the information technology companies, roaring to ever-higher peaks, and few City folk batting an eye at p/e ratios up in the sixties.

Fashion plays a prominent role in investment ratings. It is easy to get sucked in, so try to keep your feet on the ground. City backroom boys do get it wrong, and get carried away by dreams of glory for different industries. In January and February of 1997, it seemed the City was soccer crazy. Prices of the few listed companies boomed, and it seemed every club in the country was considering floating on the stockmarket. Come December, reality had returned. The Nomura Footie Index (it got so fashionable that they even invented a special index) was down 30pc. Whoops!

We all ought to have appreciated in the eighties that the personal computer boom would go bust – and it did. Simple common sense should have told anyone that the chance of such big early profits would bring a flood of competition from new entrants, bringing everyone's profit margins tumbling down. Perhaps the high technology computer-related boom of the mid-nineties will go the same way – or perhaps the market for sophisticated computers really will continue to grow.

In the wake of the 1987 Crash, I tired of telling people to sell property shares. It was clear that the City was heading for hard times, and would not be able to afford ridiculous expansion plans using expensive new offices. It was no great shakes in the forecasting stakes – simple common sense. That is a commodity which often eludes City aces as they run with the pack. Living in each other's pockets, they are easily fooled when booming profit prospects are on the lips of everyone in every wine bar within half a mile of Throgmorton Street. That is why some of the best investment managers are based in Scotland. They pride themselves on being detached from the silly gossip, and are able to take an objective view. Equally, however, it does not always pay to be too smart. It hurts to recall the profit opportunities I missed, and the wonderful tips I could have given in the eighties had I not been so cautious. Many times I looked at companies on the move, and recognised old tricks and dubious names from the early seventies. Because I thought I could spot what was happening, I kept away, quietly forecasting problems ahead. Often, I was right. Sooner or later, so many of the suspect little games, the brief fashionable stocks, fell apart. But by keeping aloof, I had missed profit opportunities galore while the game was still good.

Before the problems, there would often be 18 months or more of glorious short-term gains. You need to know what fashions are in, and when to go with them. If you can spot the emerging trend early enough, no matter how suspect, it can yield handsome returns – provided you get out before the mood changes. You can be too smart, too cautious, for your own good. My smug satisfaction at spotting the dubious nature of many situations in the eighties was spoilt when I woke up to how well others had done by playing along with the games. Of late, I have been a touch more flexible, recognising that sometimes it takes the more – shall we say, adventurous – entrepreneurs to back new ideas and get them moving.

The PEG

Popularised in this country by Jim Slater, PEG stands for Price Earnings Growth Factor. It is calculated by dividing the prospective price earnings ratio into the estimated future rate of growth in earnings. Say, for example, that the average pe is 15, and the average broking forecast of growth is 15, then the PEG is one

A low PEG is a sign that investors are ready to pay a fairly low price for future growth in earnings, while a high PEG suggests the shares are more expensive. On the whole, this system works well, and Slater has publicised it widely, while his son Mark has used it to guide the investment policy of his successful unit trust. It is an advance on the standard pe ratio because it links the pe to future earnings growth. Slater suggests that it has paid over the long term to buy on a PEG of under one. The snag, of course, is that you need access to brokers' forecasts in order to operate the system. These are available in the Slater-devised reference book, *Company REFS*, and other services listed below. While at first glance the system might appear to have an authority lacking in some others, it should not be forgotten that it relies ultimately on fallible human judgement – the rate of growth forecast by the brokers, who do get it wrong quite frequently. That said, the very popularity of the system means it is worth watching because if it prompts many investors to buy or sell, shares will move accordingly. And because the system does make pretty good sense, whatever the weakness.

Eyeing The Averages

Keep a hold on reality by eyeing the averages. The best place to find them is in the *Financial Times*. Each day it carries a detailed table headed 'FT-ACTUARIES SHARE INDICES'. It moves about the paper a bit, but is usually near the stockmarket report. This splits the market into 70 or more groups, and gives the average dividend yield, and p/e, plus other odds and ends for each group, and the market as a whole. That way you can compare, say, the yield and p/e on National Westminster Bank with the average for all of the main shares in the bank sector.

Obviously these continually shift with market moves. But if you spot one sector which is way out of line, be extra cautious. You will need a very good reason for investing in it. All too often, it means shares in that particular industry have run too far ahead. They will be pulled back in line not by a roaring boom, but by a slump – in profits, or in share prices. Since the market always tends to overdo things – up or down – that could mean dramatic losses. Similar reservations apply if you spot an individual share way out of line with the average for the group.

Prospective Problems

Be wary, too, of ambitious projections. In a rising market, those who once considered p/e ratios of 15 rather lively soon learn to live with them, and begin to feel comfortable with p/es in the 20s. Look hard. As the mood gets merrier, you may find you have switched from talking about historic p/es based on actual profits companies have already made, to prospective p/es, based on what this year's profits might be – altogether more speculative sums based on guesswork.

Any price-earnings ratio in excess of 25 needs a special explanation, and should only be attached to a very special company indeed. Of the familiar UK names, Body Shop once appeared to be able to command an astronomic rating almost indefinitely. In the last edition of this book, I warned that even Body Shop might not warrant such a rating for ever. It was growing big enough and international enough to meet the kind of organizational problems which confront all majors, and growth could slow. Sure enough, it has happened. Now Body Shop sells on a routine rating, in line with stickier prospects.

The warning about a high p/e applies no matter what the averages, no matter how buoyant the market. If p/es over 25 become common, it is a clear signal that the market is getting overheated. Everyone is liable to get sucked in, though. Early in 1986, otherwise sane and respectable fund managers were beginning to cite prospective price-earnings ratios based on projected profits for 1990. They might have been right. They might have been mad. Either way, if they believed they were basing decisions on anything other than sheer guesswork, they were fooling themselves. It is impossible to make a sensible forecast for more than two years ahead. The imponderables are just too great.

In fact, the Crash of 1987 seems to have brought most managers down to earth. In the nineties, I have seen few eager analysts projecting profits more than two years ahead, except... Well, there are always exceptions. The boom in biotechnology and pharmaceutical stocks has led to a flurry of clever estimates of what the drugs each company was developing in the nineties might be earning in the year 2000, or perhaps 2005. Take that year 2000 figure, discount it back (knock off say 30% a year), and you could get an estimate of what the wonders of 2000 were worth several years before they were anywhere near ready for sale. Or something like that. Crazy? Not altogether. High risk? Absolutely.

In August 1995, I recommended shares in Shield Diagnostic at 65p. Late in 1997, they were 750p, and we were happily trying to weigh the chances of Shield making £20m a year from each of two diagnostic products by the year 2005. It was working well in 1997, but I have to recognise that the shares price could slump if something goes badly wrong in the next few years. On the other hand, Shield did come up with very specific products for very clear markets – rather different than just guessing that some unproven idea might create a new market. By the middle of 1998, Shield shares were back under 500p, and fans were still waiting for the world to understand that profits would be brilliant in five years' time. Hope we were right.

Asset Backing – The Backstop

Once you are satisfied that the dividend yield and price-earnings ratio makes sense in the share of your choice, check the asset backing. This is the backstop. It gives you an idea of what the company might fetch if it stopped trading, the business was sold, and the borrowings repaid.

Assets were described earlier when we discussed the balance sheet. To discover the asset backing of a company, take the total value of assets – land, buildings, machinery, stocks, cash and such – deduct the liabilities – loans, tax due, creditors and so on – and you get shareholders' funds. Divide this sum by the number of Ordinary shares in issue, and you have net asset backing per share. As usual, this is not something you have to calculate yourself. A few companies actually publish it in their annual report. But your broker will check it for you.

Asset backing is not too important day-to-day. What matters most is the profits earned from those assets. No-one bothered much about the asset backing of Imperial Chemical Industries until Hanson picked up a small stake and began hovering as a possible bidder. Even then, in a company like ICI, trading profits continued to be the main issue. The Hanson initiative, though, did help prompt ICI to split itself into two – ICI and Zeneca – and that proved richly rewarding for investors. So perhaps the assets did matter, after all. Assets are always especially important where there is the chance of a bid, and these days there are precious few companies where you can rule out the possibility. So it is always comforting to know that the share of your choice can lay claim to a vast pile of assets. That can be crucial if a company is in trouble, or in one of two specialist categories - property companies or investment trusts.

The text book asset play of 1995 was chemicals group Fisons. It started the year down on its luck, with the share price little over 100p. Stuart Wallis had come in as boss in the autumn of 1994, with a hot reputation. Profit prospects were poor, and many doubted whether Fisons could make much progress. By the middle of the year, though, Wallis had made a dazzling series of deals to sell different parts of the business, generating more than £600m, while managing to keep profits in reasonable shape. As he later admitted, when he first looked at Fisons, he could see the potential, but worried whether he would be given time to reshape the company, fearing that a bidder might strike first. He had assessed the odds brilliantly. By October, Fisons had fallen for 265p to Rhône-Poulenc Rorer, the French end of an American giant. Wallis had done a wonderful job for shareholders – but the strength of the assets in Fisons was what allowed him to achieve it.

Obviously the more assets, the better. The closer those assets are to cash, the better. Look in the balance sheet to find the cash (minus overdrafts), or investments (saleable shares in other companies). There may also be a holding in an unquoted associate company, that may be in the books at a nominal value, but might be worth a great deal more if sold. Property usually comes next in the asset line-up, though in the nineties it is a more dubious benefit. The nearer London, the better, used to be the rule, and the older the date of valuation, the more scope there could be for greater value than the figures suggest. In the nineties, though, any property needs to be treated with caution. Valuations from the late eighties or early nineties could prove optimistic, especially if they relate to offices in London. Plant and machinery values are always doubtful. Though listed as an asset, much of it may be virtually worthless in a sale. Stocks (whatever the company makes, or the raw materials it makes them from) are also of uncertain worth. Clearly, last year's fashions are not worth much to a clothing company, nor Ninja Turtle toys when the 1990 boom was over. What price a warehouse full of Spice Girls dolls in 1998?

Pay particular attention to debtors, the negative side of the balance sheet. You must be scrupulous in knocking off the full weight of loans in calculating asset value. ALWAYS ASSUME THE WORST. If a loan has to be redeemed by the company under any circumstances, deduct the full cost of repayment. The worst has an uncanny knack of rolling around, just when you can least afford it. Ideally, you want a company which is trading well, with an asset backing comfortably in excess of the share price. Then you are covered both ways – either the shares sell as a promising trading situation, or someone might take a fancy to the company and bid to take over the assets and put them to better use where they can earn more profits. Such companies can be hard to find. The strongest asset situations crop up when a company has had a trading setback, and the price has fallen – just like Fisons. Disappointing profits often leave assets looking cheap. You have to decide whether the setback is temporary, and whether those assets are worthwhile. That is not easy, but at least if you pick an asset-backed recovery company, asset power will help you sleep more easily.

The Asset Exceptions – Property Companies And Investment Trusts

Shares in property companies and investment trusts usually sell for less than the value of their assets – a discount. In bad times, the discount can be as large as 60% in the case of property companies, and 35% for investment trusts – though, once again, there can be exceptions. This means you could find a property company with 100p of assets with shares at 40p or less, or an investment trust with 100p of assets whose shares are 65p. Do not get carried away thinking you have found a bargain. You might have, but the City will know about it, and there will usually be a good reason for it. Brokers have vast expensive teams of analysts specialising in different sectors. They do nothing else but look at property shares or investment trusts.

Large property share discounts will reflect worries about the viability of the company, and the accuracy of their last published valuations. In the early nineties, property companies led the list of collapses. Often, they were saddled with enormous buildings which they could not let. No-one wanted to rent them. Empty buildings are not just a useless asset, they are expensive, depreciating assets – or, rather, nasty liabilities. An empty property is costly to keep in good condition. It needs guarding, and the systems must be kept in working order. It will almost certainly have been built with borrowed money, and that will be racking up interest charges every minute.

At one stage, companies were offering rent-free periods, even paying people to use their properties, just to reduce the cost of outgoings. Until properties have a tenant, and an assured flow of rental income, their capital value is debatable. The quality of the rent roll, and the amount of the rents, really determines what someone will pay to buy a building, given that most of the buyers are insurance companies or pension funds looking for a predictable flow of rising income as time goes by.

Even by the mid-nineties, there was still a surplus of empty properties, and a millstone of debt around the necks of many property companies. Asset valuations are dubious, to put it kindly. There will be investment opportunities among property companies, but it is a sector to be treated with great caution until you can be pretty sure you know what you are doing. Even prestige office blocks in the heart of the City can be of uncertain value. Even if they are a mere 15 years old, they may not be able to take the complicated wiring and temperature systems so vital to large offices these days, or may not be able to provide the large open trading floors which are in vogue. Unless you really understand what each building might be worth, stay away.

Investment trusts are altogether different. As explained earlier, they hold shares in other companies, quoted or unquoted. They hope to boost revenue by picking companies whose dividends are growing. And hope to increase their own capital value by picking companies whose shares are rising. A number of stockbrokers have departments which follow every nuance, and can calculate the slightest change in underlying asset value of the trusts day-by-day. NatWest and SBC Warburg are probably the best. You will not be able to compete against such people in discovering new excitement. But you can do well by going with the flow, choosing shares in sectors which are making headway.

It is also worth paying attention to the investments which the trusts themselves make. Most will be delighted to send you their latest report and accounts. The best provide a complete list of their holdings, plus a thumbnail sketch of what those companies do, and why they are worth supporting. That way, you can get useful tips from some of the best-paid professionals in the investment world.

As ever, be wary of fashion. Some trusts specialise in emerging markets, particular countries, or particular commodities. They are almost always launched, or seek to raise extra capital, at or near the peak of the fashion for such things. Sometimes they do well, but more often, they should be avoided. The mid-nineties saw giant new trusts launched with a mighty hullabaloo by Mercury and Kleinwort Benson, specialising in mining stocks, and in European privatisation issues. Years later, they were still below their issue prices.

New investment trust issues are particularly tricky because they begin by selling 100p shares for 100p. But because of initial expenses, and the cost of buying shares to make up their portfolio, they might actually begin trading with assets of 95p, perhaps less. So, instead of buying the trust shares at a discount (paying less for the assets than they are worth), you are actually paying a premium (100p for 95p of assets). In order to get round this, trusts increasingly issue warrants with the new shares. These come notionally free of charge, and carry the right to buy extra shares in the trust at some future date at a specific price. The warrants might, for example, allow you to buy one share per warrant at 120p at any time between three and five years hence. The assumption is that the trust will by then have done well enough to be selling at more than 120p, so the warrants will let you buy extra shares cheap. This right has a value, so from the very beginning, the warrants themselves have a value, and can usually be bought and sold separately from the trust shares. The warrant value might be enough to make up for the loss in the asset value of the trust share itself in the early days.

As usual, take care. If you are going to get involved, take expert advice. And, as always, if you are not sure you understand it, keep out.

Reading The City Pages

It is all very well arming yourself with the standard tools – dividend yield, p/e, and asset values. But everyone can get them. They merely give you an investment road map. You must decide where you are going, and how you are going to get there. You must add your own touch, that extra ingredient which will make a particular share right for you. You need to develop a feel for the market. Try to immerse yourself in it as far as possible. You need to develop the trading instinct which will ultimately be your most important asset – except, perhaps, sheer luck. The harder you work, the luckier you get.

The simple way of getting a feel for what is happening is to read the City pages regularly. Pay particular attention to the stockmarket report. The *Financial Times*, The *Independent* and the *Daily Mail* are among the best. What you really want to know is not so much what happened yesterday, but what might happen next.

Most market reports carry unconfirmed gossip. Some is rubbish, plain and simple. Some remarkably well informed. Few market reporters are experienced analysts. They are poorly equipped to make decisions on what is good and what is bad. They rely on whoever they speak to. Market reporters are often fed stories by people who simply want to get a share moving, up or down, because they have a position in it themselves. It is worth reading *Profit Of The Plunge* (0 9480 3517 X) by bear raider Simon Cawkwell for an insight into how he seeks to use the press to his advantage though he has sometimes been extremely useful to me in my researches. So use newspapers to identify where the action is. Sometimes the market reports score splendid coups, picking up on the right rumours of a bid a day or two before it comes true. Sometimes they identify exciting new developments and personalities. Read them absorb then, sift them and – above all – question what they say. Eventually, you will develop a feel for what makes sense, and what might be sheer rumour. Do not rely totally on them as sources of share tips. Market reporters are just that – reporters – not qualified analysts.

Public Relations

Much of the gossip is planted by public relations agents employed by public companies. Some agencies work for dozens of companies. They leak stories unofficially, using the press to manipulate the market. Others simply like to impress their clients with the sheer volume of comment they can generate. Rarely do they drop bad news to journalists. Sometimes, though, they leak a diluted version to soften up market expectations if something really grim is on the way. Just now and then they leak really bad tidings so that an otherwise shocking result will not appear quite so bad when it comes. Usually, however, they give a hint of something good.

Both sides think they benefit. The reporter has a story which may move the shares the next day, making him look good. The public relations agent thinks he has done his client a good turn. It may be deplorable manipulation, but it cannot be disregarded, because it does move prices. So you have to heed it, with a suitably cynical perspective.

Keep such reservations in mind when you read the market reports. And do not forget them when you go on to the rest of the City pages. You will soon find what suits you best, making the most sense. Some Sunday pages are particularly prone to running friendly stories on companies fed to them by public relations agents. They need to fill the space somehow. Sometimes they are given extremely important exclusive stories, ones you will really need to read. Bear in mind, though, that the story will be coloured by the source. The public relations company will make sure that the journalist knows which side his bread is buttered on. Do not disregard the stories, however. The good news will often turn out to be true, and leaking it indicates which shares are being powered by a public relations push. Someone is working to move them higher – no bad thing if treated with suitable caution. A good public relations campaign can be a real asset at times.

Some journalists are especially gullible. All make mistakes. My most glaring error was to recommend Polly Peck a few months before the crash. Once his sternest critic, I had become a friend of chairman Asil Nadir through the years, and believed in his plans. I passed them to readers in the form of share recommendations, usually with success. Sadly, I did not spot the potential problems. To this day, I am ready to apologise to any who took my mistaken advice, though Nadir still swears that he will find a way of making money in future for Polly Peck shareholders. Financial journalists bear a heavy responsibility to their readers, one which some do not discharge with credit. On the whole, though, most journalists try honestly to convey what they believe to be the proper story. Rarely do they know anything approaching the whole truth. But financial journalists are important to investors. They may be ignorant, careless, and easily fooled. But they are the only genuinely independent source of advice most people can obtain. Most other sources have a financial interest in the advice they give. So stick with the press. It may be better than you think.

The *Financial Times* carries the most weight. It covers virtually every item of company and economic news, and frequently interprets it usefully. The 'Lex' column is required City reading, and can move shares sharply. It varies in quality as the contributors change – a problem which influences all newspapers. The *Daily Mail* City section is widely accepted as a more readable companion to the *Financial Times*. It mixes gossip, news and opinion freely in a fashion few others follow. It is closer to the chat you might hear over lunch in the City. My contributions have always been heavily slanted towards the private investor. I am always eager to learn of examples worth fighting for – though the pressure of helping produce a page each day means that I do not reply to letters as often as I should. But do tell me what upsets you, or excites you – I take comments from readers seriously.

The *Daily Telegraph* is a consistently intelligent commentator, with the intelligence of Neil Collins enlivened by the wit of Christopher Fildes. *The Independent* is valuable. Among Sunday papers, the *Observer* is notable for the foraging of Michael Gillard. He also contributes to the *Private Eye* column 'City Slicker', which has some of the best City scandal-mongering reports. And some of the silliest.

Pick your own tipsters. Paul Kavanagh in the *Sunday Times* and Edmond Jackson in the *Sunday Telegraph* both appear sensible to me. Be wary of the little snippets mentioning several companies. These tend to adopt a shotgun approach, allowing the papers to proclaim their tipping abilities. The winners are trumpeted, and the many failures are, needless to say, quietly forgotten.

Understanding The Price Tables

The most comprehensive price table is in the *Financial Times*. Finding individual prices can be a nightmare, thanks to the erratic nature of the sub-divisions. Read the accompanying notes carefully, however, and it can be deciphered. It tells you an impressive amount about each company. There is the middle price, the amount of any change, the high and low for the past year, the market capitalisation, dividend yield, and the p/e. There are also blobs and notes of different sorts, with boxes purporting to mark the most actively traded stocks. This does not always appear to be as accurate as it might be. In the 'Investment Trusts' section there is also a figure for net asset value (NAV) and a column to show the discount or premium reflected in the share price.

All of the broadsheets carry prices, some with numbers for phone lines which can be used during the day to get the latest price. On a Saturday, the *Financial Times* also lists actual share markings. These include several special areas, and can be useful in picking up some more obscure stocks whose prices are not readily available elsewhere.

Market Capitalisation

Market capitalisation is invaluable. It shows the value of the whole company, worked out by multiplying the number of shares in issue by the price. In an instant, it gives you an idea whether you are talking about the kind of company which has to be taken seriously, or a tiddler which could be vulnerable in hard times, or might rocket when the mood is right.

It is amazing how often enthusiasm comes crashing to earth when you realise that some would-be winner is already valued at millions more than you might have expected – or a would-be bidder is so small that it could not possibly launch the bid that the rumours suggest. Some little ones do make offers for their bigger brethren, but normally the bidder needs to be at least as big as the target company.

All The Exes

The price tables are scattered with cryptic exes. They are ex-dividend, ex-scrip, ex-rights. The ex means 'without'. If you buy a share ex-dividend (or xd), it means that you are not buying the right to a recent dividend which was declared by the company, but which has not yet been sent out. Ex-scrip (or ex cap, or merely xc) means you buy without the right to a recent scrip issue. And ex-rights (or xr) means the shares are no longer entitled to subscribe to a recent rights issue. You are not losing by these exes. Share prices will have been adjusted to reflect the loss of these benefits. Sometimes prices seem to fall sharply, but if you look more closely, you will find that they have simply gone 'ex' something. For example, shares which are ex a one-for-one scrip issue will halve in price, because there will be twice as many of them from that point. The opposite to ex is cum (meaning 'with'). That means you do buy the shares with the rights to a dividend, scrip, or rights issue.

Recent Issues

Several papers carry a table of recent issues, but the *Financial Times* has the best. It covers the price of shares in new issues, or rights issues. It offers a handy guide to the premium on shares which are trading ex-rights – telling you how much you could get if you wanted to sell your entitlement to a rights issue from a company where you are a shareholder. It can be attractive to buy these rights entitlements. They give you a way of buying in at a relatively low dealing cost, or the opportunity for a low cost short-term speculation. There is a short period – a few weeks usually – when these rights to subscribe to a rights issue are tradeable. If, say, a company launches a one- for-two rights issue at 100p when the shares are 120p, the rights will, in theory, be worth just over 13p. That can be calculated by taking the price of two shares at 120p, plus another at 100p, so that after the rights issue you have three shares which have cost 340p, or just over 113p each. So the value of your rights share is not the 100p you have to pay, but 113p.

If the shares move up in the market to 124p, a relatively modest gain, then the rights are worth 16p, a rise of almost a quarter. You calculate it by taking two shares at 124p, plus one at 100p. That equals 348p. Divide it by three to get 116p, or 16p above the price of the rights at 100p. You can see there are opportunities for fast, big profits if you are just buying the rights.

But it is high-risk investment. Look at what happens if the share price proper goes down. A fall from 120p to 116p means the rights are worth under 11p (twice 116p equals 232p, plus 100p, equals 332p. Divide 332p by three equals just under 111p, minus 100p). The fall from just under 13p (when the shares were 120p) to just under 11p means a hefty percentage loss. It is not a game to play until you have resources you can afford to risk, you know a helpful broker, and fully understand what you are doing.

Highs And Lows

Once again, the *Financial Times* has the best list of shares which have hit highs and lows for the past year in the previous trading session. Study it. Sometimes it can be frustrating. On a day when the market surges or slumps, there can be too many new highs and lows for individual names to be listed. When they are there, though, they form a useful way of picking up movers you may have missed from simply scanning the market report or the main changes. They show the shares which are quietly moving along.

Many changes will be prompted by readily accessible announcements. Others will be more subtle. They will be sparked by quiet insider dealing, people in the know buying or selling. Or by changes in broker profit forecasts. Or by a buying programme from someone building a share stake. Watch especially for those moving against the trend, shares which rise on a dull day, or fall when the market is good. Those are usually more than just casual moves. They will have a special reason. It is tempting to think that by the time shares have hit the highs or lows list, you have missed the main action. Not so. The trend is your friend, they say. If the shares have broken into new ground, the chances are that they will keep moving that way a while longer. They will start interesting others who watch the high and low lists. And once a share reaches new territory, that can have additional impact, as I explain later in dealing with chartists.

Trading Volume

The latest addition to the investors' armoury is a table in the *Financial Times* labelled 'Trading Volume in Major Stocks'. Something like it does appear elsewhere, and is well worth studying. Sadly, it still only covers some 200 leading companies. It can be misleading. Sometimes deals are inaccurately recorded, and sometimes they are done outside the system, deliberately designed to escape the net. Bear in mind, too, that the real number changing hands will be half the figure published. That figure takes in the sale and the purchase, so there is double counting.

Nonetheless, the table is a useful indication of the weight of money behind particular changes. Clearly a 2p rise on volume of 50,000 shares is less comforting than one on volume of 500,000 shares – but only in some ways. We come back to the snag of being able to interpret almost any rule in conflicting fashion.

A big rise on small trading volume might be suspect. It could be a freak, sparked because the market-maker was caught short of stock, something which may not last long. Or it could mean the market is fragile, and the price will respond quickly and dramatically to modest buying – ideal for a quick profit. Existing investors might all be firm holders, determined not to sell. Excellent. Or it could mean that if a sizeable seller comes on, there will not be buyers enough for the stock, and the price will plummet. Sometimes you will see heavy volume of four million shares or so, and hardly any price change. Buyers and sellers evenly matched, not much point in picking them up, because it will take a mighty change in attitude to move the price? Perhaps. Heavy is a relative term. Regular trades of one million shares or more mean little on most days in Marks & Spencer or Barclays Bank.

But they would be big news for something like MFI, the furniture company. And do not forget the money involved. Trading 11m shares in hotels group Queens Moat Houses at 16p involves some £880,000. Three million shares in National Westminster Bank at 1050p means around

159

£16m has changed hands. (Remember the volumes involve double counting, buying and selling the same shares, so you need to halve the disclosed figure to find the real trade). When markets were booming, some investors followed a variation on a plan devised by Nicholas Darvas, a former dancer *How I Made $2,000,000 in the Stockmarket.* He explained how he made his fortune in America by combining price moves with volume. The higher the volume when shares are rising, the better. The system looks appealing, but is hampered by the lack of easily accessible volume figures. You can, however, ask your broker to check them for you by using his SEAQ Level Two screen.

Equity Futures And Options Trading

Moves in the real market are influenced increasingly by positions in the futures market. This is a fast-moving area dominated by professional players. From time to time, futures are used to manipulate the main market, and vice versa. The *Financial Times* has the best reports of what goes on.

Traditional options are gradually being elbowed aside. I deal later with how they can be used for profit, but as a general guide, they can yield ideas for specific investment. Watch the list. Broadly speaking, call options mean someone expects a rise of 20% or more over the next three months, while a put suggests a fall. Double options mean they expect action, but are not sure whether it will be good or bad. That, though, is a vast over-simplification. Watch the list more as a way of pointing up stocks which are worth investigation, simply because some other punter is taking an interest in them. And who knows what they may know?

What The Brokers Say

Some newspapers and magazines carry regular articles summarising a few of the circulars sent out by leading stockbrokers. The *Daily Mail* has been featuring a list on Saturdays, as does the *Telegraph*. The *Investors Chronicle* has one every week. They are worth watching, simply to see what well-informed City professionals are saying. By the time they reach the press, they are often out of date. But, since they influence the market, they are important. It might be worth ringing the broker concerned for a copy of what takes your fancy. The broker might not let you have one but, by the same token, some will.

Some circulars are remarkably detailed and well-informed. Others? Well, we all have our problems – and some brokers, of course, will be closely linked to the company whose shares they are praising. Make a special point of trying to check whether they are the 'shop', or broker to the company.

Investment Magazines

There is only one investment magazine of real consequence – the *Investors Chronicle*. Weekly, it is almost essential reading. It combines general articles with features on particular companies and industries, covers anything from economics to option trading. Most useful of all are the brief analytical pieces in the second half, commenting on almost all company announcements, and analysing each new set of accounts. These analyses give a handy statement of asset values, and borrowing levels. *IC* opinions are sometimes off beam, but for the serious investor, the magazine is excellent. *Money Observer* is monthly, and a valuable source of much solid information. Others like *What Investment* or *Moneywise* are more erratic, and of limited value. Their share tips, in particular, should be approached with extreme caution. *The Small Company Investor* is an interesting newcomer. It concentrates on smaller companies and the AIM. If it stays the course, it could be very welcome.

Tip Sheets

Tip sheets – investment newsletters – can be worthwhile. The most prominent is the *Fleet Street Letter*. It is usually backed by thoughtful research, and good sense. Watch for offers of cut-price subscriptions which it runs every so often. There is also an impressive, but expensive publication called *Analyst*. Market guru Jim Slater has also launched his own investment newsletter, which cannot be ignored.

Penny Share Guide and *Penny Share Focus* are worth considering if you are seeking a gamble. They produce so many ideas that it is easy to think you should be spreading your cash everywhere in small doses, fearful of missing the next winner. All of the tip sheets spot some profitable shares, and find it easier to forget their flops. Use them as a source of possible ideas, and as a way of teaching yourself what to look out for, not as a bible to be taken totally seriously. I should declare an interest – the Chartsearch company which publishes tip sheets published earlier editions of some of my investment books. *Penny Share Focus* promoted an earlier edition of my book *How To Make A Killing In Penny Shares* (0 9480 3520 X). The most outstanding specialist magazine is *Techinvest*, a fortnightly subscription newsletter produced in Dublin. It concentrates on high technology stocks, and has an excellent record. If such an area interests you – and it should – it is essential reading. It has developed a sufficient following to be a powerful share price mover.

Market-makers subscribe to all of the tip sheets, so tip prices are usually marked up smartly before actual trading opens, and there can be a scramble to buy when the market is hot. So subscribers often pay over the odds, and might do better to wait a day or two for the temperature to cool. Some newsletters are too slow to advise subscribers when to sell. Nonetheless, a good newsletter can be worth taking when fun is in the air.

Beware of newsletters which are circulated free of charge. These are meant to lure you into buying something or other. Often they create the opening which gives some dodgy share pusher an excuse to phone you. Have absolutely nothing to do with them, especially any from overseas. Better still, send me a copy so that I can warn *Daily Mail* readers off.

Steer clear, too, of telephone share tipping lines. These attract a flurry of interest among the City professionals, who have to know what is being pushed to the mug punters. They may appear well in touch with events, but I am very uneasy about them. And they are expensive.

Oracle On The TV

If you have a TV set with Teletext, you might find the Oracle pages useful. They come free of charge, and provide a handy City news service throughout the day. It covers everything from share prices to foreign exchange rates and company announcements. It is far from comprehensive, and lags behind events, but is a useful stopgap for investors stranded at home.

Computer Systems

There are now several software programmes you can buy to use on a personal computer. I do not have experience of any of them, and several require a relatively hefty investment. ProShare has a useful list of what is available, and the *Investors Chronicle* appears to carry the greatest batch of relevant advertisements. I have gone on to the Internet, the global computer link, to try to keep track of what is on offer there. So far, I have found little of interest. Brokers are also beginning to offer their services on the Internet. And Charles Schwab has launched an internet service, in conjunction with Electronic Share Information, a company offering a variety of investment services. The Hemmington Scott Information Exchange, an Internet noticeboard, is fun.

ProShare

ProShare has been mentioned earlier as the organisation set up to encourage private investors, and act as a pressure group on their behalf. It produces several useful investment aids, and is well worth contacting to see what is currently on offer.

Other Sources

Where else can you go for clues? Your local library, for a start. Check the reference shelves, the stock of newspapers and magazines. You might find some surprising new sources of information. If, for example, the investment love of your life should be a supermarket company, cast an eye over *The Grocer*. It could give you valuable tips about what is happening, who looks good, and who is full of ideas, opening in new places. Trade papers often beat the national press to stories in their own specialist areas. Now and then, they could put you on to a real winner before the rest of the world wakes up. On the *Daily Mail*, we picked up several price-sensitive stories on Eurotunnel from the construction press. The bigger the library, the wider the range of useful publications.

Major libraries also carry Extel cards. These are produced by the Exchange Telegraph Company, but nowadays are losing their old position as standard reference sources for many stockbrokers, big investors, and newspaper offices. There is an Extel card for every public company, and additional services covering major private companies (useful when a public company is rumoured to be taking over someone private), and foreign companies.

The cards may look complicated, but will repay a little patience. They tell you what the company does, its address, the name and address of the registrars (who keep records of all shareholdings), plus a list of main subsidiary companies. They also show who is on the board, the main shareholders, how the price has moved over the years, what the balance sheet looks like, the net asset value, dividend details, and potted versions of recent announcements. The cards are updated regularly.

Extel cards record the past, and what matters to you is the future. Libraries may also carry the *Stock Exchange Weekly Official Intelligence*. That lists all share quotations, plus a variety of odds and ends. Most useful is the list of dealings by directors. The *Stock Exchange Official Yearbook* may also be there. That has basic information, company names and addresses, brief profits, and so on.

There could be some of the reference books which cover similar ground to Extel cards. Most are relatively expensive, and not worth buying unless you are a totally dedicated dealer – and then they will probably become outdated too quickly for you. They include the *Extel Handbook of Market Leaders*, and the *Hambro Company Guide*.

If you can afford it, it is well worth getting hold of *Company REFS, the Really Essential Financial Statistics*. Devised by Jim Slater, this comes in two hefty volumes, with another book which explains how to use the *REFS* – that book in itself is well worth exploring. The whole package is updated monthly, but it is possible to buy quarterly editions for a lower price. *REFS* is excellent. It comes as near to the complete company investment reference tool as you are likely to get. It gives a graph of each company's share price and, as the name promises, all of the really essential financial statistics. It marks a major advance in supplying information for the individual investor, and is published by Hemmington Scott (0171 278 7769). It also carries brokers' forecasts of profits. There are two specialist services concentrating on giving forecasts of profits across a wide range of brokers. Updated monthly, they are useful, though expensive. Ask your brokers what they say, or check major libraries for them. They are *The Estimate Directory* (0131 538 7070), and *Earnings Guide* (0171 278 7769).

If you work in the City, there is a specialised business library, which is well worth a lunch-time trip. The librarians are very helpful, and there is an enormous range of specialist publications.

Then come the companies themselves. Never hesitate to write to any which interests you. Check the registered address on an Extel card, *REFS*, or in the *Stock Exchange Yearbook*, and ask the company secretary for the latest report and accounts. Almost invariably, you will get a helpful reply. Watch, too, for newspaper advertisements of company progress. And pay attention to unit trust and investment trust advertisements. See which areas are in vogue, and watch where the money is flowing.

Write to the more successful fund managers (most family finance pages run league tables regularly). They will send reports and brochures which will show what they have been buying and selling. You can pick the brains of all manner of investment experts for the price of a postage stamp. An inventive investor need never feel alone out there. There is always a queue of City professionals seeking to impress you, and sell you their services. Just remember – they get it wrong sometimes, too.

CHAPTER EIGHT

Share Personalities

The deeper you delve, and the more you get sucked into the market, the more you find that shares are not simply boring bits of paper. They come alive. Companies and their share prices have very distinct personalities. Some you will like, others you will loathe. Try to step back and rationalise it, rather than letting it sneak up on you. Otherwise, one morning you might wake to realise you are sitting on a load of rubbish, a share portfolio which is simply not suited to the results you are trying to achieve.

Building A Portfolio

Conventional wisdom will tell you to spread your investments to reduce your risk. No share can be absolutely safe, and the most unexpected things can, and do, happen. If you hold ten different shares, the chances of them all going wrong are modest, though if the whole market collapses, all could suffer. Within that ten, you ought to have a mix of industries – not all stores or engineers, for instance. While you might be able to afford the odd small, speculative company, it is best to balance it with a solid chunk of major names, which are less likely to spring any nasty surprises.

That sort of advice would win a nod of approval from most investment advisers. Build a portfolio with a sensible, conservative profile. That is the way to do it. And yet... And yet that may not suit you at all. How can you spread your risk if you have £1,000 or £2,000 to play with? It makes no sense to split £2,000 between ten companies. And £1,000? No way. Dealing costs would eat up an enormous portion of your cash.

Even if you have the money to spread wider – say £1,000 each in ten shares – that may not suit your temperament. Picking one decent share is hard enough, let alone finding ten. One or two winners, even if they double, would not make that much of an impression on a £10,000 portfolio. Turning £10,000 into £12,000 is very nice. But it hardly sparkles with sex appeal, does it?

Through the years, I have formed the impression that many private investors want excitement. They are prepared to gamble with a modest amount of capital, taking a high risk here and there, hoping for a high return – the Polly Peck dream, if you like, where £2,500 was transformed into £1 million in three years – if you bought at the right time, held on, and sold at the right time. I know someone who did actually make millions, though he started with much more than £2,500 – though he put in so much early that he was able to take out big profits on part of his holding along the way. That may be an extreme example, but I certainly know many people who have made 25, 30, 40 times their money in a share in two or three years.

Perhaps you are ready to take more of a gamble than the experts suggest. If you really are using money you can afford to lose – you should certainly view your first foray into the stockmarket as a potential losing proposition – you might be more inclined to split your £2,000 between just two companies, or even your £10,000 between four or five. That would mean a worthwhile return if you did pick a winner.

Do not let me tempt you. My inclination is towards the more aggressive approach. You can play anyway you wish. Decide for yourself. That is what matters. Do not let anyone tell you what to do with your money. Whether you really like the thought or not, stockmarket money is gambling money. You can play it dangerously, or you can play carefully. Just so long as you are realistic, and acknowledge to yourself what you are really doing.

Blue Chips

Blue chips are the cream of the crop, shares in the biggest, best and safest companies. Marks & Spencer, British Telecom, Prudential Assurance, Imperial Chemical Industries, Great Universal Stores, those sort of names. The list changes from time to time. Every so often, even the odd blue chip gets a little cracked. At one stage, National Westminster Bank slipped off the list. In the early nineties, like all clearing banks, it had made so many foolish loans and dissipated so much capital that it could hardly be held up as a model to anyone. By the mid nineties, it sneaked back in among the blue chips again, because it survived so well, though it remained among the most lowly rated of the big banks. Blue chips are likely to have a market capitalisation in excess of £2bn, and if all of the names are not immediately familiar, they will own companies whose names are well-known.

It is possible to deal easily in large quantities of the shares of such companies. Market-makers routinely quote prices in 50,000, maybe 250,000 without altering the price. A million or two might change hands each day, many more when times are busy. Because of that, trading in them is relatively cheap, with a narrow spread between buying and selling prices. Because they are so well-established, pillars of the investment community, they are widely assumed to be safe. Can't go wrong with them, old chap.Or can you? They got the blue chip name from the highest-value chips in a poker game, and they can be quite a gamble. Look at the highs and lows in your paper, and you will see how sharply the prices move inside a year, or less. The price of Marks & Spencer moved between 489p and 685p in the first half of 1998 alone, though most of that move was down. British Telecom, though, was brilliant. Between August 1997 and July 1998 it more than doubled, topping 900p in July. In the first half of 1998, even the staid old Pru moved between 654p and 1,000p, ICI between 738p and 1244p, and GEC from a low of 338p to a high of 550p.

Those figures do not necessarily represent the extremes of what you could have made or lost. They did not move straight from the bottom to the top, or vice versa. But they do suggest that, even in a spell when the market moved from buoyant to uneasy, there were money-making opportunities in the most conventional places. You could get it wrong, of course. Late in 1995, for example, Marks & Spencer and Telecom were still way below their 1994 peak, despite a relatively strong general market. And if Hanson was a blue chip (most would have called it so in the eighties and early nineties), by the final quarter of 1995, it was under 200p, against a 1994 peak of 300p. Dismal? Certainly. Doubly depressing if you had been holding it for the long-term. Even back in the eighties, it went over 200p. By 1998, it was a shadow of its former self, and had been broken up into several pieces.

By and large, though, the lower risk reputation for blue chips is well-earned. Blue chips are safer than the average share, less likely to let you down. They have a history of building carefully and responsibly. They are well researched throughout the City. Everyone knows the broad direction of their business and their profits. They may not always go up, but if they are going to rise or fall sharply, everyone gets the message in good time to prepare for it. Though increasing US involvement in our markets can lead to sharper price changes, and the Stock Exchange Electronic Trading System has produced some alarming short-term volatility, they tend to move in fairly steady, predictable lines. Everyone has ample room to think carefully, to buy or sell without undue haste. No one will tell you that buying a blue chip was a bad mistake, even if you lose money on it. And you can sleep safe.

High Income Shares

This book is slanted towards capital growth, rather than high income situations. Fixed interest investments offer the highest return, but are said normally to lack the capital gains potential to resist the steady drip of inflation, which gradually erodes the worth of capital. In fact, check the records of high income unit trusts against the growth trusts, and you find that for total return (capital growth plus income), the high yielders do slightly better on average than the growth trusts. That reflects, of course, the good growth potential of carefully selected high interest shares. High income shares generally combine a good return with the chance of capital gain. Spotting the high return is relatively easy, though picking an all-round winner is far tougher. Look down the list of dividend yields, decide what return you want, and place strong emphasis on high profits and dividend cover. The greater the cover – the amount by which profits available for distribution exceed the cost of paying the dividend – the further profits can fall before a company is forced to cut the dividend.

Safety counts a lot with income stocks. Unfortunately, the highest income shares are the riskiest. The yield may be high because it might not be there tomorrow. Always view a 10% plus yield with suspicion. In 1986, the largest yields were in gold and oil shares. The dangers were obvious, with South Africa in turmoil, and the price of oil in retreat. By 1991, the high yielders were housebuilders and property shares – sectors deep in trouble with companies collapsing all around. Come the late nineties, really high yielders are few and far between, and the high yield sectors are not so clearly defined, with one exception. Where you see a trust with two or three classes of share, you will find high-yielding income shares. These come with the split-level trusts, clever little schemers which credit most of the capital growth from the shares they hold to a special class of capital share, while granting almost all of the income from their investments to their own income shares.

Be warned, though. There are often special conditions attached to split-level shares. The income shares, for instance, may be redeemable at a set date for little more than their nominal value. That might involve a capital loss which would reduce the value of the earlier high income. Do not shy away. Take advice from investment trust specialists. Shrewdly selected high income shares can outperform a growth portfolio, especially when income is taken into account. In an uncertain market, shares with a high yield are presented as having defensive qualities. The slightly dubious notion is that their greater dividend return will prevent them falling as far as higher fliers with only a tiny return. When the going gets tough, investors concentrate on dividend yields as a surer thing than capital growth. It sounds plausible, and has some merit. In practice, however, the income prop can get knocked away. Companies do cut dividends, and when the whole market is falling, good goes down with bad. Higher-yielders fall with the rest, and the market looks for higher returns from everything. Income stocks may not fall as far as out-of-favour growth stocks, but fall they will. It is little consolation that you may be losing less than the next investor. You will still finish down. And that is not the idea.

Where high income shares do well, they do it for the classic reason – the higher the risk, the greater the return. If they come right, the capital gain is heavier. So when you opt for a high income buy – outside the fixed interest sector – you may be taking on a riskier proposition than you realise. Do it with your eyes open. Unless you know better – and are sure of it – higher return almost invariably does mean higher risk. That brings us back to the beginning of this chapter, and spreading risk. If you really do want a high return, you ought to try to spread your risk as far as you sensibly can. Do not plunge all on one or two stocks. Try to find half a dozen high yielders, just in case one goes wrong. One almost certainly will cut its dividend. You must appreciate, though, that one dud, if it happens, will cost you enough to knock a point or two off your overall return. So the high yield might not be that tempting after all.

Growth Stocks

Growth stocks are heavenly bodies, investments everybody dreams about, shares that go on and up supported by a busy board and ever-expanding profits. You never intend, of course, to buy anything else. After all, you are not laying your money down to see it sit and do nothing. You could get that in the building society. The growth stock commands a higher price-earnings ratio than average, and gives a lower dividend yield. The idea is that you accept lower returns today in exchange for growth tomorrow. Such stocks need to be in growing industries, run by competently alert directors, ready to expand by organic growth and by acquisition.

Growth stocks are not always what they seem. Great Universal Stores, for example, long appeared to be the slumbering giant of the mail order catalogue and the High Street. It hardly ranked as fashionable. Yet it has a record of more than 40 years of unbroken growth in profits, until the 1997 profits. Beauty, though, is in the eye of the beholder. Not too many trendy eyes glanced the way of GUS through the years, though they did enjoy a great run when it became apparent that the two tier voting structure was to be changed. Towards the end of 1995 they began to return to vogue as speculation mounted over the successors to the controlling group of directors who, by the mid-nineties were ageing. In 1998, it is headed by the Lord Wolfson, who helped engineer a startling revival of Next in the years after George Davies departed, and there are many who hope he will put the gorgeous back into Gussies. Expansion by acquisition is one of the key elements in the growth game. It can mean frequent issues of highly-rated shares, perhaps supplemented by increased borrowings to mix a little cash in with any takeover bait.

The idea is that a company with a price-earnings ratio of 20 can gobble up one on a p/e of 10, and gain a fresh injection of growth. If both are the same size, a price-earnings ratio of 10 merged with one of 20 will produce a company with a price-earnings ratio of 15. Mix in the notion that the two together can save costs, and apply the premium talents of a growth stock management team to the lowly-rated acquisition, and suddenly the City can be persuaded that a p/e of 15 is too modest for this exciting new and larger animal. The City begins to start talking about synergy – one and one make three. Should this exciting growth stock really sell on a p/e of what? Shall we say 18? Shall we say 20, given a little time? So the shares perk up, and the game can start again after a pause for digestion. It is wonderful how a p/e play like that, hatched on the back of an envelope, can start a minor industrial revolution, rationalising British industry and all that – with a profit or two for bankers, brokers, directors and share punters along the way.

Using highly-rated shares as currency is a splendid way of buying other companies, their profits, assets, and potential on the cheap. Bid with cash, and it could cost 15% or more in interest charges on the cash, depending on interest rates at the time. Use high-flying shares, and the effective cost could be as low as the dividend yield on those shares – perhaps 2%. Once issued, though, shares are forever. Dividends have to be paid on them, year in, year out. And profits must be earned to pay those dividends. Bank borrowings can always be repaid to save interest charges. By the mid-nineties, companies were beginning to pay more attention to this. Several set in train programmes to repurchase significant quantities of their own shares, trimming dividend costs and cutting the price-earnings ratio.

Nonetheless, acquisitions by share issue are popular, especially when the market is good. Banks like to see companies with a large slice of risk capital in relation to borrowings. The theory is that when times get tough, companies can cut dividends to save money, so the interest paid to the banks is that much safer. Ordinary share capital is risk capital, so banks are happy to see companies expand their risk capital base. That, in turn, allows the companies to borrow more from the banks. It is all about gearing, that sort of thing. When times are good, everybody is happy.

The plusses and minuses are complex, but when a share is running, few pause to argue. For budding entrepreneurs building growth companies, the main problem can be ensuring that they do not issue too many shares, and leave themselves with too small a slice of the cake they are baking. Growth stocks are wonderful when the market is rising. Beautiful profits keep coming through, and a flow of deals makes it difficult for sceptics to analyse things too closely. The element of sustainable, organic growth can be difficult to split from the one-off profits, and the clever accounting tricks. As profits mount, so the shares are pushed up, and opportunities for yet more profitable deals emerge. For a while, it looks like a machine for perpetual motion, and everlasting share trading profits. Watch out.

Growth stocks can be forgiven one hiccup, provided the excuses are plausible. Two hiccups, though, can be fatal to the rating, and the game stops. Always remember that few stocks grow for ever. The bigger they get, the tougher it is to keep up the pace. Hanson illustrated that point vividly, too big to imagine almost any deal making a major impact – unless it involved splitting the company into smaller pieces. Deals need to be ever larger to make any real impact. Always stand by the door, ready to make your excuses and leave with a profit. Do not hesitate. Do it the minute you start to feel uneasy. If you are getting that itch, how many other investors will be feeling it too? First one out is the winner.

Recovery Stocks

Recovery stocks are simply super – provided they recover. You find them when the hard times are almost over, in industries which have fallen from favour. Housebuilders, metal bashers, and electronics seem to be perpetual favourites, but in the early nineties the list could have gone on much longer – garages, estate agents, stores, banks and so on. A few years later, and the late nineties saw engineering stocks moving down from a spell as favourites, and back towards recovery stocks as they wrestled with the impact of a strong pound on their profits. The furniture sellers and carpet retailers were perhaps the least fashionable in the late nineties, and looked set to stay that way for a while – until interest rates start falling again. Sometimes, you come across the odd exception, a company in a growth industry that has fallen on bad times for exceptional reasons. Unfortunately, it is easy to wade into a depressed company, only to discover that it has further to fall, or that it takes ages to recover.

You can trawl for suitable candidates for recovery either by choosing particular industries which you reckon are due to get better, then picking individual shares, or by finding a bombed-out share you fancy and trying to work out whether it is in the sort of business which will pick up. Do whatever suits you. Either way makes sense. On the whole, it will be harder to find a real recovery prospect unless it is in the sort of business which is plainly doing better – and in any boom sector, there are always a few laggards. Picking the right companies in the right sector could make the difference between average and special performance, though. You need to look for signs of firm management. Tough though it may be on the workers, factory closures and redundancies can be good news for investors. The amazing advance of the regional electricity companies was a prime example of this, as they shed layer after layer of the labour force.

Sales of subsidiary companies, assets outside the m 🐾 ream of the business, are also useful plusses. The action at Fisons, mentioned earlier, shows what can be achieved. Swift surgery and concentration of effort can work wonders in reviving profits. It can bring several benefits. It cuts overheads and reduces general costs, may put an end to a loss-maker which was bleeding the business, and could produce a cash injection from any assets which are sold. The talk of companies emerging leaner and fitter at the end of difficult times is right. They have been forced to look carefully at costs, and cut them to the bone. When orders pick up, that means a greater proportion of revenue flows through to profit.

Companies which have been trimming back often find there is a bonus in the pension fund. Thanks to the dreadful Robert Maxwell, this has become a hot potato. But when a workforce is reduced, surpluses tend to accumulate in the pension fund. It can be perfectly legal and proper for the company to take some benefit from this. Clearly, any company has an obligation to be fair to pensioners and employees who are still contributing to the fund. Pensions should be raised and worker benefits enhanced. But in many cases, there is still a handsome surplus which may allow the company to reduce its own contributions. In no way would I condone clawing back cash from a fund. But slimmed-down businesses often find that they can take a pension holiday, not paying into the fund, for a few years. That can be of great benefit to profits – something would-be investors should consider.

Management changes can be vital. They are engineered sometimes by the big investors, using their voting power behind the scenes to force changes of direction or actual changes in top management personnel. For my money, the big boys exercise that power too infrequently, allowing too many dud managers to linger on – and then take enormous golden handshakes when they finally do go. Watch for big pay-offs especially. Rewarding failure may be upsetting, but when it happens, there is normally a good reason for it. The institutions will not have taken such a step unless they are convinced it is necessary. They will expect to see their efforts rewarded by much better future performance. And the institutions are becoming more alive to their responsibilities, forcing more movement.

So watch for board changes. The newspapers spotlight the more significant ones. Sometimes the old team simply decides to go, selling quietly to new boys who fancy their chances of rebuilding the business. That can be particularly rewarding.

Changes at the top often push up the share price. They make a good each-way bet. Either the new team succeeds, or a bidder steps in. The changes put pressure on the company, and the new managers find they are working under the threat of a takeover if they should fail. After a few months in the hot seat, the new boys usually trot around the City, keen to say what a good job they can do, begging big shareholders to hold on while explaining a new strategy and not to become impatient. That, too, can help the shares.

Always, though, pay special attention to assets at any would-be recovery stock. If there is no recovery, the assets will count. If the company goes bust, they will determine whether anything is left for shareholders ("No" is almost invariably the answer). The assets will allow new managers to rebuild the business, or attract a bidder. Avoid companies with heavy borrowings, unless there are parts which can be sold to cut debt.

The Biotech Boys

After a dismal start more than a decade ago, biotechnology stocks provided some of the market's most sensational gains in the mid-nineties. Biotechnology is effectively biological engineering, experimenting with nature to make new products, sometimes new vegetables and such, more often drugs. Valuing them is a nightmare for the small investor, because hardly any of them make a penny profit. And it is extremely difficult to work out just what they are doing, and whether it really makes sense.

Towards the end of 1995, I calculated that the leading six British baby biostocks had a stockmarket value in excess of £1.7bn between them. Every single one was losing money. Yet all had high hopes, and had scored spectacular share price gains that year.

If you are tempted, talk to a broker who follows the sector. Beg for research notes. Ring the companies, ask for their published documents, not just the report and accounts, but any literature relating to their research. Most will be happy to help.

Then you need to try to work out how far they are from a successful product which can actually be sold, and generate revenue. It can take ten years for a successful drug to reach the market. Crucially, it has to pass all manner of regulators, with the American Federal Drug Agency toughest

of the lot. Getting past the FDA alone can sometimes take three or
four years.

Check what stage of testing the drugs are in. There are three serious
phases, each involving testing on a widening number of patients. From
phase one to phase three can take years. If the new compound reaches
phase three, it is reckoned there is a 60% or greater chance of ultimate
success. Even after phase three, though, it can take a long while before a
new drug produces revenue.

In such a situation, it is vital to check how much cash the company has
available to finance research and development. In the jargon, go for the
'burn' – the annual cost of research and development. Divide that into the
company's cash and borrowing capacity, and you can see whether the
business will run out of money before the drug generates profits.

Good progress in testing obviously helps. Most companies use test
results to help raise more money from shareholders. Many will come to
market for cash two or three times between first floating and establishing
a successful drug. No matter what they say, always reckon they will need
more cash more quickly than the original prospectus suggests.

Crucial in influencing whether they will get it is the likely market for the
prospective new drugs. Obviously there is a big difference between the sales
potential for a new cure for in-growing toenails, and the answer to arthritis.

Broking analysts try to measure the likely market and sales value of a
drug, then discount it back to the present date to arrive at a notional
current value for the shares, assuming all goes well. They will knock off
between 30% and 40% of the value for each year of waiting. It is all very
much pie in the sky, but there is little alternative.

Get it right, and the rewards can be enormous. One blockbuster drug
can be worth £1bn or more, and generate vast profits for years to come.
So it is crucial to keep an eye on the market value of the company
concerned. In some of the smaller companies especially, investors get
carried away with the dream of some wonder cure, or perhaps a diagnostic

kit which allows early detection of disease. And the value of the company can get inflated out of all proportion.

In the biotech game, then, you are venturing into relatively uncharted water, and taking an unusually high risk for high returns. Try to understand what is going on, check the competition, and check the number of drugs in the pipeline. Scotia, for example, had six in the later stages of testing in 1995, with several others further down the line. That was unusual. Some companies have only one or two. But many in the industry questioned the unusual nature of Scotia's technology, suggesting that while Scotia's oil of evening primrose-based business generated drugs with low side-effects, their ultimate efficiency might be less dramatic than others. Late in 1997, in fact, Scotia took on new management. It dumped founder Dr David Horrobin, who had devoted his career to one particular area of biotechnology, away from the herd. If his research is right, he will have created a massively-profitable business. But after he left, Scotia cut back sharply on many of his research projects. That tended to confirm the fears of those who dubbed Scotia a maverick.

Others in the City preferred a more conservative line, opting to invest in companies headed by those with a more conventional background. So check the directors and researchers. They are crucial. A background with the big pharmaceutical companies, and research supported by learned medical journals, obviously helps the investment rating. Nothing, though, is foolproof. At one stage in the mid-nineties, half of the City loved British Biotech. Seen as the flagship for the industry, it looked as if it was moving ahead with a cancer drug. Sadly, early in 1998, it all began to fall apart as one former senior researcher raised questions publicly. The board was accused of making misleading announcements. The shares, once over 300p, tumbled to 30p. Remember – all share buying is a form of gambling.

The Computer Kings

Alongside the biotech boys, the computer kings made much of the running in the mid to late nineties. Against the background of the emerging information super highway, they promised much, and proved almost as difficult as the biotech businesses to value. Once again, looking at such companies can be immensely rewarding, but totally taxing. As with biotechnology, the average investor is quickly liable to become bogged down in a slurry of incomprehensible language. All you can do is to buy an electronics dictionary, and plough through the PC magazines. In an effort to come to terms with some of it, I invested in the full kit to get on to the Internet, the global computer network. In the early stages, at least, I struggled to find much of interest, though I did begin to learn the meaning of some of the more widely used terms.

Happily, however, many of the computer and electronics stocks do actually earn profits. As the great hype machine swung into action to promote the Microsoft *Windows 95* software (the instruction kits which make computers do clever things), it was clear that companies selling more powerful personal computers and the other paraphernalia would do well. That was fairly simple. In the hardware side of it (the machines and other bits), you can gain a reasonable idea of what is going on by watching who gets which orders. Links with the big US names are important to British companies, and distribution deals around the world matter, too. The great Millennium bug hype helped software companies enormously, sending them soaring. Others benefited when IT stocks were given a separate sector in the FT indices, encouraging big funds to move into them.

The game worked beautifully for a while, but by 1997, some of the hardware companies had hit problems. And a few of the new issues had come crashing down. Shares are for buying, and selling, not holding forever. Clues to hi-tech success can be hard to pin down. The initial runaway success of shares in Memory Corporation, a small company initially floated off market, and then on the AIM in the summer of 1995, involved an act of faith. The business had a system for using defective silicon chips. Since it was not in production at first, you had to hope that it would work. Then it was necessary to try to measure whether there was a market for the product at a reasonable price, whether it could be made in bulk, and whether a steady flow of raw materials would be available at reasonable prices. All common sense. But for many investors, it meant simply taking a view on the quality of the management, and on the advisers bringing the shares to market. In fact, almost everything that could turn bad for Memory turned bad at the same time – computer chip prices tumbled, and demand slumped just as the company was gearing up to get into volume production. By 1998, Memory was still operating, but tackling a different line of the chip business. Elsewhere in the high technology game, there are information delivery companies like Dialog, and On-Demand Information.

Assessing them is hard, because their future depends on convincing sufficient customers that their systems are worth having. Similar guidelines apply to the assorted telecoms stocks which enjoyed such a vogue in 1997 and 1998. Once again, you must measure whether the business can generate good returns before it runs out of money. Try to look at the scope of what is on offer, estimate the likely market, and watch for the names of supporters and customers. It is hard for private investors to form a view of their own. Beg, steal or borrow stockbroking reports. Read them critically, and remember that brokers like to say "buy", and rarely say you should sell shares of a company they act for. And no matter how good the City experts rate the business, some of them will fail.

As in biotech stocks, watch the market capitalisations, and measure the management. And keep your fingers crossed. Such stocks can be very volatile, rising sharply on big contracts or alliances, plunging if a big name pulls out of a deal. If you are brave, though, it is worth plugging on. The big profits often come from backing fashionable stocks in fashionable areas. But be aware you are following fashion, and that fashion changes, so you must be ready to sell. Biotech and high-tech were the places to be in 1995. By 1998, the British Biotech fiasco had hammered ratings across that sector – they were already falling in 1997 – but hi-tech was still booming. The growth potential for both is vast enough to last well into the next century, but it may take a few years and a few block-busting drugs actually reaching the market for bio-tech ratings to regain their old glory.

Penny Stocks

Once upon a time, penny stocks were what the name suggests – shares selling for a few pence. Now, anything under 100p is liable to be called a penny stock. A whole industry grew up around them in the mid-eighties, with tip sheets and a unit trust. From time to time, I revise and update my book *How To Make A Killing in Penny Shares* (0 9480 3520 X) to advise those who concentrate on this very special sector.

Things are not what they used to be in the penny share game. Quite a few penny share companies went bust in the late eighties and early nineties. Many others left their fans nursing heavy losses. But after the shake-out, there are many more companies back in the old-style penny groove, with prices down to 10p or less.

The excitement began to come alive again in the mid-nineties. Should the boom get under way, the penny stock sector will be the hot one to be in. There are bargains there. Many low-priced companies were poor performers in the late eighties and the early nineties. But lots of good ones were dragged down with the dross. Many received an injection of ambitious new management.

Penny shares are appealing because they appear to give you more for your money. Buying 5,000 shares for 10p each seems much better than spending the same £500 on 100 shares at £5 each. There are snags, of course. The dealing spread – the difference between the price you pay and the price you get when you sell – is bigger, and works against you. Shares with a middle price of £5 might well be 495p to sell, 505p to buy – a spread of 10p, or 2%. The 10p shares might well be 9p to sell, 11p to buy – a spread of 2p, or 20%. Your penny stock has to work much harder before you clear dealing costs and make a profit.

It is not all bad. When a penny share moves, it moves much faster than a heavier-priced rival, because it takes proportionately bigger strides. On a 10p share, the next middle price up will be 10½p, a theoretical 5% gain (though still a long way from making money). The £5 share may have moved up to 505p, a gain of 1%. When a share is sliding, a penny stock seems to race away from you. A fall from 10p to 9p middle price means that the shares which may have cost 11p will only fetch 8p if you sell – a hefty loss with the first mark-down. All the while, the investment fundamentals remain the same for a penny stock as for a heavyweight. A share selling at 10p is theoretically worth the same as one selling at £5 if both are selling on a price earnings ratio of 20, and a dividend yield of 2%.

The lesson comes home clearly when there is a scrip issue or a share split. If your £5 share had a nominal value originally of £1, and the board decided to split each £1 nominal share into ten shares of 10p nominal value, the price would then fall to 50p for each share – but since there would then be ten of them for every one held previously, there would be no real change in the value of the company. Suddenly, though, the £5 share is a 50p penny share. There is merit in the argument that penny shares have more room to grow than the big boys. It is a little deceptive, in truth, a bit of a cheat. Though it is generally applied to penny stocks, it should more accurately be used on small companies. It fits usually because penny stocks tend to be smallish companies. Look at ICI. That is unlikely to grow ten-fold over the next decade. A low-priced, penny stock company just might, and in much less than ten years. It might more easily go bust, too. Penny share fans are really saying that they have found a gambling counter which might take off, and are backing that instead of some big, established company in a more mature stage of development, with much lower risk. The old maxim – high risk, high reward – creeps back again.

That is not to knock penny shares. I am a firm fan. They can be terrific fun, and wonderfully rewarding. But many are in small, highly speculative companies. Just be sure you understand that.

Much of their attraction, in the end, comes back to the psychological factor – and more speculative stockbrokers are always keen to follow low-priced shares. They know they will find more takers for them among private clients than for the heavyweights. The more takers, the higher the share price will rise.

Penny shares slumped dramatically in the Crash of '87, often shedding half of their value quickly, then drifting still lower. Unlike some of the leaders, which also tumbled heavily, some penny shares still ended that year with a good profit. Because they had risen so far, they had plenty of room to fall, and still come out ahead. The long, slow grind into the nineties gradually took its toll of the brightest winners, however. It became harder to sell them in any decent quantity, and the prices dribbled ever lower.

Nonetheless, the eighties created a whole new breed of penny share punters. They are still out there, waiting for the right conditions to try again. Any half-decent penny share company always finds a ready audience. Never have I subscribed to the City opinion about the small punters being fools who always rush in at the top. Many wait, staying out of the market until they are reasonably sure that they have a fair chance of winning. Penny shares will be there, providing fun and profits galore all through the nineties.

CHAPTER NINE

The Shell Game

Five times a night or not, company directors are only human. They are in the great stockmarket game for much the same reasons as you are – the fun and the money. They only begin to tune in to the notion of a knighthood, building a business for posterity, the good of the nation and all that other ego-boosting stuff in their later years. Having fun and making money amount to very nearly the same thing for most company directors. So long as they are making the money for their company and building a rising share price, then the interests of directors and their investors coincide nicely. That is the angle for investors to watch – the way the money goes.

Making money retains a fascination for company promoters long after it would satisfy the wildest dreams of most people. The first million matters because that is spending stuff, money to live on. The next however many tens of millions matter, too, because by then the promoters have been trapped by the game. Every extra pound is another point gained. The money itself may not matter, but the score certainly does. And if you have built up a thriving public company, you are concerned about playing the game – taking on all-comers, and beating them.

Brilliant money-making players pop up every so often at the head of a new issue, and we have already explored how to get a piece of the new issue action. Just as often, though, the real movers try their hand at shaking up an old company in the shell game. Spotting candidate companies for the shell game can be one of the most rewarding of all stockmarket moves.

Shells come in all shapes and sizes, generally the smaller the better. The idea is to take control of a company which is going nowhere much, put an unquoted business in, and use it as a base on which to build. The companies going in will generally be too young or small to gain a quotation in their own right. Put a group of them together under bright management and you can build an exciting business fast – and highly profitably.

A staple of the eighties, this technique has lost none of its allure in the nineties. As the economy has gained ground, and the market has regained confidence, new management teams with ambitious ideas have been moving quietly into small companies galore. Make no mistake. The fun hardly stopped, even in the gloomiest days of the late eighties and the early nineties.

The First Clues

Would-be shell promoters want a company where they can buy control, or perhaps a 29.9% stake, as cheaply as possible. Profits may not be too important, but ideally the target company will have some assets, preferably cash, or assets which can be turned into cash fairly easily – share stakes, a subsidiary or two which might be sold, perhaps property. Often the shell will have hit a poor trading patch under established directors who are getting long in the tooth and lack the heart for the wholesale reconstruction required to whip the business back into shape.

The new promoter may start quietly building a small share stake. Anything over 2.9% has to be announced publicly. Who is to say, though, that a few friends – totally unconnected and unaware of any plan so far as the Takeover Code is concerned, you understand – may not pick up a small stake or two as well?

188

Step two is to try to get the board to sell a few more shares. Watch for announcements of stakes changing hands. Everyone keeps an eye out for them. And sometimes prices soar as soon as a new 3% plus investor appears. However, there is a risk in leaping in after a big rise. The new would-be hero may be blocked by the board, or unable to buy more shares without the price running too far ahead. In some cases, it may all be a bluff. Someone might pick a stake and make their presence known in the hope of pushing the price up and making a quick and profitable sale. Sometimes, the lack of a price surge after news of a stake may be disturbing. It may mean the market men know nothing much is going to happen. Or you might just have spotted one that they have missed. Try to make doubly sure. Usually, however, the patient investor will come to little harm by seeing the professionals move in first, even if it means paying a shade more. Look upon it as an insurance policy.

The next big step comes when the new promoter moves in publicly. This will involve either buying shares from the board and making a bid for the rest, or selling a company to the quoted one in return for sufficient shares to yield control. Either option is promising. If there is a full cash bid, it will usually be way below the share price, and holders will not be expected to take it. Under Takeover Panel rules, such a bid has to be made by anyone with more than 29.9%. If it comes, check who is underwriting it – providing the cash. That will give a clue to the muscle behind the new promoter.

If a company is being sold in, watch who is providing the professional advice – the bankers, stockbrokers, and auditors. The bigger the names, the better. Check, too, if they are staying on as advisers. The right names will be more acceptable to the City in future deals, and it is important to get them involved as early as possible.

In some cases, you will find that the new promoter is going to end up with 29.9% or less of the shell. That will mean that no bid is intended, and either the target company is too big for the newcomer to bid for fully, or perhaps further share issues will follow in time. Either way, the action will be starting.

Reading The Plans

Obviously, it is worth watching for anything the new team has to say. The type of company being sold in will usually indicate the intended area of expansion. At this stage, it does not greatly matter what is offered for public consumption. You really only need clear assurances that expansion is on the menu. Organic growth (growth from within a company) is fine for established operators, but you want newcomers to make it clear they are planning to grow by buying businesses. It is quicker that way. Stock Exchange rules sometimes make it difficult to signal the real plan. Companies are supposed to stay in the same line of business, and any radical change may need to be made in stages. Any big deal must be approached slowly. Minnows are not allowed to swallow whales without a mass of red tape, so small fish have to be fattened carefully before the big bite, for fear of frightening the authorities. No matter how implausible the official story, the mere arrival of someone new will be enough to generate interest. Enterprising players rarely get beyond stage one without lining up well-informed support for the next stage. As usual, the insiders know best, so a rising share price will usually tell you whether good things are on the way. It may not mean that all shareholders are given equal access to information, but insiders have their uses – and the money to back promising newcomers who may have big ideas. So watch where the money goes.

What you want is a hungry newcomer, keen to make his fortune by buying businesses. Unfortunately, hungry newcomers are not allowed to advertise their intentions too openly in documents to shareholders, but they can give a few clues.

Spotting The Hungry Young Men

Look hard at any potted career history in company documents, and note the age of the new chief executive. Under 28 is suspect – he may be too flash, too inexperienced, and out to make a quick buck at any price. Over 56 may simply be over the hill, and have left it too late to make real money in the game, unless he is a veteran who has played it successfully in the past – or comes in alongside bright, younger talent. Ideally, you want someone with a measure of experience, and time, ambition and energy enough to build something big – a hungry young man. If he has worked with major companies, or at the feet of the previous generation of company promoters, he might be just right – and could bring valuable support from his old associate – covertly or quite openly.

Beware of anyone linked to previous duds. In this game, it rarely pays to give a loser a second chance. Do look very carefully at potted career histories. They are especially useful in the AIM companies, because those have to give details of past problems. And watch if people below board level have hit trouble in the past – in AIM companies they might be important players, sitting just below board level in order to avoid disclosing past troubles.

Most important, see how the new player and his team take their share stake. Watch what they have paid, either by buying shares or the value put on shares they are taking in exchange for anything they are pumping in. Check, too, whether there are restrictions on when they can sell their shares, and if they have options to take more, perhaps linked to profit targets. You want them to be made to hold on to their shares as long as possible, and the longer it takes for them to earn big money on their options, the better. Long-term commitment is what you want. So check what prices they will pay, and when they will get their extra shares. Comb the fine print at the back of the document, looking through the material contracts to see if they have done other deals for shares. Work out the price they have paid. And scan their contracts of employment to see whether they are on a slice of profits. The deeper they are committed, the harder they will work. Price points or profit targets when they take more shares will give you the best glimpse of what is expected, how they see the company developing. You can bet they have not set targets they do not think they can reach. It may take extra application, but it is worth sitting down with a calculator and working out the detail of what it all could mean to them. Do not take the percentages and multiples on trust, and guess whether they look generous. Do the arithmetic. It can be quite staggering. Sometimes you will be astonished just how large a take the new team may plan, if they achieve their top targets. Through the years, I have been horrified how few shareholders – large or small – actually bother. The answers can be breathtaking – though as a new shareholder you may want to applaud, not complain. Greed may be good, so long as you get a share. Just so long as there is enough left in the pot for the outside shareholders as well.

Danger Signals

In a rising market, the honeymoon will normally last about six months, or until the first sizeable deal – whichever comes first. If nothing has happened after nine months, beware. Something is wrong. Sell, unless you can establish very sound reasons for staying on.

Now and then, a promising shell is used to float smallish companies dominated by family directors with little experience outside their own business. Tread carefully. That kind of deal will set the family up nicely, and rakes in large fees for the original finders of the shell and those who got in before the action started. However, there may be no great follow-through, as the family sit with the prestige of a public company, selling shares from time to time and watching their business grow quietly, without plans for dynamic growth.

Reconstructions

Managed carefully, a successful shell can be built into a stockmarket monster. Profits from picking the right one and sticking with it can be enormous. Pizza Express, where Luke Johnson and friends persuaded long-time owner Peter Boizot to sell his restaurant chain into the remains of a small investment trust, is perhaps the best-known of the nineties successes. The remnants of the shell company changed hands at 9p in the early nineties. By 1998, the shares had hit 950p.

There were many less spectacular, but highly-rewarding examples. Paul Levinson and his family backed Lance Yates to put his casual clothing business into Hay & Robertson, and saw the shares rocket more than 15-fold in the mid-nineties. Greg Hutchings, who learnt his trade with Hanson, did brilliantly at Tomkins for many years, until it got too big to make such progress, and worried the City by taking on baker Rank Hovis McDougall. Sir Nigel Rudd and Brian McGowan built Williams Holdings into a first-class, almost blue-chip, company.

There are many others. They have yielded enormous profits for those who backed them on the way up. And that is all that need concern you – hitching a ride up. What you want is a share trading profit, not part of a monument to endure forever. Take your profits and kiss it goodbye. Purists might argue over definitions. Some big winners might appear more like reconstructions than shells. But the principles are the same – spot a modest business which is not going anywhere, reshape it and pump in new companies to generate growth. The reconstruction may be a little harder to spot because the chosen company might not appear such an obvious case for treatment, and the first deal might not be particularly attractive. But such companies are well worth seeking, whatever you call them.

Fund-Raising

Definitions are for dictionaries. They do not matter to the share trader. What you want is action, in a shell or a reconstructed company. Either way, if you miss the first stages, you may be able to clamber aboard when the first major fund-raising exercise is launched. Most new boys with big ideas will soon want more cash. It makes life easier in a myriad of ways. The popular method of raising cash is by a rights issue – offering new shares to existing investors at a special price. This expands the capital base, widening the scope for bank and other borrowings. It also allows the promoter, or his backers, to raise their share stake on the cheap. The price of the rights issue will usually be pitched well below the market price, but well above the real worth of the business. It is a classic means of using the market, translating hope into hard cash, which can then be employed – if all goes well – to justify that hope, and generate a still fatter premium for still more hope.

The impact of a fund-raising move depends on the state of the market. It might well be timed to accompany a kitchen sink exercise. Unless the market is in good shape, and well attuned to what is happening, that might knock the price a bit, and create a real buying opportunity.

The kitchen sink exercise is a time-honoured ritual. The new management goes in, looks around, clucks, and decides that things were really much worse than expected. So they take an axe to everything in sight. Assets are written down, stock values chopped, provisions are set aside for redundancy and reorganisation, and the grimmest view possible is attached to previous trading. Perhaps employing new auditors, anything which might be taken as a loss is thrown in. The published figures are absolutely dreadful, and the new managers sit smiling, hand on heart, saying they have taken the responsible view, and had a real accounting clear-out, tossing out all of the old management's skeletons. As a public relations move, it is sound. It makes a virtue out of necessity, and perhaps creates a wonderful opportunity for further advancement. Tucked away in the accounting clear-out will be the kind of tough treatment which may overstate the damage, leaving room for some losses to be written back quietly as profits in the future. That flatters the new boy, gives him time to breathe, extra scope for looking good. And it may persuade Stock Exchange officials and others that the new share issue price should not be pitched too high, or make a few unsophisticated investors feel things are really so bad that it is not worth supporting. That way, some shareholders will not take up their rights, leaving the new team to buy them as underwriters. Either way, the home team gets a good chunk of extra stock at a bargain rate – though only they know how much of a bargain.

So do not be put off by the kitchen sink stuff. Concentrate. WATCH THE WAY THE MONEY FLOWS. If the new team is putting more cash in, that means more than anything they say. Words are cheap, cash is precious. They are out to make money for themselves first, their chums second, and their advisers next. Shareholders are there to be used. But if they stay awake, they can do very nicely, too.

It does not always work quite that way. Fund-raising may send the price up at first, if the market is roaring. Then it will tend to sit quietly for a spell, awaiting the next move. That is the time to buy. If you got in early, always take up your rights issues if you can. Fund-raising is the surest of all signs that the new team is serious, and set for action. THEY WILL NOT BE PUTTING MONEY IN UNLESS THEY EXPECT TO MAKE A PROFIT ON IT.

The Public Relations Push

As the first big fund-raising hits, it should begin to attract attention in the City pages. This will be an encouraging sign that the insiders are playing the game. City public relations firms galore are employed to see that the press gets the latest company announcements and documents. The agencies vary from sophisticated postmen to outright share-pushers who cultivate journalists with a view to persuading them to be nice about their clients. The idea is to create a good, positive image, and discourage adverse comment. They push out gossip which ranges from solid insider information to wild dreams based on pure invention. Used sensibly, public relations can help everyone. Inevitably, it goes over the top at times, and one or two public relations agents become the kiss of death, pushing losers or short-term spiv operators.

The outside investor may be unaware of this. Watch, though, for repeated mentions in market reports, where it is easier to place uncritical plugs. At one stage before Blue Arrow went wrong, chief executive Tony Berry seemed to appear there almost every day. *The Times* adored George Walker, the Brent Walker boss, and he was a real favourite with market reporters. Small company man Bobby 'The Bear' Morton is another who cultivates the stockmarket reporters. Keep a critical eye open. Too many rumours supported by little substance may suggest the wrong kind of public relations push. What you want is the more analytical journalists backing up the chat with careful reasoning, firmer projections of profits. And where newspapers carry stockbroker tips, you want to see 'buy' recommendations from the better-established broking houses.

All such comments, of course, should be put firmly in context. If you are chasing quick profits in a frothy market, you may be delighted by any puffery, and happy to ride on it. Good enough. But, once again, be under no illusions. If you are playing the short-term game, be ready to sell on the first setback.

What You Want To See

Once aboard, stay for the ride so long as it feels good. What you want to see are:

- an increase in earnings per share with each deal

- each deal generating cash, via the company which is being bought, or through selling assets, or through other fund-raising
- rising dividends
- directors raising their share stake by new purchases or options
- a price-earnings ratio which holds above the average
- a stable core of top managers
- a stable set of top City advisers
- sizeable share stakes spread among big City investors
- at least one significant deal every nine months
- projections of rising profits in 'buy' notes from stockbrokers
- the name of the chief executive or chairman attracting sensible press comment.

What You Do Not Want To See

Investment fashions change. The economy may turn down, or your superstar promoter could stumble, so watch for the danger signs. The things you do not want are almost a mirror image of the positive signs listed above. You do not want:

- deals which cut earnings per share
- increasing debt
- higher stocks and work in progress
- large share sales by the board
- static dividends
- a price earnings ratio down to a single figure
- constant management changes
- changes in City advisers
- long periods without expansion news
- innovative ways of raising cash by new-fangled pieces of paper
- the top man joining other boards, taking a seat on Government bodies, the CBI, or City authorities

- directors telling the press the shares are cheap
- a move to new headquarters in Mayfair or Docklands
- talk of going into financial services
- the top man winning any award as something or other of the year.

Tread carefully, too, once the market capitalisation exceeds £500 million. By then it may be more difficult to find suitable targets to buy. Tread even more gently when the capitalisation goes over £1bn. The company may still prosper, but the shares are much less likely to double or treble in a year. They may still do nicely, but the earlier excitement will have faded. Early fans may be taking profits, many big investors will already have shares enough, and future growth may involve issuing lots of shares in an unwelcome takeover which could attract damaging comment from the target company. If you stay with the shares, you might be best advised to take some profits. This may no longer be the go-go stock you bought originally.

More Warning Signals

Everyone has their own danger signs. Bill Mackey was a partner in top accountants Ernst & Whinney, and the man appointed receiver to countless company collapses, public and private. His warning signals may appear to be tongue in cheek, but they are well worth heeding nonetheless. Down the years, they have proved remarkably prescient. He frowned at:

- directors driving Rolls-Royces with personalised number plates
- a fountain in the reception area
- a flagpole outside the factory
- the Queen's Award for Industry – UK only
- the chairman honoured for services to industry
- new offices opened by the Prime Minister
- an unqualified or elderly accountant (a real killer that one)

- products which are market leaders
- 'Hi-tech' in the company name
- an audit partner who grew up with the company
- a politician well known for public works as chairman
- satisfied personnel with no strike record
- a recently-announced technological breakthrough
- whizkid chairman
- winners of *The Accountant* award for the best report and accounts
- a picture in the accounts of the chairman getting out of a helicopter
- new company offices in China.

Yet More Danger Signs

In the nineties, we might substitute a Bentley Turbo for the Rolls-Royce in Bill Mackey's list. What should we add?

- a staff magazine with more than two pictures of the chairman
- report and accounts too large or strangely shaped to fit normal files
- soft focus colour pictures of the board behind semi-transparent protective sheets
- shareholder meetings close to Christmas or New Year's Eve, at 10 in the morning or on Friday afternoon
- shareholder meetings closed to the press
- directors who do not appear or answer questions at annual meetings
- the chairman's yacht
- chairman or chief executive on the board of a football club
- the chairman or chief executive in the Nigel Dempster column of the *Daily Mail*
- any director who plays polo
- any director who claims to play polo with the Prince of Wales, or to be his friend
- any company with some sort of Royal on the board.

CHAPTER TEN

The Bid Bonanza

Gone are the days when a takeover bid was a major event. After a quiet spell in the early nineties, they came back in vogue in the mid-nineties, and have stayed there. Now no company can consider itself safe. Some of the most famous names in British industry succumbed in the recession hit eighties – tobacco giant Imperial Group, Scotch whisky aristocrat Distillers, performance car builder Jaguar, and High Street chains like Currys, Debenhams, and British Home Stores.

In the nineties, Midland Bank has gone to a Far Eastern owner, the Trustee Savings Bank has been snapped up, the Savoy has gone to the Americans, and even the National Westminster may have gone by the time you read this, and the regional electricity companies have all been on the bid list.

If you are a share trader, forget the debate about whether bids are good for Britain, good for industry, or serve the consumer well. While the system lasts, what matters to the active investor is the chance of big, quick profits. A bid is the great bonus, a short-cut to capital gains which might have taken years if left to profits growth alone. Never mind industrial strategy – enjoy the soaring share price.

That bid-and-damn-it philosophy applies all across the City, no matter what the mouthpieces may pretend. Bankers and brokers have departments combing company records, looking for suitable bid targets, companies they can help break up, sell, float, or manipulate in some way. The whole thing is fee-driven. They have vastly expensive offices and staff desperate to earn money advising companies. So they must generate corporate action. All of the top merchant banks and brokers – and especially the aggressive Americans – circulate schemes suggesting one company might take on another. And how established companies might be broken up, complete with computations of how profitable it might be to the management. So the big boys are working for you, doing all they can to stimulate bids. Some of the most beautiful shares on the market belong to growing companies which have bid prospects thrown in. Choose carefully, and you have a triple winner – a share which rises because trading is good and profits are rising, a share which bobs higher on rumours of a bid, and – best of all – a share which leaps when a bid actually appears.

Spotting A Bid Stock

Finding such a stock can be hard, but not impossible. There are many clues. Unfortunately, there are no guarantees. Some stocks remain bid stocks for 20 years or more, always the bridesmaid and never the bride. It would be tempting fate to mention the names here. The faithful cling to them still, convinced that the offer will have arrived by the time you read this – or pretty soon, anyway.

The ideal bid stock will have a good profits record, heavy asset backing, a fair spread of investors without large blocks of stock stuck in the hands of a small number of long-term holders, and a slice of a growing section of industry. That is pretty near the ideal stock, let alone a bid stock. Find any two of those qualities, and you really could be in with a fair chance.

Strategic Stakeholders

As we move through the nineties, businesses holding strategic stakes in growth industries have become real takeover targets. In March 1995, I tipped shares of Unipalm in the *Daily Mail* at 118p. I did so because it was the only quoted way into the booming new global computer information network – the Internet. Unipalm provided the means for companies and individuals to get onto the Net. It was a boom area, and though profits were tiny, Unipalm was an important player.

In all honesty, I did not initially appreciate quite how important a player, though from the beginning I suggested that someone could take it over because it had a big market share which must eventually appeal to a giant. It received a bid worth around 450p just seven months later, and in the fun and games, I was able to advise *Daily Mail* readers to sell half of their stake at over 500p. It later topped 850p. Terrific.

Unipalm, though, was only one among many stocks moving up in 1995 because it had a big piece of a growing market, and was coveted by a still larger player. For all of 1995, Thorn EMI was buoyed by suggestions that one of the global media giants would bid for it to acquire the music business, the last significant saleable stake in a giant industry. That, alone, came to have a market value in excess of the worth of the whole of the business just a year or two earlier. With Thorn EMI, though, as with any investment, you needed to stay awake. The company split into two, and instead of leaving the two parts more vulnerable to bids, that simply marked the start of a sad decline in the shares of both companies. Eventually, the unglamorous Thorn bit, with the TV rentals and such, did get taken out, but at a disappointing price. All down the line, there were smaller bids and deals as go-ahead companies sought to pick up extra market shares in particular niche industries. If you were number one in the sprocket-building business, why not buy the number two or number three in order to achieve economies of scale? It makes sense – and creates profitable opportunities for investors who pick the right companies. Study the annual report carefully. You can never be sure, but be on the alert for any promising subsidiary in a growth industry. That might be enough to attract a bid for the whole company.

Profit Margins

Look, too, for established names which have gone off the boil. Profit margins may be important here. You can do simple margin sums by dividing pre-tax profits into sales or turnover. If other companies in the same line of business are making larger margins, ask yourself why. Your company might be inefficient, or there might be one or two bad bits making losses, or tiny returns, tucked away among the good. Either way, unless they are in shrinking industries, they could attract a livelier competitor who might want to buy the turnover to boost margins (and profits) to his own level. Or perhaps simply to close down and sell the loss-makers.

Capital Returns

Returns on capital are trickier. Retailers are fond of checking how much trading space their rivals own, and calculating sales per square foot. If they themselves get a higher return, they may be interested in bidding. That reasoning sparked the Burton bid for the Debenhams department stores, and the Dixons bid for Currys. Others look at brand names, which are often in the balance sheet at a low figure. They calculate their worth under different management, with more attention given to maximising profits, or perhaps with greater investment in new products under established names. Most companies have spotted this one. There has been keen debate about the correct way of valuing brands. Some companies have slapped high figures in their balance sheet for what are, essentially, intangible assets. It makes sense for some companies – and is a downright liberty for others.

Tired Families

Families who have controlled a company for years and lost their motivation or touch are fair game for bidders. Sometimes the younger generation does not follow their parents into the business, and the original directors opt out and seek a bidder so they can slip quietly into retirement. It is hard, however, to distinguish between large holders who are determined to hang on, and those ready to go.

Bomb-Blasted Business

Bomb-blasted businesses are really our old friends, recovery stocks, in a slightly different guise. A bad year or two may have shattered the share price, and the management may lack the nerve or verve to put the business back together again. Look for companies which have grown fat with assets, have over-expanded, or are weighed down by loss-makers and heavy borrowings. There may be opportunities for selling either good businesses to slash borrowings, or bad ones to eliminate losses. If borrowings come down, the interest burden can be lifted, and profits may leap.

Share Stakes

Many bidders telegraph their intentions by picking up a share stake before they actually bid. It is not completely daft. Sometimes it destabilises the shareholder list, and puts a company in play. Speculative buyers pick up blocks of shares, and are more ready to sell to a bidder, making it harder for the company to defend itself. Watch the City pages for news of stakes. They will spark a flurry of interest and the price will rise. If the company looks right, go in then. It might be our old friend, the shell promoter. Or it could be a fully-fledged bidder. The bidder might sit for a few months, allowing the price to settle back, and you might be able to buy more cheaply on a dull day. They always come, sooner or later. Try for shares in companies with price-earnings ratios around the average for their sector, with reasonable trading prospects. That way, you might be able to ride the bid roundabout without an additional entry fee. Even if the first stakeholder does not bid, there is always the chance he will sell to another bidder. Once a stake has been announced, there are always chances – if no bid appears, you will get periodic bursts of action as the market speculates that something is about to happen. The fly boys may be stuck, but they are expert at generating rumours so they can scramble out.

Leaks

In theory, bids should come like a bolt from the blue. In practice, illegal or not, insiders get to work in four bids out of five, and nibble at the shares. The press, especially the market reports, give the best guide. Watch, too, for shares which keep edging to new highs or hold steady on days when all about them are falling. Someone knows something.

Study comments which are reported in response to bid rumours. A flat 'No comment' is pretty imperturbable, but it is astonishing how often company representatives give a clue, unwittingly or not. Any reservation at all can be the sign of an honest person who cannot admit what is afoot but will not offer a bare-faced lie. Even so, bare-faced lies do pop out from time to time. That is part of the reason for employing public relations agents. They parrot what they are told. It can be dismissed later by the company as a mistake, or a misunderstanding. So the most vehement denial may not be the end of the story. It may be a deliberate attempt to mislead, or it may even be that the press is ahead of the game, and the company itself has not yet learnt of the bid which is on its way. You are on dangerous ground, though, buying bid stocks on leaks from friends in the business. If your source knows for sure, it is illegal to tell you, and illegal for you to act on the tip. If your source does not know for sure, you could be buying shares which are being run up by market men spreading the story so that they can sell. You could be buying a pup.

Study, too, the comments from the bidder. Once a bidder has said the offer is final, that is it. Under panel rules, that company can make no higher bid. The first bid price is rarely the last.

What To Do When The Bid Comes

If you have shares when a bid comes, hallelujah. Life is suddenly bright and beautiful. Sit back and enjoy it. You may be bombarded with circulars, but the more the merrier. The more attention you receive, the higher the final bid is likely to be.

Until the closing stages, all you need worry about is the Monopolies Commission. These days, most bidders seek quiet guidance first, and do not move unless they know that they are likely to escape a reference to the Commission. The system is not infallible, however, and some bids do get referred. If a reference seems likely, sell straight away. It can mean a six-month delay, or, more likely, will prompt the bidder to walk away. Otherwise do nothing until the last possible moment.

The waiting game is the winning game in a bid. Make your decision just before the very last closing date, never by the first. Once a bidder has sent an offer document to shareholders, they have 60 days. If they have not won by then, they cannot try again for a year. Nowadays, though, counter-bidding and general jiggery-pokery introduce all manner of complexities, and bids can drag on for months and months. The first bidder may not be the winning bidder. You should act eventually, however. Do not let a bid slip by without doing something – unless, of course, it is for shares in the kind of shell company we touched on earlier. Those sort of bid shares you must keep. If they choose, successful bidders can force you to take their bid once acceptances are over 90% of the share capital for which the offer was made. Watch this. By then you may have no option but to take the shares they are offering. Any cash alternative, if there was one, may have closed earlier.

Taking The Cash Bid

Your tax position will probably be the most important factor in deciding whether to take cash or shares. Once you take cash, you have effectively sold as far as the tax man is concerned, so you may have incurred a capital gains tax liability. This will only matter if your total gains in that tax year are above the annual free allowance. Before you choose cash, check the market price. The value of the bidder's paper (shares) offer may have pushed your shares above the cash alternative, so you might do better selling in the market.

There is one important exception. If you have shares in a qualifying AIM company, you do not have to pay capital gains tax if you sell in a bid, provided you reinvest the proceeds in another qualifying AIM or similar company within three years. Check this with your broker. The rules are uncertain following Labour changes.

Accepting Shares

If you accept shares in a bid, you defer your liability to capital gains tax until you sell those shares. This can be a big advantage. You need to be sure, however, that the shares are worth keeping. Look to see what price the cash alternative puts on them (effectively the price the bidder's shares are being underwritten at). This gives you an idea of what the institutions think they are worth. They will not want to see them below that. Check, too, what your income will be if you take shares. Many bids incorporate fixed-interest stock as part of the bid currency. That is done to make sure that shareholders do not end up with a lower dividend income by accepting. If income is what you want, you might do better taking the cash, and reinvesting in other high yielders. Bear in mind that if you take part fixed-interest capital and part Ordinary shares, you will have two lots of dealing expenses if you sell later.

Turning Down A Bid

At times, you might think it worth turning down a bid. Most shareholders feel a certain allegiance to their directors, and take more notice of them than of the bidder. The defending board will produce a flurry of promises which the City will expect them to keep. Usually, shares in a company which has fought off a bid fall when the offer lapses. But if the board has put up a strong enough case, they might attract a permanently higher rating. In many cases, the original bidder, or perhaps another, pops up again. Obviously, if the losing bidder has accumulated a sizeable share stake, further action is likely, eventually.

Buying When A Bid Arrives

No matter how dedicated a detective you might be, you cannot spot bid stocks to order. Do not despair. If you have the nerve – and usually you do not need much of it – you can still do well buying after the bid arrives. This became increasingly popular in the eighties as merger mania gripped the market. It was fuelled by events in America, where people like Sir James Goldsmith bought blocks of stock in companies, then were paid extra to go away. Ivan Boesky made a remarkable reputation as an arbitrageur, making massive profits by buying shares after the first bid appeared. Later, of course, he was exposed as a cheat and an insider dealer. But the message struck home – the first bid is rarely the final, highest bid. Buy when an offer first appears, and you could still profit. The financial muscle of the US arbitrageurs allowed them to help shape events. The small investor cannot do that, but there is ample scope for profit. The chances of losing are modest, if you are careful not to pay too much over the original offer price. At least you are assured of action.

What Bid Language Really Means

Obviously, an agreed bid is no use to you, apart from giving you an initial profit. There is no reason for the shares to rise above the offer, no chance of making more. Most bids, though, are disputed, and the more bitter the dispute, the better. So you need to read between the lines when the combatants start talking.

Under the rules of the Takeover Panel, bidders are not allowed to describe their offer as 'final' until near the very end. Before then, there is always the chance that they will pay more, no matter how much they huff and puff. There is an almost automatic assumption that the first bid is a sighting shot, meant to draw the defence and to measure more accurately what it might really take to win. So disregard what the bidder may say, until the offer is final.

Almost any bid which is not agreed at the very beginning will turn into a battle. The first statement from the target company will give an important clue to their attitude. If it follows almost immediately after the terms of the offer, and talks of inadequate, unsuitable terms, they are planning a tough fight. If the first response takes a day or two, or simply advises shareholders to do nothing for the moment, that also means a fight is on, but perhaps the defender is not in quite so strong a position – they need to think carefully before blasting off. The routine has become much more familiar, however, and some of the craftier players now simply take extra time to think before saying anything.

As ever, the press is a crucial source of information. Look for signs that the two sides have had preliminary talks. If they have, and the bidder is going ahead without agreement, the fight could be really bitter. The two sides have already established that they cannot get on. Watch, too, for any hint of another bidder, or a white knight – a friendly counter-bidder. Try to judge the emphasis on independence, and whether there could be readiness to sell to someone other than the first bidder. Check whether the bidder has a share stake, or if there are other stakeholders who might enter the fray. Watch how many shares defending directors control, and whether they really count. Particular institutions have a habit of supporting boards – Britannic Assurance (strong in Midlands engineering companies), and unit trust group M & G are especially prominent, though in the late nineties pressure to perform after a poor run of investment gains has prompted M & G to start accepting bids more readily. The more shares which look like backing the board, the more likely the bidder will have to pay extra.

Directors have a natural inclination to fight for their jobs. That angle serves the interests of shareholders, provided it does not get out of hand. In the end, however, they have an obligation to take a good bid. The institutions recognise this. They themselves must work in the best interests of their shareholders and policyholders. The victims most likely to put up a strong fight or attract another bid are the best quality companies. The bigger the asset backing, the bigger the bid. The better the profits record, the higher the worth of the company. Any bid should automatically offer a premium for control, so any company should expect to be taken out for at least 1½ times the average price-earnings ratio for the sector.

The Bankers To Back

Last but by no means least in deciding bid strategy is the identity of the merchant banks and brokers involved. League tables change. In the mid-eighties, Morgan Grenfell was top of the banking league, thanks largely to the innovative and imaginative abilities of corporate finance man Roger Seelig. He ended up in court as a result of the Guinness affair, and Morgan's star waned. Hill Samuel was another to take a knock, this time from the Takeover Panel, in a bid defence. The whole bank ended up being taken over by the Trustee Savings Bank, now itself taken over. But you need a tough fighter, ready to go to the limit in a bid defence. Top names in the nineties include Warburg, Kleinwort Benson, Rothschild, Lazard Brothers, Schroders and NatWest.

Buying After A Winning Bid

Should you buy shares of the winner after a winning bid? This works sometimes as the market realises what a good deal the bidder has got. And if you had shares in the company which was taken over and you took cash, it might be a good idea to buy into the victorious group if there is a slide in the price after the bid and you think your company went cheap. That worked well with Granada after it bought Forte.

Often shares sit quietly for a while as the market absorbs the extra capital, and as the directors get down to sorting out their acquisition. Give it a few months, maybe three or four, then take a look. If, however, your winning bidder is a shell company, or one being built quickly by ambitious new managers, the quiet spell after the bid may be the time to buy. Sooner or later, the next bid proposition will be lined up, and the bidder will need to get the shares motoring to help finance it. Around that time – what a coincidence – reports will start filtering out to big City investors, and through the company's brokers, recounting just what a wonderful deal the previous bid has proved to be. Pick a sufficiently aggressive company, and it can make sense to buy in the wake of a winning bid.

CHAPTER ELEVEN

The Streetwise Share-Trader

Learning about the stockmarket and share trading never stops. Commit every line, every comma, of this book to heart, and you will be on the way to making a killing in the share jungle. But there will still be much more to learn. The more you understand the theory, the better. There are guides galore to show how things ought to work, but they are no substitute for experience and the personal touch. And this only you can add.

All along, I have tried to flesh out theory with insight into what really happens, tricks of the trade. Theories give a rough guide, the rules which work until someone spots a smarter way. They are valuable because they tell you roughly how everyone else will approach things. The crowd pushes shares up or down. You want to anticipate what the crowd will do, get there first, and take advantage of it – a step ahead of the action. You are taking on all-comers. When you do, it helps to become streetwise, alert to everything around you, alive to the impact of changing moods and the way everyday events influence companies and share prices. After a while, it becomes natural, instinctive. The streetwise share trader develops a feel for how people react, the way prices respond, how the more routine developments – and the most improbable events – can influence shares.

Backing The Man

It takes no great genius to appreciate that backing the right man is a formula for successful investment. It has been explained several times already in this book, especially when looking at shell companies and reconstructions. It matters just as much in big companies as small ones. Sir John Harvey-Jones had a radical impact on Imperial Chemical Industries. With his straggly hair, garish kipper ties and energetic, abrasive style, he showed that there was much in ICI which warranted change. It impressed the City no end, and sent the shares to new peaks. A few years after he had gone, people began questioning his achievements. Never mind. For the alert investor, who had ridden the rise and sold before the slump, Sir John had been a man to follow.

In the High Street in the mid-eighties, a similar picture developed, but in more flamboyant style. Sir Terence Conran at Storehouse, Sir Ralph Halpern at Burton Group, and George Davies at Next all revolutionised their companies. So did Gerald Ratner before his unfortunate joke about selling poor quality products. While they were on top, the shares enjoyed massive gains. All are long gone, and their strategies look wildly over-ambitious with hindsight. The shares slumped eventually. But while they were hot, they were really hot. In the stockmarket, nothing lasts forever.

The great long distance runners, of course, were Lord Hanson and the late Lord White at Hanson, and Lord Weinstock at GEC. They have lost their edge, perhaps because their creations have grown too big to move swiftly, and are being broken apart. In their heyday, they were all marvellous. Already, I have mentioned Greg Hutchings at Tomkins, and Sir Nigel Rudd and Brian McGowan at Williams Holdings as leaders of the next generation of big winners, now settling into boring middle-age.

There are many more, coming up behind. David Jones has triumphed in rebuilding Next. Stuart Wallis did a marvellous job at Fisons, and will win instant support wherever he surfaces next. Gerry Robinson and his bold expansion of Granada by acquisition has been impressive. Sir Clive Thompson has set himself a target of 20 per cent annual growth at Rentokil, and managed to meet it until the summer of 1998.

On a smaller scale, one-time stockbroker Luke Johnson has been behind some startling winners. In the early nineties, it became fashionable to decry the efforts of individual entrepreneurs, attack one-man-band businesses, and sing the praises of supervision by a strong board, with a split between the functions of chairman and chief executive, and ample squads of non-executive directors on hand. Companies pay homage to the Cadbury Committee and the code of corporate governance, reinforced by Sir Richard Greenbury's rules on executive rewards, with Sir Ronnie Hampel working away on another code to make it all more cumbersome. I have my doubts. This is a response to the many failures to hit the recession years. With a few exceptions, government by committee does not work so well. For the aggressive share player, the big winners are still most likely to come from companies associated with one strong, determined individual.

Almost every stockmarket winner is associated with a driving personality at the top. The earlier you spot them, the better. You can do well by a shrewd selection of big companies, but the real excitement is in small to medium situations which are picking up speed. Pick the right man in the right company, and you could see the price double or treble in the first year, and again in the second. You will not get that sort of performance from too many industrial giants. Remember, though, that smaller companies and one-man-bands do carry higher risks.

Using Your Instincts

Sorting the prospective high-flyer from the common or garden director is not easy. Follow your instincts. If what he says and does seems sensible, back him. If it does not, do not be persuaded. Instinct and common sense are great investment tools. Time and again, they prove to be the winners. No matter what others may say, if the new hero strikes you as a shifty character who rarely gives a straight answer, keep clear. EVERY CON-MAN HAS TO HAVE A STORY, has to be able to persuade people to believe in him if he is going to be able to rip them off. This may sound unduly cynical, the sour reaction of a hard-bitten journalist. Perhaps it is. In 36 years of reporting financial affairs, I have met hundreds of company promoters who have come unstuck, from the monstrous Maxwell to the most piffling piranhas. They were either out to take shareholders for a ride, or simply totally incapable of delivering the delights they promised. Every one had a fan club. Every one appeared to know all of the answers. So they should. No investor on the outside can understand what is going on inside a company nearly so well as the person in charge.

Often the promoters themselves believe what they are saying, as they are saying it. They have a shining self-belief, faith in themselves and their schemes, a conviction that somehow it will all work out. Step back and think about what they are saying. Sometimes the cracks appear very quickly. A few minutes spent analysing what they actually promise, in the quiet, on your own, can give you a very different view.

Remember how someone was convincing enough in the late eighties to persuade people to back a company devoted to farming goats, and how it all fell apart? Ostriches lost unwise investors a lot of money in the nineties. If you ever bought one, and stopped to think how often you used it a second or third time, you would have ducked the mid-nineties vogue for companies publishing CD-ROMs, the discs which brought books and pictures to personal computers. The novelty wore off almost before you unpacked them, and a string of companies making them hit trouble almost as soon as they gained a share listing. And the mugs never seem to tire of pumping money into dodgy futures and foreign exchange deals. My scepticism is hard-earned. I have listened to the promises, and watched the problems break in their wake. Then I have read the letters from disillusioned investors who have lost their savings. It can be shattering. After a while, believing becomes the most difficult thing of all.

It would be quite wrong, though, to pretend that I get it right every time. Every so often, I get taken in, and find myself believing something which turns out to be fatally flawed. It happens, no matter how much I try to heed my own warning signs. There are other times when I realise that I have been unduly harsh about some scheme which is relatively well-founded. That is a mistake I make less frequently, the sort of mistake all of us must accept. Every time, err on the side of caution. It is no great loss if you miss the odd good thing. You lose nothing real, no cash. If you do back a dud, you will know what you have lost – real money.

The man to follow is the man you can believe in. You need someone with personality and a plan, someone who makes sense, someone ambitious and – above all – someone whose own fortune depends on the success of the company and the shares.

Time and again, it does come down to instinct. Never neglect it. Never let it be overruled by the idea that so many clever chaps in the City see it differently. If the so-called experts never got it wrong, there would never be any suspect schemes, never any company collapses or scandals. How many times have I heard mining promoters emphasise that their estimates of reserves are backed by independent geologists? And how many times has the company failed ? And, to hear promoters talk, you might think that a big name accounting firm never ever audited the accounts of any enterprise which went belly-up a few months later. Pull the other one, please. Never give the suspect the benefit of the doubt. No matter how glittering the prize, there will always be another coming along later.

Making The Meeting

Once you have backed your high-flyer and bought his shares, make an effort to meet him. The annual meeting is your best opportunity, though while a company is growing fast, there may be several extraordinary meetings for investors to approve deals. Try to go to one. The annual meeting especially is the one occasion each year when this budding captain of industry is answerable to you as a shareholder, one of the owners of the company.

You may be unsure about confronting some well-known name, a man of power and repute. Grit your teeth. He will be nervous, too. Company directors are used to telling others what to do, demanding answers to their questions. A shrewdly-posed question at an annual meeting can catch them off guard. Many directors rehearse replies to all likely questions, with advisers quizzing them ahead of the meeting, especially if something controversial is on the agenda.

Do not be put off. Do not be rude. Be polite, but firm. Frame your question with a compliment. Listen to the answer. If it does not make sense, or avoids the question, do not hesitate to come back. All too often, shareholders are overcome by nerves, too shy to pick up obvious evasions. Do not let it happen to you. You deserve a proper reply. You have taken the trouble to buy the shares, and attend the meeting. You have every right to be treated politely and intelligently. If you are not, learn from it. Ask yourself if this is a man and a company you should trust with your money. Make any question brief, clear, and to the point. It does not have to be clever. A simple query about progress may be enough. Anything sensible will make a mark, and the chances are that the chairman or some director will come to talk to you about it afterwards.

Even Robert Maxwell used to do that sometimes, though he found it a strain to suppress his impatience and to exude charm for more than a brief spell. Always stay behind at the end of a meeting and chat to as many directors as you can. It gives you an excellent chance of weighing up the people who are responsible for your investment. Most genuinely welcome your interest. If they do not treat you as you think they should, beware. They are fools, and badly-advised fools at that. In the last resort, if you feel you have something really important to raise, ring the City office of the *Daily Mail* and tell us to come along to listen to your questions.

Using Your Eyes And Ears

Many companies use annual meetings to display their products and services. This can give a valuable impression of what is really going on, and can ensure that you know what the company really does. That will help day-to-day investment judgements. It is routine for the streetwise share trader to be picking up investment information no matter what they are doing. You can stumble across share tips anywhere, at any time, if you are alert enough to appreciate them.

The transformation of stuffy old menswear group J. Hepworth into high-flying fashion chain Next happened in the High Street for all to see. Drab Hepworth shops closed, and the clean lines of Next replaced them. A casual glance at the fashion spreads in the papers confirmed that Next boss George Davies was impressing everyone. If you backed him at the beginning, you could have multiplied your money five-fold. Perhaps you were smart enough to spot it going off the rails, with too many stores, conflicting brands, and so on. And then, believe it or not, you could have multiplied your money more than twenty-fold inside five or six years as Next turned round again, and came right under David Jones.

Even Alan Sugar enjoyed his few moments in the limelight as investors picked up on his remarkable ability in the early days to produce low-priced versions of computers and electrical goods.

The spread of the monster Wetherspoon pubs across the country gave signals that something good was happening in the nineties, though for a while, the trends to spot were mostly the other way. Keeping your eyes open produced warnings galore. There was Ratners with the never-ending cut-price offers. There were stores with sale after sale, bank branches closing, housebuilders slashing prices and offering low-cost mortgages.

On the bright side, though, there were opportunities developing. The rise of direct selling insurance by Direct Line helped power Royal Bank of Scotland shares to new peaks. The really smart punter would have spotted, of course, that the competition moved in everywhere after a few years, hitting Direct Line's profit growth. The launch of *Windows 95*, the Microsoft computer software operating system, did great things for companies like P & P and Datrontech, supplying computer systems and the accessories which go with them. Then they hit problems as microchip prices slumped. On a global scale, the Gulf War killed an already flagging tourist business, hammering groups with central London hotels. British Airways suffered badly, too, for a while. That merely created a buying opportunity as world travel later picked up anew. Share tips – to buy or sell – are all around. You simply need to notice them, and think what they might mean.

Listening To The Gossip

Gossip may come your way at your local, or from neighbours on the train. A friend of a friend said chaps from another company have been crawling all over the works, a new plant is being planned, or a massive order is on the way, or uncle was told by someone who works in the City that someone is planning a takeover – but don't pass it on.

Do not trust the tip. Try to check it, by all means. Careless talk costs money. Employees are rarely good at judging the impact of events, real or imaginary, on shares in their own company. They may well be out of touch with the market, and have no idea what the City is expecting, or knows already. A big development might mean more jobs, and sound good to the workers, but might mean a cashflow shortage in the company, or lower profits for a while. Bid whispers might be right – who knows? More often than not, they are wrong. Anyone who really knows about a bid is breaking the law by passing the word on, if they expect someone to buy shares as a result. If the tip is right, the chances are that the City has already heard it. You could be Tail-End Charlie, the last mug buyer.

Perhaps the most significant exception is where information has been released to unions,or staff meetings. This should not go outside the plant or office, but it does. More often than not, it is advance warning of bad news, trouble or staff cutbacks. There was a classic example early in 1992, when I heard that staff in the Ratners jewellery group (now Signet) were to be addressed by area managers. Christmas trading had been grim, and cuts were in the air. In the next trading session, the shares fell 20%. Be careful. Best rely on your stockbroker for share gossip. Ask him or her about the rumours you have heard. He will have some idea of whether what you heard makes sense, and whether it will make a difference to the share price.

Director Dealing

It has become fashionable to watch the way directors trade their shares. Several services publish charts based on boardroom trading, and attempt to analyse what this means for prices. They make some questionable judgements, but the information itself is interesting. Directors should have a better idea than most of how the company is performing. Their trading is more likely than not to get the trend right – but it is by no means infallible.

Directors and their families are not allowed to deal in the two months ahead of scheduled company announcements – interim and preliminary profit statements. Nor when they know price sensitive news is on the way. So sometimes they are forced to buy or sell at inconvenient, inopportune moments. And the routine excuses of needing to sell to pay off overdrafts, meet family needs, other personal reasons can be quite genuine. Publications like *The Estimate Directory* and *Company REFS* offer a useful monitoring service.

Directors' dealings are reported in several newspapers, with a regular Saturday slot in the *Financial Times*. You can get the same information, sometimes slightly earlier, sometimes later, from the *Stock Exchange Weekly Official Intelligence* in larger libraries.

What The Chairman Really Means

There is something about running a public company that brings out the pomposity in people. Even the most down-to-earth directors can get a touch pretentious when they write to shareholders in the name of the company. The words get in the way of what they mean to say.

It is not made any easier by a bewildering array of Stock Exchange, Takeover Panel, Companies Act, and Financial Services Act obstacles. Sometimes, it seems, merely opening your mouth can be an offence. Or perhaps the chairman does have something to hide, and finds fluffing his meaning helps. Either way, you need to decode the message, or perhaps clarify it in a chat after the annual meeting.

The future is what matters most. Look hard at anything under the heading 'Prospects' for reservations, qualifications, or modifications. They will not be there by accident. The wording will be intended to give the chairman an excuse to say "I warned you" if something should go wrong, even if he has said something like "Prospects appear excellent, and the company will continue to grow strongly while demand is sustained." Excuse me. "While demand is sustained?" What does that mean? Is it a sneaky way of saying that we do not know what is happening to orders, they may not stretch too far ahead, and we could be in trouble if they fall?

Talk of 'continuing growth' could refer to sales, trading profits, pre-tax profits, or earnings. What matters most is earnings per share. 'Expansion' is another vague word. It could be good. But does it mean issuing lots of shares? Or will existing businesses do better and grow? If there was heavy capital spending last year, will it bring higher profits this year? Or will there be a hefty depreciation charge to hit profits? Is expansion of sales concealing a fall in profits?

If there is no mention of growth, will there be any? Chairmen should give some guidance in the report, or at the annual meeting. What is left unsaid could be more important than what is said. Talk of rationalisation means some part of the business is not going well. Will closing or cutting it back mean an exceptional charge? Will it threaten the dividend?

Mention of 'increased competition' almost invariably means lower margins and falling profits. Does it mean actual losses? 'Market share' can be tricky, too. Is the market itself growing? Or is the company seeing lower sales, and raising market share by clinging on in a market which is falling? 'Currency changes' may influence profits, and could mean assets have to be written down – or up.

Total candour is rare indeed when it means explaining to investors that things are going wrong, and the business is falling apart. Companies almost always put the best interpretation they can on any given situation. So if you are worried, and the message is not clear to you, never hesitate to ask. It is your money at stake.

Creative Accounting

You can be sure the chairman will want to steer clear of questions about creative accounting. Any hint of accounting matters, and he will pass them to the finance director, or the auditors. You may get precious little satisfaction or sense out of them.

In these sophisticated times, it can come as a shock to be told that company profits, duly audited by the nation's finest and most expensive accountancy brains and certified as complying with the Companies Act, may be far from what they seem. Companies have great flexibility in deciding what is, and what is not, a profit or a loss. It is all due to accounting standards, and can be quite baffling for even the most advanced investors.

Because relatively few really understand accounting, it does not have a vast impact on share prices, even across the City. It often hovers somewhere between fact and fiction, a vague impression that some accounts are not to be trusted quite so much as others. A full understanding might help you avoid some of the dodgier companies, but their problems will generally be spotted elsewhere in time for you to heed the warning of a falling share price, and to sell them. Concentrate on the cash flow. The cash generated after paying dividends and capital spending is important in financing the company's future growth. If there is plenty of cash coming into the business, all is probably well. Watch to see that the cashflow from operating activities – not the one-off sales – is roughly the same as the profits generated by trading activities. If cash coming in from operations is lower than the operating profits, it is a signal to look more carefully. There may have been some creative accounting. Cashflow is hard to fiddle in the accounts. So is the tax bill. If the company is paying little tax, perhaps it is actually making little real profit. For the average investor, it may be enough to listen for talk about things like off-balance sheet financing. That means the company is arranging borrowings in associated companies in a fashion which does not show up readily in the published report and accounts. The company may have mortgaged the future more heavily than you realise, and may be legally responsible for more debt than you imagined, if things go wrong. In future, this should be less of a problem. New accounting standards, set up to tackle many of the more obvious tricks, decree that such borrowings should now be in the accounts.

Companies can juggle with the allocation of costs, capitalising them. This means the cost of work is assumed to have added value to an asset, and can be written into the balance sheet as a plus, instead of being taken off profits as a minus. Wonderful. The most commonly capitalised item is interest – the cost of the money property companies borrow while they are building something, and which they expect to recover when the completed building is eventually sold. That works well, until the building has to be sold at a loss. There used to be a great game of extraordinary items and exceptional items. Because they are a one-off, and would not normally happen again, the idea was that they should not be allowed to distort the real trend, so they were not included on the face of the profit and loss account. Now they are there, up front. If you sell a factory, the gain is there. If you close one down, the cost is there. And so on. It makes calculating the normal flow of profits a little more tricky, but it does make sense.

Then there are provisions. These little beauties crop up frequently when a company has been active in acquiring others. The buyer makes a provision against the cost of reorganising the newly-bought business. In subsequent years, it can gradually take these provisions back, setting them off against the costs which are actually incurred, as they arise. The scope for taking running costs out of the profit and loss account, and thus transforming them into a less sensitive balance sheet item, is wonderful. Too many losses, of course, dent the profit record and the share rating. Busy companies would not be able to persuade the City to back them to make more bids.

There are games galore a shrewd finance director can play, all with the blessing of accountants. The main worry comes when the games start attracting comment, and begin to undermine the share price. Sometimes, of course, the tricks build the equivalent of an unexploded bomb, storing up potential problems that could lead to massive losses if it all goes wrong. The Maxwell accounts were a classic example. Without too much skill, you could examine the profits of around £150m sceptically, take off all of the dubious amounts which were not quite what they seemed, and you ended up with losses. For most purposes, you need not worry too much. It only really counts when the City begins to worry about what is going on, and it hits the share price. When that starts, do not wait. Sell at once. It will only get worse.

Talking To Your Broker

Talking to your stockbroker, if you have one, can be an art in itself. Never forget, they have an angle. They live on the commission they earn buying and selling shares, so they like you to trade. They also live on capital gains from trading shares for themselves, so there are times when it will suit them for you to buy a particular share to help push the price up. And since Big Bang, the shares they suggest you buy might be owned by their firm – though they should tell you. So remember our earlier note about the difference between agents and principals. Agents act for you, and do not hold shares themselves. Principals act for you, but may set the prices and may own the shares you buy or sell.

If a broker comes up with a share for you to buy, ask why? There may be a written report on it from the research department, with profit projections, dividend forecasts, price-earnings ratios, asset value, and so on. Such reports can be brilliant. Or they may be third-rate. Try to talk to the analysts, and note what they say. Ask whether there are any special sellers about, who they might be, and how many there are. If they are part of a large line, perhaps someone interesting – a director or a major shareholder – is selling. Why? Usually, of course, the shares will not be coming from anywhere special, and your broker will deal in the normal way through a market-maker.

In general, it is not a good idea to trade on your broker's gossip, unless you know the broker extremely well. A newcomer, anxious to impress, may give you their best ideas, but their inexperience may tell. More senior brokers will give the best ideas to their biggest clients first. And remember, brokers take less risk when they deal for themselves, because they pay no commission, and are in touch minute by minute. Today's favourite may be old news for them tomorrow. They may have been in and moved on out, while you are still wondering what is happening.

If you contact a broker with an idea, ask what they think and what the research department makes of it. Several bigger firms provide predictions across a remarkable range of companies, either in books which are regularly updated, or on computer screens. You may get a frosty response if you are a small trader, but it is worth trying. Ask your broker to check the price and size (the number of shares you can trade in) with all of the market-makers (prices do differ a little from place to place). A good broker will do this automatically, getting the best for you.

What Your Broker Really Means

Informed, independent and urbane though they may appear, brokers are merely tradesmen, there to do your bidding. You pay the bill. But they also often owe a duty to some of the companies whose shares they trade. All quoted companies have a stockbroking firm to advise them. That firm will usually produce reports on the company's progress, and be the best-informed source of profit forecasts. Most often, comment will be favourable. The verdict will rarely be 'Sell'. That could cost the broker a valuable customer, and a handy retainer.

Even if your broker is not an official broker to a particular company, the research department has to tread delicately. Whatever brokers may say in private, they have to be careful about their public stance – witness the remarkable ability of Smith New Court (now taken over by Americans Merrill Lynch) to act for Robert Maxwell while quietly telling valued customers to sell the shares.

Stockbroking analysts can ask penetrating questions of companies, and some are impressively well-informed. Unlike financial journalists, they cannot try to insist on answers. They rely for their information on the company's goodwill. So when it comes to making less than glowing comments, brokers must be careful. If they tell clients to sell, or point to a problem, that company may refuse to speak to the analyst again. Analysts need to be able to talk to companies to get the extra, inside information which will allow them to give advice.

Make no mistake, company brokers ARE given inside information. They are used deliberately to channel good news to the big investors. Or, when the company itself cannot be seen to do it directly, they are encouraged to soften the blow of bad news by filtering the word quietly around the City. The upshot of all this is that brokers often speak in riddles. Written comments sometimes appear in a code, because it would be unwise to say what they really mean. On other occasions, they simply get so tangled in clever technical analysis that they are almost incapable of putting it into plain English, or assessing what it means as far as the share price is concerned.

So look at brokers' circulars with a jaundiced eye, and talk to them with care. They can be invaluable. But sometimes you need to try to decipher the real message. Only slightly tongue-in-cheek, this may help.

- *Strong Buy...* My neck is on the line if we do not get the price up.
- *Buy...* Should be all right.
- *Buy for income...* Do not expect much capital gain.
- *Buy for the long term...* Something may turn up.
- *Buy/Hold...* We are brokers to the company. They would be upset if we did not say "buy".
- *Look to buy...* It may go down, so do not touch it now.
- *Buy for recovery...* We hope the fall has stopped.
- *Take Overweight Position...* Probably a buy, but we do not want anyone to criticise us if it goes down.
- *Undervalued Opportunity...* Nothing has happened for ages. The directors say the shares are too low. They always say that.
- *Strong Hold...* Who knows?
- *Hold...* Nothing happening. Sell.
- *Weak hold...* Sell at once.
- *Reduce Weighting...* Sell the lot.
- *Look to sell...* May go up a little. Get out if you have any sense.

- *Good technical position...* Our chartist thinks it looks cheap, but what does he know?
- *Weak technical position...* Our chartist says it is dear. Who knows?
- *Our forecast is being raised...* The company swears business is good, and another broker has raised his forecast.
- *Our forecast is being reduced...* We got it wrong. We have already told our best clients to sell.
- *Bid possibilities are in the price for nothing...* Take a gamble
- *Ambitious expansion programme...* Watch for a flood of new shares.

Setting Limits

Always give your broker clear instructions on the number of shares to trade, and what you expect to pay or get. Be sure whether they are to deal 'at best' – whatever price they can get – or 'on limits', only at a price you set. Following the introduction of the Stock Exchange Electronic Trading System (SETS) under which deals in the bigger companies are matched by computer, it has become crucial not to tell your broker to deal at best, but to specify careful limits. If you do not give limits, there is a chance you might end up on the automatic system, paying a wildly erratic price for shares. It has been particularly dangerous and volatile in the opening half hour, and the closing 30 minutes. If you do set limits, make them clear, and be prepared not to trade if your broker cannot meet them.

Sometimes they will be able to leave your limits with the market-maker, perhaps for days, and he will deal if the price hits them. This gives dealers a useful target, and can help you get a better price, but it does not always work. Where you are trying to buy shares with a wide spread between buying and selling price, it may be worth setting limits close to the middle price. Give your broker something to work for, if they will take such an order.

Make it clear, too, whether your broker can deal at their discretion, or only on your instructions. Good brokers can save you money by trading quickly if they see an opportunity, and use their discretion on individual trades. But you need to trust each other, and it is no good giving brokers discretion and complaining if their judgement turns out wrong. Do not give anyone blanket discretion to trade all of your spare cash, or all of your portfolio. That way, you may find you are pumped full of the old rubbish the firm needs to shift. Do not give discretion to anyone who approaches you over the phone with investment ideas. And never deposit cash with a broker you do not know well, and leave them to deal with it. If you sell something, try to make sure the cash comes back to you. If you leave it on account with the broker, get clear written undertakings of where it is left, and what claim you have to it, no matter how safe and convenient the broker may suggest the system may be. Previously, I have advised against leaving money on deposit with a broker. These days, though, the faster settlement system means it can make sense, and most brokers have formalised arrangements with respectable banking houses.

Narrow Markets

Never buy more shares than the market-maker will normally trade at the stated price. If you do, it could be difficult to sell. You may not be able to deal at the market price, especially if prices are falling. If the price quoted is in 5,000 shares, do not buy 10,000 unless you are ready to take an extra risk, and prepared to be patient about getting out.

If the market-makers quote a price for a relatively small package, with a wide spread between buying and selling rates – say, more than 5% – take extra care. You have found a narrow market stock. This can be advantageous when the price is rising, because it responds sharply to modest buying. Whereas you can trade in £250,000 worth of ICI shares without the price blinking, there are shares which move 5% or more on a deal worth £1,000. Many more move 5% on deals worth £5,000. These are generally shares in small, speculative companies. But not always.

Narrow market shares are killers when the price turns down. This usually happens more rapidly and savagely than a rise. The moment they sense extra selling, market-makers hammer the price. They do not want to get caught holding stock in a little company which attracts modest trade, and which may spring a nasty surprise.

It is a brave, or foolish, investor who weighs in heavily for a narrow market stock. Seeing it go up, it can be tempting to buy more. Be warned. The real disaster for small punters and other gamblers in the Crash of 1987 was finding that they literally could not sell some companies at any price. If your broker says your favourite stock is a narrow market, think again. You need to be doubly sure when you walk on the wild side.

Cheap At The Price

Hard to believe, but there are brokers who will peddle you the line that certain shares are cheap because they were once much dearer. You hear it from unsophisticated investors, and naive journalists, too. Perhaps weariness takes over and they stop thinking. Do not get caught. If you study the highs and lows, and see that a share is 100p below its peak, it is tempting to think that it might go back up again one day. After all, somebody once thought it worth 100p extra, and actually paid it. It must have looked right then. Perhaps it just drifted back by chance? Forget it. Shares do fall out of favour, and prices do suffer from neglect at times. But there is usually a reason. Usually, the business is going wrong. Somebody else knows it. Circumstances have changed. If the price goes back towards the peak, there will be sellers all the way up, relieved at the chance to break even and write off a mistake.

Listen To The Price

Listen to what the share price is telling you. It is a valuable lesson. Before you buy, watch for a while. Get a feel for the range it trades in, how sharply it rises, the way it falls. Watch closely on days when the market is moving strongly one way or another. If it falls when all else is rising, be wary. If it rises when others fall, or holds steady, someone may be accumulating stock, confident enough to pick it up through thick and thin. Smart dealers know how to build a stake without attracting attention. They try to buy when the market is falling, lay off to let sellers come in, and pick up stock again when the price slips.

Get your broker to try to check with the market-maker. A good broker may be able to wheedle out whether the buying is consistently from one source. He may even glean some idea of price parameters. When the big boys are buying, you may be able to tag along just for the ride.

Shares do tend to get a momentum going. Do not fight it. If a share keeps sliding gently, be suspicious. If you are determined to buy, wait for it to find a level. It is worth sacrificing 10% or so to make sure the fall is over. 'Never try to catch a falling knife' is the market cliche. Let someone else risk buying at the bottom. Equally, there are times when a rise goes steadily on and up. It is always hard to guess where it will stop. Stay with it while it lasts, if you can time it correctly.

Double Bottoms and Plunging Necklines – The Charts

There are people who live by charts, who swear they tell you the true share story. They shut their eyes to fundamentals – such things as profits and dividends – and watch dots or crosses on graph paper, and reckon the real action is there, plain to see.

It is easy to mock. One of the noisiest names in the business used his charts to recommend one company less than a fortnight before the receiver moved in. Had he spoken to the brokers, or looked at the accounts, he would have known what dire straits the company was in before he recommended it. Now he checks the fundamentals before going overboard on chart tips.

There is another side to the coin. Jim Slater, the share king of the sixties and early seventies, was asked at one annual meeting of Slater Walker what he thought of chartists who said his shares were too high. He answered scornfully that chartists tended to have ragged raincoats and big overdrafts. A few years later, Slater Walker crashed. Jim himself became our best-known minus millionaire for a while.

Now, of course, he is a massively successful investment guru. As ever, well worth listening to. But charts can be a valuable aid, if you are first familiar with the investment basics. They do give an idea of what other investors think, and sometimes show what the insiders are doing. Once you have found an interesting share, there is no harm in seeing what the charts say. Most brokers have a chartist tucked away. And you can watch for their views in the press, or in specialist services.

What Chartists Do

Chartists draw patterns around share price moves. Some follow the closing price each day, marking it on a vertical scale, with the time period on the horizontal. Others make bar charts, placing a little vertical line to cover the high and low trading range for the day, with a horizontal line for the closing level.

Point and figure charts are more ambitious. These focus on significant price movements, with a vertical row of crosses for each worthwhile gain, and noughts for each fall. There is no set timescale. A new column is formed with each change of direction. The chartist sees a pattern in the dots and lines. A double bottom shows a price falling to a low, rising, and finally falling back to that low. This might mean the shares will go no lower. It might mean someone is buying at a particular level, and this the chart watcher can follow.

On the other hand, a double bottom might become a triple bottom. Or even a false bottom, followed by a lower bottom. Turn bottoms upside down, and they become plunging necklines, which catch the eye of the chartist in a falling market. A neckline is a support level below a head and shoulders formation. Leave it to the experts to determine what that is, along with flags, spear points, rectangles, reverse heads and shoulders, and all the other exotica.

Around all of these, chartists arrive at conclusions on trends and momentum. Ask, and you may be told a trend is a trend until it stops. That sums up a great deal about chart watching. It gives a glimpse of what is going on, sort of, but it is of limited use for what you really want to know – what happens next.

The Value Of Charts

Charts do count, however, because people pay attention to them. No matter how daft it may seem, anything is important if it prompts people to buy or sell. Talk about support points and resistance levels means chartists think it will be important if a share – or perhaps the market – moves beyond a particular level. They may be telling clients that if the FTSE index falls below 4,500, an important support has been breached and a slump could follow. Some clients may take notice and sell, so the prediction becomes self-fulfilling. You may not heed it, but it is as well to be aware of what is going on.

Where a share is rising, signs that it once hovered around a particular price may indicate a potential resistance level, where many bought earlier, saw a fall, and got out when they got their money back. It may be significant if the price goes above this resistance. Potential sellers may be exhausted, and future buyers could find the shares in shorter supply, so they will rise more rapidly. In a falling market, the reverse may happen. If a share drops through a support level, where there have been ready buyers in the past, potential new buyers may be put off, and sellers will hit the price harder.

Such an outline does scant justice to what has become a very sophisticated affair, but it will suffice for many investors. Chartists would be more convincing if they could muster greater agreement among themselves over the meaning of charts. Ask half a dozen about the same chart, and you could get six different views. That, as they say, is what makes a market. If you want to learn more, the classic chartist text book is *Technical Analysis of Stock Trends*, by Edwards & McGee. Easier to understand, though, and highly recommended is *Charters On Charting* by David Charters (0 7134 8389 X).

No One Left To Buy

Charts can help clarify some of the rules the professionals keep in mind, especially relating to the particular characteristics some shares develop. It all goes back to instinct, developing a feel. Watch, and you will see how some shares never make much progress, no matter how impressive the fundamentals. Year in, year out, analysts used to estimate that the asset value of the multinational Lonrho was four or five times greater than the share price, that profits were rising, and that the dividend yield was into double figures, way above average. Nevertheless, the shares stuck in a narrow trading range. You either loved or hated Lonrho chief executive, the late Tiny Rowland. In 1985, Lonrho began to power ahead, breaking out of the price trap, pushing up in 1986. After years of stagnation, they had found a new generation of buyers, young fund managers ready to buy a high-yielder with prejudice from long-established City doubts about the company. Until then, every believer had the shares. The rest did not want to know at any price. There was no one left to buy, no matter how bright the business looked.

They got it wrong, of course. Lonrho never managed a sustained advance, and it all ended in tears for Tiny when he was forced out by one of his proteges, Dieter Bock. Through most of the nineties, Greg Hutchings must have been scratching his head about his Tomkins share price. Whatever he did, it never seemed able to sustain much of a re-rating.

Shares do run out of buyers. They learn to live with their rating. The market grows used to seeing some shares on a low p/e, and others on a high one. They get left alone, indiscriminately. It can take a major change to shift perceptions. Only the big boys will bring it about. Watch for it starting, and try to ride with it then. Stay away until you are sure the change is coming.

Late News

Be wary of announcements which come late. Bad figures almost invariably take longer to add up than good ones. Companies often announce in advance the date of profit statements, but there is no firm rule. Usually, they roll around at about the same point each year, so keep an eye on your diary. Any statement more than three weeks overdue should be viewed with suspicion. Ask your broker if he knows the reason. Or try ringing the company secretary. It might be safest not to wait. If in doubt, sell out.

One Product Companies

Take special care with one product companies, or companies which depend for a large slice of their business on one customer. There are not too many about these days. But when the competition comes along, as it surely will, they can crumble fast.

And be imaginative. Ratners the jewellers may not strike you immediately as the retail equivalent of a one product company. But in the UK and the US, it got stuck with a down-market cut-price image, even though it had a number of better-class stores. When the fun started to fade for cheaper jewellery, the impact was devastating. Suddenly chairman Gerald Ratner found himself hoist on his own petard, condemned all round as the cut-price king, with nowhere to go but down.

Quarter Days

The opportunities may be limited, but it is as well to remember that big investors can act strangely towards the end of each quarter – 31 March, 30 June, 30 September, and 31 December. It sounds silly, but in the weeks ahead of these dates, they tend to throw out smaller companies, or shares which have been doing badly.

Most of the trustees who watch over pension funds and so on tend to glance at investment schedules which are often compiled at the end of each quarter. Rather than have to explain to the pensions committee or the insurance board why they are holding a particular loser, or some controversial company, fund managers dump them in advance. Out of sight, out of mind. If they are not on the investment list, the trustees are none the wiser, and ask no awkward questions. It is easier for fund managers to hide their mistakes, to take a loss, setting it off against profits elsewhere. That means there are sometimes special buying opportunities as quarter days approach – or sometimes after there is a change of manager in a particular fund. It is outrageous the way in which perfectly good stocks are sometimes dumped at silly prices, all in one lot, when a careful and patient selling programme would realise better prices. That cuts the value of your pension and mine, perhaps. So you might find that your favourite stock has a bad patch for no apparent reason. Or there might be a good buying opportunity. Never imagine that perfect logic has anything to do with the way fund managers operate.

Changing Brokers

Something similar can happen when a company changes brokers. Often it is a good sign. The company will only change for a good reason. Usually, it will be because it is fed up with the old broker not doing enough to promote the shares, leaving the price to perform below board expectations. Sometimes, though, the broker will be disappointed with the company. That can be especially bad news, because brokers do not easily abandon the retainer they are paid for their efforts.

Either way, though, changing brokers can mean an unsettling patch for the shares. The old broking house may start selling the shares out of unit trusts it manages, and from client accounts where it has discretionary management rights. There might be a good reason to do it, it might be spite, or more probably it is a way of freeing cash to invest into another client company. That way, the broker can gain some goodwill with someone, let alone the extra commissions generated by selling one company and buying shares in another.

If the new broker is more powerful than the old one, the depressing effect may not make itself felt, initially. The new house will be anxious to impress the company, and is likely to encourage clients to buy. And may be able to generate more interesting deals. You may never spot that this is going on – but keep an eye open, just in case.

CHAPTER TWELVE

The Crucial Move – Selling Shares

It is easy to buy a share, much harder to sell it. Somehow parting with an investment is a more emotional affair than picking it in the first place. Investors can be remarkably patient with a tipster who gets it wrong. Tell someone to take profits on a favourite which promptly goes higher, and the complaints come loud and long. I know it. Hell hath no fury like a winner scorned.

Selling, though, is the essential second half of any successful investment deal. It is no good spotting winner after winner if you are hanging on when the market turns, and everything you have made takes a hefty dive. The only profits which count are the ones you take, the ones you bank by selling winners while you are ahead. Paper profits are for the birds. There is one classic, all-time investment rule. CUT YOUR LOSSES QUICKLY, AND LET YOUR PROFITS RUN. Everybody knows it. Almost everyone ignores it. There is a natural tendency to sell winners to indulge losers – to do just the opposite of what you should. Investors are surprisingly devoted to duds, reluctant to accept that they have got it wrong, and that the best way out is the quickest.

Cutting Your Losses

Do it. CUT YOUR LOSSES. Experts count themselves content if they pick six winners out of ten – anything better is a bonus. It may sound wimpish, until you try to do it. It may even be a trifle conservative in a bull market, when almost everything is rising. But it is not unrealistic. Pick more winners than losers, and you must come out ahead unless you are stupid. You become stupid by keeping losers until the bitter end. You will certainly come out ahead if you make it an unbudging rule to sell losers while the losses are small, and to hold winners while the profits are piling up.

Think about it. Put £1,000 each into ten shares. Lose 20% on five, and your £5,000 is down to £4,000. Make 20% on the other five, and that £5,000 is up to £6,000 – no gain, no loss (though dealing expenses leave you down). Your £10,000 is worth £10,000. But lose 20% on four of the ten, and you see a £4,000 stake down to £3,200. Gain 20% on the other six, and that £6,000 stake is up to £7,200. In total, your £10,000 has risen to £10,400. Four mistakes out of six, and you are still ahead. Not bad. If, of course, one of your six winners has gained more than 20%, you are doing still better. Your gains can be infinite, sky high, but your losses never need to be much more than 20% because you have decided to swing the odds in your favour by selling at a 20% loss, no matter what. It is up to you. It is obvious, so elementary that it hardly needs saying. Sadly, years of talking to investors, reading their letters, listening to their excuses, make it plain that few people heed it. CUT, CUT, CUT YOUR LOSSES QUICKLY.

Everyone will have their own idea of what cutting losses quickly means. Time hardly matters. Linger as long as you like, but move swiftly once the loss starts to mount. It sounds like a cop-out, but YOU MUST SET A SELLING TARGET. Promise yourself to sell if your shares fall beyond a certain level. Set this selling point when you buy. Set it sensibly. Make it between 10% and 20% below your buying price, less if you are an aggressive investor, more perhaps if you are in unusually volatile shares or penny shares. At this point, it is tempting to start screaming: "I have just given you the best investment advice you will ever get. It is worth a fortune – if you follow it. It is the most important thing in this whole book". Yet most investors ignore it.

How do I know? Week after week there are calls or letters to my office at the *Daily Mail.* They come from readers who have bought shares tipped in my Investment Extra column, and who did not sell when they fell through the stop-loss level I try to publish every four or five weeks if there is sufficient space. Charming, sensible people, most of them, they want reassurance. They like to feel that they have a special insight, an extra streak of luck. Because they did not sell when the share started falling, they want to believe that, just this time, it will turn out right after all. Sometimes it does. More often, it does not.

Often I find it hard talking to them. At times, they are sitting on a big winner, but are seeing their profits drift away. Some are on a loser – one of my tips which went wrong, or which did not score much of a gain before the stop-loss was used. Sometimes I am inclined to agree that the stock in question should not have fallen, and might bounce back. Often I am wrong, and that proves to be largely wishful thinking. Nine times out of ten, when a share falls through my stop-loss level, I stop following it. So I am not sufficiently in touch to give properly informed advice. I am guessing.

Readers rang about Utility Cable, a share I tipped in the *Daily Mail* in November 1993, and one of the early ventures by former stockbroking analyst Luke Johnson and his partners. I had admired Luke's tough approach to investment analysis, and we had become pals, lunching regularly. I had long watched his progress, feeling sure he would hit some winners eventually. This move involved taking over the rump of a small investment trust, then injecting a cable-laying company into it. It was a brilliant success. I tipped it at the equivalent to 6p, well after Johnson's interest had been made public, and told readers to sell through my stop loss at 30p in June 1994. Anyone who did so (it was possible to buy and to sell at those prices) would have multiplied their money five times over in eight months. In fact, anyone operating the stop-loss system for themselves, trailing the price up penny for penny on each rise, would have done still better, because the shares briefly touched almost 40p. Some greedy readers, inevitably, did not sell when it fell through 30p. Several brokers were still recommending the shares as a buy then. A year later, Utility Cable was under 20p – still looking like a growth business, but somehow sadly out of favour. By early 1998, it was down to 2½p. At 30p, the stop-loss system had cut through the chat, and imposed a winning discipline upon those who followed it. This is an old example. There have been many, many more in the years since I returned to share tipping. If you are interested – or want to learn still more about the stop-loss – there are further examples in my book *How to Beat The Bear Market* (0 7134 8494 2).

One of the greatest merits of the system is that it stops you leaving your money at risk on the strength of mere guesswork. You should invest out of conviction – only buy something you feel sure must be right. That does not mean you will always get it right. The stop-loss does prevent half-baked emotions getting in the way. If a share falls through your stop loss, sell it, and forget it. No point in carrying on a hopeless love affair. No one buys a share with the idea of losing money. The sensible investor admits the possibility. Keep a stop-loss figure in your head. Ask your broker about it. Some brokers will take stop-loss levels, and try to work with them. Others may rely on you to tell them when you should sell. Do it.

The Stop-Loss System

Prudent investors will go further than simply placing a stop-loss order to prevent large losses. Although it takes some of the romance out of investment, eliminating the thrill of imagining you are flying brilliantly by the seat of your pants, you should operate a fully-fledged stop-loss system – to cover winners and losers. Never mind that it is called a stop-loss system. It might as well be called a save-profits system. Or anything you like. Just follow it.

It may sound a trifle complicated, but once you get used to the idea, it is simplicity itself. It also has the virtue of encouraging you to watch prices each day, so you develop a better feel for what is happening. When you buy a share, set a price at which you will sell should it fall, following the simple stop-loss rule outlined above. As the price rises, move your potential selling point up behind it – a trailing stop-loss. Never cheat. NEVER, NEVER LOWER YOUR STOP-LOSS PRICE. Say you buy at 100p. Set your first stop-loss price at 80p. If it falls that far, sell, and write that share off. If the price rises to 110p, raise your stop-loss level to 90p. If it goes to 120p, trail the stop-loss price up behind it to 100p. And so on and so forth.

If the shares go to 150p, your stop-loss price should be 130p. Then if there is a market slump, or something goes wrong with that particular share, you will have sold at 130p to clinch a 30% profit. You may have missed the top, but you will not be left worried and miserable, with no profit at all, if the price slides back to 100p – or 90p, or less.

The disadvantage of the system is clear. You never get out at the top. And selling at the top really can give you a warm, superior glow. Remember, though, the old market legend about the Rothschild who made his fortune by selling too soon – but at a profit. The system is not infallible – no system is. There are times when it will take you out of super stocks too soon. It may leave you nursing a loss on a potential winner which takes off the instant you sell it. Just such a thing happened in the mid-eighties when I wrote a tipping column in the *Daily Mail* on a Saturday. I fancied Alan Sugar's Amstrad just as he introduced his big-selling word processor, and tipped the shares. Within weeks, I was forced to apologise, and suggested readers should follow my advice and take a stop-loss of just under 20%, selling in the 70p range. Almost immediately after, Amstrad took off like a rocket. I had spotted one of the year's big success stories, but got my timing completely wrong, and managed to advise millions of *Daily Mail* readers on how to lose money on it. Great.

That never shook my faith in the system. I gave up that tipping column in 1986 worried about the frothy nature of the market. I started tipping again in October 1992, after we left the ERM – and will stop when I become convinced the market is too frothy. In 1986 it did not seem right tipping shares when things could so easily go wrong. My timing was a bit off, but only slightly. The Great Crash did not happen until October 1987, though the market peaked some months earlier. When the Crash came, I was relieved that no *Daily Mail* reader should have been left with massive losses on my tips. Everyone should have used the stop-loss system to cut losses quickly, or should have trailed the selling level up as the shares went higher. Most should have been able to get out at a useful profit.

Smart? Not really. Elementary. But, above all, a responsible approach to share tipping. Sadly, I overlooked it later with Polly Peck. I had picked Polly as my share of the year for 1990, and suggested a stop-loss price. Anyone who followed that would have got out with a good profit before Polly tumbled in the autumn. Fine. Foolishly, I tipped Polly again in June 1990, near the peak, without suggesting a stop-loss. As the crisis hit, I found it hard to believe the shares would not bounce. Instead of advising readers to cut losses, I suggested holding on. The shares were suspended, and now look worthless. It was a stupid mistake. I had forgotten my own rule, became blinded by past success tipping the stock, and too much influenced by my regard for chairman Asil Nadir.

It is easy to make mistakes, and easy to see them later with hindsight. I tell the Polly Peck story to remind me of a particularly painful one, and to hammer home the stop-loss message. It is tempting to plead that certain stocks are special. Forget it. Stick to the system, no matter what. It is much the safest way to play.

It would be possible to quote one example after another, back to the early seventies when I started using the system. Bob Beckman, the source of so many valuable investment pointers, taught me about it. In truth, it was a lesson I ignored in my personal investments until the late eighties. Then I began to follow it. Though there was one period when I regretted selling stock just before a rally, a few months later I was blessing it. Selling saved me a handsome sum.

Do it, and it will ensure that you come out ahead, provided you pick more winners than losers. This simple system means your losses are relatively small, and your gains are bigger. You will still lose money when you get things wrong. The system ignores dealing costs, which take a bite out of all of your investments. And there may be times when you cannot sell at your stop-loss, because the price falls too quickly. Do not be deflected. Sell at the highest price you can, once your stop-loss level has been breached.

You can introduce a degree of refinement if the market is edgy, or if you are playing a particularly volatile stock. Clearly, slower-moving shares do not always require a full 20% discount when you set the stop-loss. It might be better to set a stop-loss 10%, or 15% below the buying price.You can refine the system as your profits grow. Obviously a 20% discount of 20p on a 100p price is equivalent to a 10% discount by the time the price rises to 200p. You might be happy to accept that finer margin. Or you might want to reset the stop-loss at 160p. Cutting the stop-loss in that way is not unreasonable when you are on a big winner and are tempted to stay with it. But never abandon the stop-loss altogether.On the other hand, you might grow more nervous as the price goes higher. You might want a tighter stop-loss. If the market is overheating, it might be sensible to close all of your stop-loss settings tighter behind the price, bidding goodbye at the first real setback. Use your own judgement.

If you are playing penny shares, where prices move in chunks of 10% or 20% a time, you obviously have to set a wider stop-loss margin, perhaps up to 50%. And if you are playing especially volatile stocks, where the price moves sharply up or down at regular intervals, you need a similarly wider margin. Use your own judgement. But do stick to a system. One reader wrote to me with his own variation. He used three stop-loss points – selling a third of his stake when the loss was 10%, a third when it was 20%, and another third when it was 30%. That way, he got out at an average loss of 20%. He felt he avoided selling too much, too soon, just in case the loser might bounce. Fine. If he felt happy with it, good enough. So long as you use the system, you can vary it to accommodate your own preferences, just so long as you do sell. His triple-whammy was, however, incurring three lots of dealing costs.

Selling Half

There are other selling systems. Most popular is the notion of selling half when a share doubles. Pick a big winner, and you can end up with one stock dominating your portfolio, exposing you to a potential disaster if it goes wrong. It is a nice problem to have. The traditional approach presents this as a great danger, insisting that you really ought to sell half so that your original holding has cost you nothing. Then you have a free ride, no worries, and can reinvest your profit in something else. Nonsense. That is no way to make a killing. Finding a real winner is not easy. When you do, stick with it. The market always tends to overdo things, and your rocket may well soar to a silly height before it begins to fade. You could see the price multiply three or four-fold, maybe much more. Never sell a share while it is still flying.

The stop-loss system is the ideal way of making the most of such a star. Do not get off until it starts to fall. By all means cheat. Once a share has doubled, allow more leeway and trail the stop-loss behind at a bigger discount, if you fancy. Bigger profits allow a more relaxed approach.

But you must sell when it begins to fail. Never fall blindly in love with a share. Try asking yourself if you would buy it if you had just stumbled across it for the first time. That can be a very sobering exercise. Suddenly you realise you may be sitting with a share with a p/e of 30 or more, not something you would touch normally – and certainly the kind of rating which will discourage potential new buyers, the ones you need to push the price still higher.

Sell Signals

Unless you have a system, deciding when to sell is a real problem. No bell rings when a share hits the top. Try turning upside down the rules you used when you decided to buy. Ask yourself if what attracted you then still holds good. If the p/e has grown too far out of line with the average for the sector, or the yield has shrunk, you may wonder whether you should hold on. When you sell, you will need to find a buyer, someone who thinks the shares are a bargain. If the averages are too far out of line, that might be difficult.

Watch the price momentum, too. You do not need a system to understand that once a share hits a peak and begins to stutter, it has lost momentum. You have to judge how long that will last, and whether it will regain momentum. Logically it may not make much sense, but potential buyers are attracted to a rising share. They see the strong price as a demonstration of confidence – if others are buying, they must know something. And when a price starts to fall, there is always a nasty feeling that someone knows something bad that you cannot see. That may be right.

The Private Investor's Advantages

The private investor has a few important advantages over the big boys, especially when it comes to selling. You are responsible to no one but yourself. There is no committee to report to, no trustees checking what you do, no shareholders, fundholders, policyholders. You get it wrong, or you get it right. No one is going to censure you, demote you, fire you. You do not have to be in the fashionable stocks of the day, nor must you avoid certain sectors which are out of favour. Press comment need not matter. No one is going to say you cannot do just what you want.

That can be worth a lot. It is part of the invaluable flexibility you have as a small investor. YOU DO NOT HAVE TO BE IN THE MARKET WHEN THINGS LOOK BAD. Big investors have to keep much of their money there all of the time. They have to take the long view. There is considered to be nowhere else big enough to take their cash. They are always ready to recommend patience to others. They do not want everyone else to sell while they are stuck in.

If they all withdrew – or tried to – the stockmarket would be finished. Prices would crash, and their own performance would be hammered. They would be slitting their own throats, lining themselves up for redundancy. Everyone has an angle, remember? Their angle is that they need to get prices up and keep them up, to keep their jobs. Their power to manipulate the market to that end may be limited by economic circumstance, and they cannot be absolute dictators. But they can go a long way towards it.

You have no such worries. And you can buy and sell much more easily. Large investors have trouble buying all of the shares they seek sometimes, and have to be wary of pushing prices up against themselves. Crucially, they can have real trouble selling. They have such a large position in so many shares that they would wallop the price out of sight if they tried to unload. When they have 3% or more of a company, every move has to be reported. Imagine the impact of a major investor cutting his stake in a market leader from 4.5% to 3% when the going turned tougher. That would smash the price. The big boys cannot always do what they know they should. You can.

They also get caught by the inside information which often helps them. Once they know something is going on, they are supposed not to sell. Though there are obvious fuzzy areas around the edges, that can be a burden. They may know bad news is coming, but they have to sit tight, and must plod on, backing any reconstruction, when they know it might take years for the price to recover.

There are no such inhibitions for the private investor. The news may come a little later, and the price may have started to fall, but the individual can kiss a dud goodbye quickly, leaving it to struggle. The small player is rarely locked in. FLEXIBILITY IS WORTH A FORTUNE. Make the most of it.

If In Doubt, Sell Out

Conventional claptrap about whether the market takes too much of a short-term view need not trouble you. Always err on the side of safety. IF IN DOUBT, SELL OUT.

The notion that the long-term investor does better than the quick in-and-out merchant has always seemed highly dubious. If making profits is your prime concern, there is no merit in holding for ten years while the market goes through an up cycle, back down, and then up again – just before it turns down. The cycles do exist. Take advantage of them, even if you only switch into cash and earn boring fixed-interest in the dull phase. Better that than to see capital values crashing. Cash will buy you so much more at the bottom than at the top. The long-term holder only does better than the in-and-out merchant (who does incur more dealing costs) if the stayer picks a good stock, and the sprinter does one dud deal after another. Common sense says so.

If you do take a long-term view, then, be absolutely certain that you have picked a winner. And be ready to face hefty losses as you go. And – be honest – acknowledge that you cannot be absolutely certain of anything in the investment game. The best stocks move with the market. At some stage, almost all will be well below their peak.

Who knows whether you will be around to benefit from holding long-term? How can you possibly judge whether circumstances will not change radically along the way? There are examples galore of how easy it is to get caught. By 1997, some of our leading property companies were still looking lifeless, though most other top shares had long emerged from the troubles of the late eighties and early nineties. It had become clear that even properties built 10 or 15 years ago could be sadly out of date. Massive office tower blocks in the best places in the City became much less attractive as the new information highway took hold. Even relatively modern blocks were becoming white elephants. Investors who had hung on in the belief that they weren't making land any more, and that properties on prime sites must eventually come good were suffering a sorry disappointment.

And there were yet other punters who had pinned their hopes on the perceived quality of management at Hanson leading to a strong recovery in the share price. By the end of 1995, Hanson shares were their lowest of the decade. A similar tale of advancing years also took its toll on GEC. And who remembers that old icon of the eighties, Trafalgar House? Only you can decide what suits you. Always err on the side of safety. October 1987 made nonsense of a lot of long-term resolutions. Gains which had taken years to accumulate were wiped out in a couple of days. Stocks did rally, and the market was hitting new peaks four years later. But many leaders had not recovered, and hundreds of medium to small stocks were still in a sorry state. Every day you are in the market, you are taking a risk. THE LONGER YOU HOLD, THE GREATER THE RISK. Who knows what is over the horizon? Do not be content to sit with a share which is quietly slipping away. Put a price limit, or a time limit, on your patience. Decide how far you will let it fall before you sell, or how long you will wait for a rise. If the price is becalmed, then begins to ease, sell. Ask yourself if you would not be doing better in something else. Take your cash and keep it safe while you worry.

Never forget the opportunity cost. If your cash is dozing off in some moribund stock, you are not making gains with it. How much better it could be if you were to sell, and take the opportunity to slap it into something livelier. What about all of the opportunities you lose by sitting still and doing nothing?

It is wrong to rush from one stock to another, of course. But shares often tell you when to sell. If you are awake, the main signal usually comes from the price itself. Watch if it fails to go up, or slips when others are rising. Unless you know why it is not responding, sell.

A Market Slump

If you think the whole market is heading for a fall, sell everything, no matter how bright the prospects may be for your favourite. Few shares buck a falling market. It is easy to get caught up watching individual prices, and to miss the signs of a general slump. Watch the indices, the FTSE 100 Share index. Watch predictions in the press, talk of economic gloom, a sterling crisis, a change of government. Take your money and run to a building society or the National Savings Investment Account until the storm blows over.

Cutting The Risk

It is easy to dismiss the stop loss system as a gloomy business, a negative force. That would be wrong. A sensible selling policy actually reduces risk, and in doing so, becomes a positive force. The shares which produce the highest returns are often those which carry the greatest risks. By deciding to sell on a fall of, say, 20% you are reducing that risk. So you can invest in rather racier, more speculative stocks with greater comfort, knowing you will sell should they fall to hit your stop loss point. By reducing the risk element in a potential big winner, you have swung the odds in your favour. Think about it.

251

Watching The Competition

There may be individual sell signs from the competition. If one brewer gives notice of a bad summer, others will be suffering. If terrorist bombs keep them away from the Savoy, other hotel companies will be feeling the pain, too. Look for allied industries. When house sales slump, it is not just housebuilders who get hurt. Estate agents, brickmakers, kitchen companies, carpet makers, do-it-yourself firms also feel the pinch. So do the banks, building societies, and second mortgage companies.

Boardroom Bust-Ups

A boardroom bust-up can be a sell sign. There may be bad profits to come, and someone is carrying the can. Generally, though, it is good news. The problems will normally have been spotted already in the market, and there will be relief that something is being done. Or the split could make the company more vulnerable to a bid, especially if the change involves anyone with a significant share stake.

Sell Ahead Of An Announcement

Always be prepared to sell ahead of a company announcement, rather than after it. The market almost always overdoes things. Anticipation is the most rewarding part of most investment – unless you spot a bid. Each Saturday or Monday, most City pages list the main board meetings in the week ahead. Prices frequently rise in the weeks before the meetings, if all is going well. Check, and if you are trading for the short-term, or thinking of selling, do it ahead of the announcement.

By the time you see it in the newspapers, any news will be known all over the City, and the shares will have reacted. You will often find that others bought in anticipation, and sold once the news appeared. That is why many shares fall on what seems to be good news. It would have taken something extra special to bring a further gain.

Selling On A Tip

Every now and then, shares take a great leap forward for no apparent reason. They may have been tipped in a newsletter, in the press, or by some stockbroker. If a good broker is getting behind them, stay aboard. If it is a tip sheet, or some press pundit, read what they have to say, and make up your own mind. It may be a good selling opportunity, taking advantage of a temporary surge while the tipster's fans climb aboard. For that reason, think twice before selling on a Friday. The weekend press usually carries a shower of tips, and your share could open with a nice Monday morning boost.

Sell In May

The market is full of old sayings. Most make some sense. 'Sell in May and go away' is a favourite. It has worked more often than not in recent years. Because the tax year ends early in April, some investors wait to take profits in the new tax year, shunting tax payments a year further forward, or using up the gains-free exemption for the new year. As May winds on, the City sneaks into summer. People go on holiday, Parliament is quiet, there is Wimbledon, Ascot, Henley, and a host of free tickets and parties to tempt fund managers from their desks. Most companies end their financial year on 31 December, or 31 March. The December year-end brigade report profits around March and April. March year-end profits tend to come out by the middle of June, so midsummer is quieter for company news. If you do sell in May, think about buying towards the second half of August. Business begins to return to normal in September.

Watch, too, for press comment on general market timing. David

Schwartz is frequently quoted on the best times to buy and sell, analysing trends month by month, week by week. He has a newsletter, and produces *The Schwartz Stock Market Handbook* (Burleigh Publishing Company).

Betting Against The Crowd

Contrary thinking, or betting against the crowd, is another favourite. It usually gains most prominence as a sign to sell.

Often it is used as a sneer to mock the small investor, with the suggestion that when the small players arrive in force, it is time for professionals to sell. It has become such a cliche that the idea is losing appeal. But it can work if applied carefully. The bigger the crowd, the fewer there are left to join in. Share prices need a constant flow of new buyers to push them up. Be careful, though. The crowd creates the winners. So contrary thinking requires caution. Use it to make sure that you look hard before leaping on any bandwagon. Check where it started rolling. The further it has come, the nearer the end it will be. Try not to be last aboard. Sensible contrary thinking does not mean you automatically do the opposite to the crowd. It should mean you are prepared to consider both sides before making a move.

Selling Short

It is easy to deal with selling short – DO NOT DO IT. Do not even think about it until you have a vast investment fortune to fall back on, and are far too sophisticated to need help from anything this book can bring you.

Professionals can make money selling short, especially in a falling market. The short seller finds a share he thinks is too high, sells, and hopes to buy it back at a lower price. He is selling shares he does not own. 'He who sells what isn't his'n must buy it back or go to prison' runs the classic old Wall Street trader rule. Sooner or later, he will have to buy an equivalent number to complete the trade. If they rise, he still has to buy them, and loses money doing it. In buying, he pushes the price up against himself, especially if he is not able to buy his full complement in one fell swoop.

See how it works. The seller knocks out, say, 1,000 Dixons at 640p. He does not own those shares. If they fall to, say, 600p, he can buy 1,000 to complete the deal. He has made profits of 40p a share, or £400, before expenses. However, if he has sold at 640p, and Dixons rise, he may have to buy at 680p. He loses 40p a share, or £400, plus expenses. When you buy a share, you can only lose as much as you have spent. Losing the lot, of course, is pretty grim. But sell short, and you cannot tell how much you might lose. Say you sell short of a share at 100p, and it suddenly gets a bid. It could rocket to 200p. You have to buy, at any price. If the market should become tight, you might have to buy at 300p, 400p, or more. That is an extreme example. But it does happen. I have watched at least two situations where the price has more than doubled as a result of a killer bear squeeze.

In the early nineties, there was considerable publicity for a group said to sell shares, and then spread rumours, seeking to push the price down to buy back at a profit. The name 'Evil Knievil' was pinned to one such operator. In 1995, he stepped into the open. An accountant called Simon Cawkwell, he has written a fascinating book *Profit Of The Plunge* (0 9480 3517 X). I know he operates extremely carefully, confining his attentions to companies where there is an inherent problem, a weak spot which could bring the price tumbling down at any time. He hit the headlines when misguided Maxwell groupies in the financial press (yes, there were some) supported Maxwell's bleatings about the way his shares were being sold. Cawkwell, though, was right. He and I swapped information about Maxwell in the year or so before the publisher's plunge, when I wrote a series of *Daily Mail* pieces warning of the possibility of meltdown in

Maxwell shares. Cawkwell launched successful bear raids on Polly Peck, Tiphook, building products group Spring Ram, and discount retailer Amber Day. Do not bet against the bears. If they hit a stock you hold, the odds are that they know much more than you do. It may well be foolish to bet against them. Play safe and sell.

Covered Bears

You can go part of the way towards selling short by becoming a 'covered bear'. The covered bear picks a company where he already holds shares, and sells an equivalent number to his holding, hoping to buy them back at a lower price. If they do not fall, he is covered because he can deliver the shares he owns, completing the trade. It only makes sense if you expect shares you are holding to take a temporary dip, and then recover. Otherwise you should sell the lot, and forget them.

Averaging

Now and then, averaging intrudes on the scene. It is popular among unit trust managers, who see it as a handy selling tool when markets are flat. What fun, the story runs, to spend a set amount each month. When prices are low, it will buy more units, or more shares. When prices rise, you will feel the benefit, because you will have cheap units alongside the more expensive ones. It has a certain logic if you want a regular savings plan. Use it to accumulate unit or investment trusts.

Others suggest that it is a good means of making the best of a long-term share stake. It is not for the serious trader. It is simply another means of postponing a decision to take a loss. On the surface, it looks good. Buy 500 shares at 100p each, and another 500 when they have fallen to 50p, then the price only has to rise to 75p for you to be breaking even on your 1,000 shares.

Forget it. You should have sold your 100p loser at 80p. If it has halved, something is clearly wrong. It could take an age before the price recovers. You may be tossing good money after bad.

Pyramiding

Pyramiding resembles averaging in reverse. Averaging tends to arise when prices are falling, pyramiding deals with rising prices. The idea is that if you buy, say 500 shares at 100p and they rise to 125p, you should ride your winner. Buy more. When your first 500 shares hit 125p, you have a paper profit of £125. If you buy another 200 shares at 125p, you will have invested a total of £750, and will hold 700 shares costing an average of just over 107p each. You will still have a profit on the lot, thanks to the safety margin from your first successful purchase. You will have more shares to profit from if they carry on up. If they fall, you can sell quickly before there is a loss.

It is an aggressive strategy which may appeal to some. Only try it if you are ready to watch prices like a hawk. They can turn quickly. You could get caught with more shares than you had intended, and a price tumbling too fast to sell while you are ahead. Pyramiding, though, has more to commend it than averaging. At least you are trying to make the most of a winner, instead of nursing a loser.

CHAPTER THIRTEEN

Gilts, Loans And Other Games

Not everything on the Stock Exchange revolves around shares. More than three-quarters of stockmarket turnover by value is in Government Securities, or gilts as they are generally called. Over £1bn can change hands in a single day. When interest rates are moving sharply, they can generate useful capital gains or nasty losses, though they are widely presented as the safer end of Stock Exchange trading. Through the first half of 1998, when interest rates rose in line with market expectations, scarcely a single gilt with a life of less than ten years traded outside a range of ten points, high to low. It is not always so serene. In the first four months of 1986, when interest rates were falling sharply, some gilts scored gains of 20 points or more – heady stuff. The shorter the date to redemption, the less dramatic the moves.

Gilt-Edged Securities

Government securities are known as gilt-edged securities – gilts, for short – because they are backed by the Government, the most reliable borrower of all, the one who (supposedly) can never go bust. Gilts are the prime source of funding for the Public Sector Borrowing Requirement (PSBR), the cash the State borrows to fund the economy. Insurance companies, pension funds and such are the biggest buyers, using them to lock in a guaranteed return to meet future liabilities. The price of gilts is always so much per £100 of stock, and £100 is the nominal value. That nominal value has a real meaning for most gilts. Unlike shares, most gilts are repaid at nominal value at or between specific dates. You get £100 from the Government for every £100 nominal you hold – except in the case of undated gilts, which may never be repaid. So if, in 1997, you bought Treasury 6% 1999 at 97, you would be repaid at £100 for each £97 worth in the year 1999.

Flat Yields

The price of gilts is determined largely by interest rates. When rates fall, gilt prices rise. When rates rise, gilts fall. Buy a gilt with a 10% coupon (the nominal interest rate it pays), standing at 100, and it gives a flat yield of 10%. If interest rates fall, the gilt price may rise to 110, where it would yield 9.09% (10 divided by 110, multiplied by 100). If interest rates rise to 12%, the gilt price would fall to 83, where it would yield 12% (10 divided by 83, multiplied by 100).

Redemption Yields

Values are complicated by the life of the gilt. Those with up to five years before they are repaid are called 'shorts'. Those with five to 15 years of life left are 'mediums', and those with more than 15 years left are 'longs'. A small number of stocks with no specific redemption date are 'undated'. They include the notorious War Loan, which may never be repaid.

Take, for example, 12.5% Treasury Stock 2003-2005. This has a coupon of 12.5%, and will be repaid at £100 between 2003 and 2005 (assume repayment will be at the last possible date). Because gilts sell above or below their nominal value, the repayment date is important, and influences value. The time factor is taken into account. Linked to the flat yield, it gives the redemption yield, the most widely-used reference point.

Clearly, if a stock is standing at 105, and will be repaid at 100 in a year's time, holders will lose £5 capital. They will require extra income to make up for that. Conversely, if a stock is at 95, and will be redeemed at 100 in a year's time, the holders will get a capital gain of £5, and can expect less interest because of it. Gains or losses on repayment are effectively incorporated into interest payments to arrive at the redemption yield.

Tax Benefits

The attractions of gilts are generally related to the tax position of the purchaser. Redemption yields have generally been quoted gross – before deducting tax. Only non-taxpayers get the full amount. So non-taxpayers would pick stocks with high flat yields. High taxpayers would plump for low coupon stocks with a much greater element of built-in capital gain to redemption. From April, 1996, the Government has allowed gilts to be treated in a more sophisticated fashion. There is to be a new gilts strip market, aimed mainly at professional investors, tailored to suit their particular needs and, hopefully, to attract more overseas buyers. Gilt strips will be created by stripping the interest payments away from the principal of a conventional gilt, and trading each component separately. No capital gains tax is payable by individuals with holdings of less than £200,000 nominal value. A husband and wife could, then, have £400,000 nominal of gilts without tax problems. Two low coupon gilts especially popular with individual investors – Funding 31/2% 1999-04 and Treasury 51/2% 2008-12 – also remain outside the tax net. Because the market is dominated by professionals, however, anyone playing in gilts will need professional advice. The needs of the big players might influence the market in ways which could influence private investors.

Index-Linked Gilts

There is another gilt complication. Since 1985, the Government has been issuing index-linked gilts. Their capital repayment value rises automatically in line with inflation, as measured by the retail price index. The coupon, or nominal interest rate, is a 'real' return. It may look low at 2% or 3%, but you actually get that 2% or 3% without having to worry about the inroads inflation makes on your capital. Because of this, an index-linked gilt may sometimes be more attractive than a conventional gilt with a similar coupon. There are index-linked gilts to cover most people's preferred time-span – short, medium, or long – and some ought to be attractive to high taxpayers. However, falling inflation rates have left index-linked gilts behind conventional ones in the quest for capital gains in many years. Somehow, they have never quite caught the imagination as they might have done.

Buying Gilts

Trading in gilts can be complex. If you want to do it – and there are times when it may offer a haven from a stormy share market – consult a broker who understands such matters. Most firms have experts on tap.

If you want to do it yourself, go to the Post Office. Many gilts can be traded over the counter with extremely low dealing costs. Gilts bought through the Post Office Register have another important advantage. The dividends are paid without tax being taken off. This saves complications for low rate taxpayers, who otherwise have to go through the tedious business of reclaiming tax. And it gives you the use of the taxable portion of the dividend for longer. It does not mean gilt dividends are free of income tax. You have to declare the interest, and pay tax on it.

Gains From Gilts

Buy gilts at the right time, and they allow you to lock in a high fixed return with safety, sometimes for a very long period. If you buy when interest rates are high, and sell when they are lower, you can also secure sizeable capital gains, free of capital gains tax up to the limit. Generally, the longer the time to redemption, the more volatile the capital value. Except with index-linked gilts, though, you face the threat of inflation, and if you get your timing wrong, could also be hit by capital losses.

Buoyant share markets usually take place against a background of steady or falling interest rates, and hence steady or rising gilt prices. When gilts make money, shares are offering opportunities, too. Pick the right share, and you will leave the best gilt standing. Unless you think low interest rates and falling inflation are here to stay, you should think hard before buying gilts when interest rates are under 9%. You are then likely to be near the bottom of the interest rate cycle, and could face capital losses when rates rise.

Convertible Loan Stocks

There is a halfway house between the sober-sided fixed-interest market and the thrills and spills of Ordinary shares – the convertible loan stock.

Convertible loan stocks carry a fixed rate of interest, a date when they will be repaid at £100 for every £100 nominal, and the opportunity to convert into Ordinary shares at certain dates. The number of shares you can switch into is fixed, and when convertibles are first issued, the terms normally let you into the Ordinary shares at a premium to the market price. Say the Ordinary shares stand at 40p, when the convertible is issued. That convertible may allow you to switch in three years' time into 200 Ordinary shares for every £100 of convertible loan stock – equivalent to buying 200 Ordinary shares at 50p each in three years' time. You will not be able to switch right away. After three years, the hope is that the Ordinary shares will have risen to 50p or more.

The best convertibles have a long conversion run – the chance of switching into shares over several years – but the first conversion date should not be too distant. You may be able to find convertibles which let you into the Ordinary shares below the current price, and give you a higher dividend return than the Ordinary shares in the meantime. Sometimes, of course, such apparent bargains signal something is wrong. But convertibles do occasionally get overlooked when there is a run in the shares, and sometimes a poor market in the convertible lets the price drift out of line. Pick a good one, and you get capital gains and a high return.

The theory is that the superior income on convertibles is a shelter from uncertainties in the shares. Be careful. This works sometimes, but a weak share price makes for a poor convertible price. A few points of extra interest is no consolation if your capital value tumbles as the company hits trouble. Normally you should never buy a convertible unless you are sure the shares themselves are worth buying.

In a recession, there are sometimes interesting possibilities for real punters. Shares might slump, dragging the convertible down so far that it yields well into double figures. Some of the companies will be in trouble, reliant on bankers to get through the next year or two. In such cases, there is no point in buying the shares. They will have no chance of capital repayment if the company fails. The convertible might. You should switch out of Ordinary shares into the convertible, if you think the company has a chance. Any capital gain will come to the convertible first, not to the Ordinary share.

This is another area where expert advice is worthwhile. Make sure you understand the conversion rights properly before buying. Some stocks are only partly convertible. Be sure not to let the convertible run past the conversion date without switching. That would leave you with a boring fixed-interest stock, and that is no joke.

Preference Points

Preference stocks are often forgotten. On the face of it, they have little to offer. They bear a fixed rate of interest, and rank ahead of Ordinary shares in their claim on dividends and assets.

The fun starts when a company hits hard times, and suspends preference dividends. Most preference capital is cumulative, which means holders are entitled to receive all of the back dividends they missed before a company can resume dividends to Ordinary shareholders. It takes a little nerve, but if you can spot cumulative preference stocks in a company with generous asset backing and the chance of a trading recovery, you could do very nicely. You could get a big slice of accumulated back dividends. Or you might find that the directors need to eliminate the preference capital in a reconstruction, and will repay it on generous terms.

Most preference stocks trade at well below their nominal value, so any capital reconstruction is likely to mean a big profit. Preference stocks also tend to be overlooked in bid battles. They get taken over in a footnote to the main event, often at a handsome price. You might be able to buy a preference stock at £40, and see it repaid at £100.

Preference stocks are not for everyone. They can take years to come good, and can be difficult to buy and sell. But do not write them off completely. Anyone who followed my *Daily Mail* column will have done well by following my recommendation for the preference stock of retirement home builder McCarthy & Stone. Spotting that the company looked like coming good, and had assets enough to cover the value of the preference shares in any event, I recommended it though it was paying no dividends. Investors trebled their money inside 18 months as the company returned to health.

Warrants

Warrants are fancy, flash relatives to convertibles. They lack the income, but can open the way for a super, low-cost, long-term gamble. They are usually created as part of some more ambitious financing package. They act as long-life options, carrying the right to subscribe for new shares at a set price (the exercise price) in the future. In theory, their value is calculated by reference to the price at which they allow you to buy new shares, and the date on which they can be bought. In practice, it is determined partly by supply and demand. Several warrants sell at prices above or below what the backroom boys impute their worth to be, using mathematical models.

How Warrants Can Be Big Winners

If you pay 20p for a warrant to subscribe for one new share at 100p, you are effectively paying 120p for that share. Generally, adding the warrant price to the share price means you will be paying a premium over the current price, which may be, say, 105p. But the warrants may not perhaps be exercisable until some future date, when the price may be above 120p. Whatever happens, the warrant subscription price will not change, so you only pay 100p for the new share by exercising the warrant. If the market price is 200p by then, the warrant will be worth 100p (200p minus the 100p subscription price).

That means the warrants will have gone up five-fold from your 20p purchase price, while the shares have not quite doubled from 105p. The gearing is terrific. Because the warrants only cost you 20p, when buying the shares would have cost you 105p a time, you will have been able to buy the rights to capital gains on five times as many shares. You will have done much better in the warrants than the shares, although you miss out on the dividends.

A well-selected warrant can be a wonderful winner, though they can fall dramatically, bringing hefty losses in a flash if you get them wrong. Some run for 10 years or more, giving a low-priced way of buying into a growth company without tying up a lot of capital for a long time. Alternatively, they can allow you to have a much bigger interest for the same outlay – buying five warrants at 20p for every one share at 105p. You should pay careful attention to the life of a warrant, as well as the conversion premium. Obviously, the longer a warrant has before the final exercise date, the more time it has to gather value from the underlying share. As that time runs out, so prospective buyers will be less attracted to the warrant. If you hold a warrant to the exercise date, and the price at which it puts you into the Ordinary shares is above the price of the shares themselves, that warrant will expire valueless. It is unwise to hold a warrant until the bitter end.

Market men like to use a prime piece of jargon when talking warrants – the capital fulcrum point. This is simply another way of working out how much the underlying share will have to rise before the warrant becomes worth exercising. Say you buy a warrant for 10p with the right to buy shares at 100p in two years. When you bought, the shares were 90p. They would have to rise to 110p inside two years for you to show a profit on the warrant, if held to the bitter end. That is around 11% a year. So the warrant has an 11% capital fulcrum point, or fulcrum.

Volatility influences value as well. The more volatile the underlying share, the greater the chance of bigger profits or losses in the warrant itself. In a bull market, volatility obviously adds more to the potential worth of the warrant. Once again, this is a market for the specialist. Big brokers have departments watching warrants. They are especially popular among investment trusts, where they offer a long-distance punt on the general direction of markets. Do not be put off by initial complications. You can select one, and back it yourself, no matter what the experts might say. The danger is that warrant issues tend to be small, and the market in them can be tight. This difficulty in dealing freely in large amounts puts some big investors off. It means that when prices are rising, warrants can rise sharply – but when they fall, it can be difficult, even almost impossible, to sell. Prices fall dramatically, and losses are heavy.

Financial advisers Hargreaves Lansdown (01179 767767) have a department specialising in warrants, and produce a useful booklet on the subject. Andrew McHattie (01275 855558) produces a warrant newsletter and other useful services. He is the author of *The Investor's Guide to Warrants*, a sophisticated and expensive book published by Pitman. Recommended reading if you are going to get seriously into warrants.

Do be warned, though, that you need to take any warrant purchase seriously. Prices can fall sharply simply because they go out of fashion – though that creates a buying opportunity for the brave.

Perhaps the best-known warrant player was Terry Ramsden, a trader who was reputed to have made hundreds of millions spotting opportunities in Japanese warrants. He regularly hit the gossip columns, buying into a football club, and owning a string of racehorses, becoming one of the biggest punters in the racing game. He came badly unstuck, lost a fortune, and ended up in court, discredited. Later, he went to jail. The Japanese warrants got some of their own back.

Zero Coupon Shares And Bonds

Relative newcomers to the UK, zero coupon bonds and preference stocks can be handy when you want to lock into a high return over a predictable period, but do not need current income. They are suited to high rate taxpayers looking ahead to retirement. Zeros offer no fixed rate of interest, no dividend. They sell at a substantial discount to the eventual redemption price, and the interest is effectively contained in the capital appreciation which accrues as redemption approaches. Most zero preference shares have been issued by investment trusts, and their ultimate value is influenced partly by how secure the performance of the trust may be. Effectively they translate income, which would be taxable, into capital gains which may escape tax if the gains are below annual exemption levels. Because they rank ahead of Ordinary shares when a trust is wound up, they ought to be relatively secure. You need to check how well the notional interest rate is covered by revenue.

Traditional Options

The glamorous and dangerous traded option market has grabbed the headlines in recent years, but traditional options still plod along, and can be a useful weapon for the gambler – a way to play in relatively large numbers of shares without laying down a fortune. Options carry the right to buy or sell a share at a set price – the 'strike' price – at some future date. Most conventional Stock Exchange options run for three months. They carry the right to buy (call options), to sell (put options), or to buy or sell (double options). Traditional options themselves cannot be bought or sold.

It is possible to negotiate an option in most shares, at a cost of between 8% and 15% of the market price for calls and puts, roughly double that for doubles. When you buy, you pay stockbroking commission on the full value of the shares under option, even if you later abandon the option. When you exercise the option – use it – you pay no extra commission.

The cost of an option can only be set off against capital gains tax if it is exercised. So sometimes it is as well to exercise an option even it involves a small trading loss.

Options can be expensive, but they do give you control of a lot of stock – far more than you could otherwise afford – let you walk away if you get it wrong, losing only the cost of your option. Get it wrong, and you cannot lose more than your option money and the commission, whatever happens. So you know your downside from the beginning.

How A Call Option Works

If you believe that, say, housebuilder Bloggs Developments will soar in the next three months, you can buy a call option on 1,000 shares. The market price may be 179p to 182p, and a call costs 17p for each share. The strike price – the price at your option will let you buy Bloggs shares – will be 182p. Add 17p to 182p, plus £35 dealing costs, and you are breaking even when Bloggs top 202½p. For every 1p that Bloggs rise thereafter, you make a profit of £10.

The following calculation may make this clearer:

Outgoings

Buy 1,000 Bloggs call options at 17p

Cost £170

Dealing charges   £35

Exercise option, buy 1,000 Bloggs at 182p

Cost £1,820

Total buying costs   £2,025

Break-even price for Bloggs option is 202½p a share

(£2,025 divided by 1,000)

Receipts

Sell 1,000 Bloggs at 203½p   £2,035

So 1p rise in Bloggs share price equals £10 profit.

At any time during the three-month life of the option, you could exercise it, buy 1,000 Bloggs, sell them in the market, and take your profit. Most option players have no intention of using the option to buy the shares and keep them – though sometimes people can add quietly to share stakes that way.

It may be tempting to take up the shares when an option is not going your way. Resist it. Take the loss, and write it off. Do not commit more money to a losing trade.

Put Options

Put options are like calls, but geared to a fall in the price. You may think Bloggs will drop significantly over the next three months. A put option costing 17p will buy the right to sell Bloggs during those three months at the strike price. The strike price will be 179p. The total cost of 1,000 put options will be £204, including dealing charges. So you need Bloggs to fall by just over 20p before you break even. For every 1p fall thereafter, you make £10 profit.

If Bloggs fall to 145p middle price, and you are able to buy 1,000 shares at 146p, you will be able to exercise your right to sell those 1,000 shares at 179p. That is a profit of 33p a share. Multiply 33p by 1,000, and you have £330. Deduct the option cost of £204, leaving a profit of £126. The whole exercise is like buying a share, and selling it later at a profit. All you have done is reversed the order, buying at a low price, and selling at the higher price fixed in advance with the option.

In the Bloggs put example, only £204 was at risk, and it yielded a profit of £126, a high percentage return inside three months. Avoid fairly stolid shares, and you might just be able to generate such fun. What you really need is a volatile stock, one which moves sharply up or down.

Double Options

Double options are expensive. They give the right to buy or sell at the strike price over a three-month period. Most punters will not bother.

Protecting Profits With Options

Options are not just for gambling. They can be used to protect profits. If you fear the market may tumble, but cannot bear to part with some old favourite, you can have your cake and eat it – at a price. Sell the shares, and buy a call option in them. That way you unlock your capital, and can place it somewhere safe to sit out the storm. Get it wrong, and you can use your option to buy back into your favourite at the strike price, even if it has gone racing ahead. If the market does tumble, and your share with it, all you have lost is your option money – and that is covered partly by the interest you have been earning on the capital you took out.

Stand the exercise on its head, and you can use options to protect a profit, too. If you fear a flop-out, you can keep the shares (wrong, wrong, wrong – remember the stop-loss chapter) and buy a put. If the fall comes, you will make money on the put to compensate for what you have lost on the shares. This only makes sense, of course, if your shares recover. Otherwise you would have been better with a straightforward sale.

These option protection policies are for the faint-hearted investor. Anyone who paid attention in the earlier part of the book will have little truck with them. Far better to cut losses quickly, and hope to buy back more cheaply later. Have the courage of your convictions.

Taking Option Money

Similar considerations apply, less forcefully, to taking option money. If this sounds too confusing, skip it. Never get into anything you do not understand. But for every option someone buys, someone is selling.

If you buy a call, someone takes that call money in return for agreeing for three months to sell shares if you should exercise that call. Because there is a market-maker in the middle, taking his turn, the taker of option money does not get the full amount the buyer is paying. So while it might cost 17p to buy a call in Bloggs, someone taking that call money might get only 12p. If the call is not exercised, you do not sell your Bloggs shares, and get 12p for what turns out to be nothing. The snag is that, if Bloggs soars, the stock will be taken away. You are effectively forced to sell at the 182p strike price, plus 12p, when the shares have soared over 200p. All sorts of plays can be constructed around taking option money. It may be possible to take call, put or double option money at the same time, and so on.

Conventional options can be used in clever combinations, but require careful understanding and a quick eye for an opportunity. If you want to try it, be sure your broker knows what they are doing. To this extent be guided by your broker.

Playing The Market With A Bookie

It is possible to gamble in the share market through IG Index, the City's own bookmaker. IG Index takes bets on market moves, and dealing costs can be less than stockmarket commissions. Profits are free of tax. Watch out, though. The bets can have quite a downside if they go wrong. Check the rules carefully.

Tax

Tax. Do not worry about it. Concentrate on making the gains. The first £6,800 of realised gains is exempt from tax for the tax year 1998-1999. The figure is changed most years, and the Labour Government is set to make more radical changes. You pay tax at your top rate on gains over the exemption limit.

Before you count the profits, you can knock off any losses realised in that tax year. Both husband and wife are eligible for the gains allowance, so it makes sense for married couples to split their portfolio between

them. You can also invest through a tax free Personal Equity Plan –
though that will disappear in 1999 under Labour plans, to be replaced by
an Individual Savings Account. There may be room for most average
investors to shelter a reasonable amount from tax. It is worth taking some
profits towards the year-end to make the most of your exemption limit, if
it suits you. Do not let tax planning dictate your investment decisions.

Bed And Breakfast

If you are doing well, it might make sense to 'bed and breakfast' some
profits, or establish some losses. This used to be a good wheeze, but
Chancellor Gordon Brown has effectively put an end to it. Some brokers
claim they can still do something like it, but be careful. Elaborate schemes
are rarely worth the trouble and risk.

Perks

Everyone loves something for nothing. No matter how trivial the gifts,
shareholders flock to annual meetings where something is being given
away. And they love shares which provide special privileges – perks – to
investors. They range from cheap trips on Cunard liners to handsome
reductions on houses from Barratt Developments or Bellway, and take in
cheap cars, meals, books and much else. The list changes all the time.
Some companies require investors to own 1,000 shares, some have no
minimum. Several brokers offer booklets listing all current perks.
Hargreaves Lansdown among them. Obviously, no one who has waded
through this book would be so foolish as to buy shares in a dud company
just to get the perks. Would they?

CHAPTER FOURTEEN

Traded Options

Welcome. Glad you have got this far through the book. It is time to leave, time to slot the book on the shelf, and use it to refresh your mind now and then. You can skip this chapter with my blessing.

It is here because, somehow, I feel it ought to be in any book talking about the share jungle. Really, though, it is not for you. Traded options are best left alone. If you want to know the basics, this chapter will help. But it does not attempt to offer any sophisticated advice. It would be wrong of me to try to do so. I have played around in traded options from time to time, and probably came out about even. But it is very much a market for specialists, and those who can watch the market closely, day to day. It would be wrong to pretend this book can offer any special insights, because I have not dealt enough in this market to gain any. So read on if you wish. But take care.

Stock Exchange officials and brokers will tell you the Traded Options Market offers an invaluable means of controlling and reducing risk – a sensible way for sophisticated investors to protect themselves, and perhaps make more money. Quite so. What they might forget to mention is that this is the hottest spot on the share-gambling scene. You can take a modest amount and, if you are good, lucky – or have inside information – you might multiply it ten-fold. And the most you can lose, unless you play an especially risky way, is your original stake money. Most of the dealers are young, quick-witted and aggressive. Corporate raiders sometimes use it to build quiet stakes in target companies, hitting traded options before they begin buying the shares. No matter how they may deny it, insider action also happens in traded options. And big investment houses use it to help manipulate prices in the real stockmarket.

It allows individuals to punt relatively small amounts of cash and control much larger chunks of shares. Get it right, and you can – literally – buy for 1p, and sell for 10p within weeks, maybe less. Winning odds of ten to one are not that common – but they do happen. The chances of doubling your money are very much better. Make no mistake, though. The risks of losing are high. The old warning has to be hammered home. Do not play traded options with money you cannot afford to lose. YOU WILL LOSE. Start with a limited amount of fun money. If you can afford it, set aside £1,000, and be prepared to kiss it goodbye. Look upon it as the cost of learning – and even then, learning only your first few lessons. Perhaps you will be lucky. Perhaps you will not lose your first £1,000. Maybe the odds will be kind.

In 1989, one player using a broker in Manchester took a few thousand pounds, and made £3m in traded options very quickly. The last I heard, he had lost a good chunk of it, and gambled £900,000 on the FTSE index traded options. A few weeks later, he must have been over £1m ahead again. Terrific. But how many of us would play that way? Our punter must have had nerves of steel, or a skull of solid concrete. The temptation to cash in and sit on the winnings long before £1m would have been irresistible to most people. It seems foolish not to suggest that anyone who gets, say, £100,000 ahead should not take most of their profits, tuck them away, and sit on their hands for at least three months. That way, you might regain some sensible perspective on the value of money, instead of getting caught up in romantic nonsense about riding a winning streak. Our anonymous gambler, though, represents the glorious dream. If you are very good, or very lucky, you can make a quick fortune in traded options. I cannot make a serious attempt to analyse the sophisticated strategies which some investment houses use. They are backed by computer power and experts who devote every waking minute to exploiting small anomalies between option rates and share prices. Expensive and extremely complicated books will give you some guidance on that. It is not for us. However, one book which does set out to explain traded options in relatively simplistic terms is *Traded Options – A Private Investor's Guide* by journalist Peter Temple (0 7134 8445 4).

As a starter, I can only try to show how relatively simple strategies can be used to make high returns, and how the most unsophisticated play can yield big profits, if you pick the right stock at the right time. In the end, that matters most – picking the right share. As ever, do not allow yourself to be intimidated by the idea that traded options are always too complicated. They can be used as simple gambling counters by anyone prepared to devote time and thought to mastering how they work. Move at your own pace. Never try anything which baffles you, just because someone else says it is good (though you will only really begin to get to grips with traded options by actually doing a deal or two). Never be put off by suggestions that this is a market for the big boys alone.

It is not. Traded options can be as simple or as complicated as you want to make them. The small investor can use them to make big profits - with shrewd trading, or with sheer good luck. But they do involve FAST-MOVING, QUICK-STRIKING, HIGH-RISK.

What Are Traded Options?

Traded options are broadly similar to the conventional options covered earlier. A call gives the right to buy certain shares at a fixed price during the life of that option. A put option gives the right to sell the shares at a fixed price during the life of that option. The buyer of the option does not have to exercise it. At its daftest, the buyer can walk away, forget about it, write it off. The buyer has absolutely no cash commitment beyond the cost of the option (and, of course, the dealing expenses, which amount to standard stockbroking levels).

Where traded options differ from conventional options is that the options themselves can be bought and sold – traded – during their life. Traded options, then, are like mini-shares, with a value of their own. This is potentially an enormous advantage. At any time in the life of a traded option, you can sell it. So even if you buy a traded option which does not work out, there is the chance of avoiding a total loss – provided you act before it falls too far, or gets too close to the end of its life.

How Long Traded Options Last

Wonderful. And this need be no desperate, breakneck sprint. Some traded options have a decent life, enough to allow you to take a considered view of what to do if the price starts moving against you.

Traded options are created with a clearly-defined life span, with regular expiry dates. These are fixed at three-monthly intervals, so each option runs for either three months, six months, or nine months. When one three-month cycle ends, a new option is introduced, expiring nine months out. For example, Superstock International may start with options which expire in April, July, and October. At a predetermined date in April, all of the Superstock April traded options will expire. A new series will be introduced, with an expiry date in January of the following year – nine months hence. When you deal, it is important to check the actual expiry date. Your broker should be able to give you a calendar. Expiry dates are normally in the second half of the relevant month.

What The Prices Mean

Look at a display of traded option prices, and there is more than one set
of prices for each expiry date. For each call (buy) and put (sell) option,
there will options with at least two fixed expiry – or exercise – prices
(often more) at each of the three expiry dates. When they start life, these
options will be set at prices either side of the then current market price
of the underlying share. So if Superstock shares are trading at 130p, there
will be traded options at 120p and 140p, one with a life of three
months, another expiring in six months' time, and another after nine
months. That way, you will have a simple table when a new options share
is introduced. Superstock will have traded options – both puts and calls
– looking like this:

April	July	October
120p	120p	120p
140p	140p	140p

If Superstock shares leap above 140p, and stay there for a certain number
of days, the Traded Options Market will create a new series of options
expiring at 160p. If the price falls below 120p, a new series will be
brought in at 110p. It is a routine facility to keep the market working. It
means that after a spell of up and down activity in Superstock, the
original traded options table could look like this:

April	July	October
110p	110p	110p
120p	120p	120p
140p	140p	140p
160p	160p	160p

While the exercise prices rise by 10p in the lower brackets, they go up by 20p above 140p. That, again, is routine. The higher a price, the less the proportional impact of a 10p change. Correspondingly, when the share price gets above 300p, option exercise prices are set 30p apart.

Exercise Prices

The lists above simply cover what are called the exercise prices. If you decide to use your right to buy or sell the actual shares, you are exercising the option. The price you buy or sell the shares at is the exercise price. So, in the table above, there are options which allow you to buy (call) or sell (put) shares in Superstock at either 110p, 120p, 140p, or 160p – at the expiry date either in April, July, or October.

Premiums

Exercise prices are not the ones which matter most. They are only a label. They simply describe the option you are buying. So the Superstock July 120p call gives you the right to buy shares in Superstock at 120p in July. And the Superstock October 140p put gives you the right to sell Superstock shares at 140p in October.

What really counts is what you pay when you buy the options, or what you get when you sell. That is called the premium, and determines whether you make a profit or a loss. In most newspapers which carry traded option prices, the premium is listed in the sections to the right, under the **Calls** heading, or under the **Puts** heading. Those **Calls** and **Puts** sections themselves are divided into three for the three-month, six-month, or nine-month expiry dates. A typical newspaper display of traded options in Superstock, with the current share price in brackets beneath the company name, might look as follows:

OPTION	Exercise		CALLS			PUTS		
	Price	Apr	Jul	Oct		Apr	Jul	Oct
Superstock	110p	24p	29p	36p		1p	3p	5p
(128p)	120p	13p	17p	20p		5p	9p	12p
	140p	6p	8p	10p		18p	23p	27p
	160p	1p	2p	3p		36p	40p	44p

Looking at the **Calls**, this shows that if you want the right to buy shares in Superstock for 110p in April, it will cost 24p a share. You are effectively betting that Superstock shares will rise from their current 128p to more than 134p (the 110p exercise price, plus the 24p premium) before your option expires in April.

If you buy Superstock October 140p calls, it will cost 10p. You are betting that, before your option expires nearly nine months away in October, Superstock shares will rise to more than 150p (the 140p exercise price, plus the 10p premium). And so on.

Scanning the **Puts**, for 9p you can buy an option to sell Superstock at 120p in July. You would be betting that the Superstock price will fall below 111p (the 120p exercise price, minus the 9p premium) before the option runs out in July.

Or if you buy the October 160p puts for 44p, you will be gambling on the price falling below 116p (160p exercise price, minus 44p) before October.

Contracts – The Trading Unit

There is a minimum size for each deal. That is called a contract, and each contract normally represents an option on 1,000 shares. This varies occasionally, but usually only for shares with a price over £10. Then each contract normally involves 100 shares.

As a result, each 1p of option premium normally translates into a cost of £10 for each contract (1,000 multiplied by 1p equals £10). So our Superstock April 110p calls at 24p premium will cost £240 for each contract, the October 140p calls at 10p will cost £100 a contract, the July 120p puts at 9p will cost £90 for one contract, and the October 160p puts at 44p will cost £440 for each contract. The same multiple comes through to your profits and losses. For every contract, each 1p change in the premium means you have made or lost £10.

A Simple Profit Play

Study the table. Think about it. Once you know what the figures mean, it is fairly simple. At its most basic, that tells you all you need to know. If you think a particular share is going to rise or fall, and if there are traded options in it (quite a big 'if' that, though additional shares are being brought into the net all of the time), you can control a far larger number of those shares by using traded options than by buying the shares. If you are betting on a rise, buy a call. To bet on a fall, buy a put.

Go back to our Superstock price table. If you expect a big rise in the next six months, and you have £600 to gamble, you can buy about 468 shares at 128p each. Or you can buy three July 120p call contracts for £170 a time (the premium is 17p, but each contract is for 1,000 shares, so each contract costs £170) to control 3,000 shares, with £90 left over. Because you have three contracts, each 1p price change means you gain or lose £30.

Say you get it just about right, and Superstock shares touch 140p. By buying the shares, you will have made a profit of just over £56 (multiply 468 by 12p equals £56.16p). By buying the options, you will have made £90 (the 120p call options should have risen from 17p to at least 20p to match the 140p market price, a rise of 3p. Each 1p change is worth £10 a contract. Three contracts are worth £30 for each 1p change. Multiply £30 by three equals £90). And you still have the £90 you did not invest.

The arithmetic looks better the higher your shares rise. Say Superstock went to 145p. Then the shares would show a profit of just under £90. Your traded options would be £240 ahead (profit of 8p on each contract. Multiply £30 by eight equals £240). Plus £90 not invested.

And if Superstock touched 150p, the options look still further ahead. The gain on buying the shares would have been nearly £103. But the traded option profit would have been £390 (profit of 13p on option, so multiply £30 by 13 equals £390), plus £90 not invested.

Terrific? Perhaps. We have ignored the cost of buying and selling. That would have cut profits sharply, especially at the lower level of gains. More important, the traded option player has taken a vastly greater risk than the share buyer. If the Superstock price had not moved over the six months, the share buyer would still have had shares worth just under £600. The option player would have lost every penny, except the £90 he did not spend.

If Superstock shares had fallen to, say, 110p, the share buyer would have an investment worth £514, a loss of around £86. Again, the traded option punter would have lost every penny, and be nursing only the £90 left over. Thankfully, the fall in the share price would not have brought any extra liability. That is the crucial advantage of traded options – if you stick to buying calls or puts, you cannot lose more than your stake money.

Make no mistake, it is easy to lose that stake money. The figures above look persuasive. But many small traded option punters do get wiped out quickly – though the fun lasts longer than the 3.30 at Epsom. Or last Saturday's Lottery ticket.

Buy a traded call in a bid target, and you can clean up when the bid comes. No complication. The shares rise, and the options with them. Usually, options gains are in massively greater proportions than profits on the shares. The lucky, or well-informed, sell the options and waltz off with an enormous haul. Easy.

Normally it is not as simple as that. Option prices do not go up in a straight line, linked to the underlying share price. Sometimes the shares rise, and the call options fall. Usually this is a result of the interaction between the two main elements which determine the level of an option price – the intrinsic value, and the time value. Sometimes there is an element of market manipulation, of course.

Intrinsic Value

Go back to our Superstock options. The premium on the Superstock April 110p call is 24p, while the share price is 128p. In theory, you could exercise the option, take the shares for 110p, and sell them for 128p, a gain of 18p. That 18p is known as the intrinsic value – the locked-in gain, if you like. Since the option costs 24p, of course, that 18p is not profit. It covers much of the premium you are paying.

In The Money

An option which has an intrinsic value – or an exercise price below the market price of the underlying share – is said to be 'in the money'.

Out Of The Money

By contrast, look at the Superstock April 140p call, with a premium of 6p. The exercise price is above the underlying share price of 128p. There is no immediate built-in gain. Such an option is 'out of the money'. Logically enough, if the option exercise price is the same as the underlying share price, the option is 'at the money'. So if Superstock shares were 140p in the market, the April 140p calls would be 'at the money'.

Time Value

Option premiums are not just determined, however, by the price of the underlying shares. They are also determined by how long the option has to run – the time value. Clearly, time has a very real value for option traders, and the more time there is before the option expires, the greater the value.

Go back again to our first example, Superstock April 110p calls, with a premium of 24p. With Superstock shares at 128p, the option is 'in the money', and has an intrinsic value of 18p. The other 6p of the premium is accounted for by time value – what you pay for the chance that the shares will rise above 128p (and effectively above 134p) before the option expires in April.

Time value does not run out evenly over the life of the option. Experts use a fancy formula to determine it, but all you need to know is that the value declines at an accelerating rate as it approaches the end of life. So you need to keep it very much in mind, especially when you get within 30 days of the end.

Volatility

Option prices are also partly determined by volatility, the violence and frequency with which share prices move. Looking at conventional options, I suggested that Bloggs was a relatively unexciting example, because the shares were pretty stolid. They do not move sharply enough, often enough. What you want, above all, is price action. You can get a good clue to the chances by studying past price movements – no guarantees, of course. When something exceptional has taken place – a bid, or news of a profit slump – you clearly must take it into account in measuring activity. Option experts have systems for measuring volatility, and helping determine whether particular option rates are good or bad value. Obviously, an option in a stock which normally fluctuates busily holds more promise of reward than a sluggard, and so the option rate may be higher. Keep it in mind, and ask your broker to check volatility before buying.

The Mathematics

Assessing volatility brings us to the brink of the more sophisticated stuff. Professional option traders run a variety of factors into their judgement of option values. They use complex mathematical formulae. Best-known is the Black-Scholes model. I do not understand it. Many of the users do not. If you want to know, most options brokers will give you a quick view of how Black-Scholes rates your prospective punt. You do not have to know what it means – but listen to what they say if they tell you it is working against you. Do not ignore the advice. It means that the professionals will be guided by it, and will tend to steer clear of your option if it looks too expensive. You could be right – if there is a bid, or your underlying reason for buying is spot on – but you would be paying over the odds for your bet, your traded option.

Dividends

Dividend payments also complicate the issue. The notion is that option prices take account of dividends well ahead of their payment date. Share prices fall when they go ex-dividend when the buyer of the shares is no longer entitled to collect the latest dividend cheque. It forms a prearranged and well understood fall in the share price. It will drive call option prices down, and raise the value of put options. Because everyone knows about it in advance, it may not have any great impact. It should have been taken into account in setting the price. And a dividend of 1p on a share selling at 250p will not matter much in any case. But the market does not always have it fully covered. A 5p dividend on a 100p share could make a big difference to a call option near the end of its life. So keep an eye out for dividends.

Writing Options

Our examples of how call and put options work have demonstrated the chance of making money by straightforward option purchases when you think a share is going to rise or fall. But there is another important aspect to options – writing them. An options writer simply sells the put or call which someone else buys. Go back to our Superstock table. If you write an April 120p call, you earn a 13p premium. If you write a 140p July put, you take a 23p premium. And so on.

Writing Covered Calls

What you are doing is effectively betting that, as above, Superstock will not go above 133p before the April expiry date, or fall below 117p before the July date. If you hold the shares, writing a call is a handy way of generating extra income, so long as they do not move out of line, and the option is exercised against you, forcing you to give up the stock. Money for almost nothing. As an option writer, what you really want is a share that goes nowhere much while the option is open – the opposite to the volatile stock you wanted when buying a put or call.

Writing an option also acts as a possible way of selling above the current price. Writing that April 120p call for a 13p premium means you are ready to sell at 133p, when the market price is 128p. If you are prepared to take a longer view, using our table, you could have sold (or written) an October 120p call for 20p, effectively getting out at 140p. The careful investor, of course, would be sure to hold the shares until October, just in case they did have to be delivered. If the option is not exercised, you will still have the shares, in addition to your 20p premium.

If you are nervous about the market, it is a way of generating extra protection. Again, using the 13p premium on an April 120p, you can see the price fall from the market level of 128p to 115p before it has taken a toll on your investment.

Naked Writing

You can play the same game without holding the shares. It is risky – very risky – and can lead to unquantified losses. When you sell a call, or write one, you are called a naked writer if you do not hold the underlying stock. If it works, and the option simply lapses, it could mean you get the premium for nothing. If the shares do not rise all of the way to cover the full premium, you can still buy the stock and cover yourself without courting disaster.

But what if the unexpected should happen? What if Superstock gets a bid at 250p early in April? The share price will rise to 250p, perhaps 260p if there is speculation on a counter-bid. The April 120p call could rocket to 135p, maybe more. The option could be exercised against you, and you have to deliver stock you have not got. You would have to go into the market and pay 260p. Since all that you have received is the 13p premium, you will have to find an extra 247p a share. Disastrous. You could, of course, buy a traded option call to cover yourself. That would cost 135p, say, leaving you to find 122p above the 13p premium you took. That, in fact, is what you would do. But, what a mess. Gambling to make a 13p profit, you have ended up losing 122p, almost ten times your money. DO NOT DO IT.

Sensibly, the market rules try to guard against reckless naked writing. Those who write options are required to pledge collateral to the value of a margin requirement. This is related to the underlying share price, and the option exercise price being calculated as 20% of the value of the underlying contract size, plus or minus the amount the option is in or out of the money. Complicated? Sure. Your broker will tell you. But if just thinking about it puts you off, great.

Writing Puts

The same sort of reasoning applies to writing puts. Effectively, there is no such thing as a covered put writer. In theory, whether you hold the shares or not, you could have a block put on you, forcing you to buy. That will happen when the shares have gone down, so you will end up with an extra lot of duds – not what you intended. Because you have taken a premium when you sold, or wrote, the put, that will reduce your purchase price. Anyone who writes put options must be happy to buy the stock at below the current level. You have to be able to lay your hands on the cash. Will you really want to be landed with a lot of the shares when the price is tumbling? Maybe not. So be careful.

What really happens, in most cases, is that the put writer has to buy the put option back in the market, effectively neutralising his liability. That can be expensive, with the put price rising as the share price tumbles. So beware.

Straddles, Spreads And So On

There are all sorts of strategies which can be devised by using a combination of options. A straddle involves buying a put and a call with the same exercise price and expiry date. Or you can use a spread, exploiting relative discrepancies between option prices within the same class. The opportunities are endless, and require careful, detailed understanding. Do not try them until you really know what you are doing. Leading brokers have handy guides, which they may send to you. It is common to hear punters complaining about the way the market operates. Market-makers are accused of running very wide spreads between buy and sell prices, and of failing to move rates properly in response to underlying share price changes. What would you expect? Real life on the option market is not simple. Everyone is out to make a profit. Do not imagine things will run just as you expect them.

Above all, remember the basics. No matter how clever the option trade may seem, and how cheap the rate looks, you have to get the share direction right first. Do not lose sight of trading in the underlying company. In the end, that is the most important influence. And then, CUT LOSSES QUICKLY, AND RUN YOUR PROFITS. Because there is a limited life to options, it is hard to operate a stop-loss system. But do not be silly and let your emotions rule your head. You will come unstuck far faster as a fool in the options market than you will by playing shares alone.

Playing Footsie

There is one special facility in the options market which is unrivalled by the share game. You can take a view on the overall direction of share prices by playing Footsie, the FTSE 100 Share index. There are Footsie options contracts which operate in much the same fashion as options on individual shares. You can buy options on the index running several months ahead. You are betting on which way the index will move. Obviously, you do not get a basket of shares if you exercise the option, simply the cash difference between your price and the FTSE level. Playing the Footsie can be useful when you are worried about a possible market slump. Or if you think there may be a rise, but are not quite ready to plunge in yet. Above all, it can be a great insurance policy, allowing you either to sit with your shares and cover a general market move, or to sell your portfolio, bank the cash, and keep an interest in the market at low cost through a Footsie option. Talk to your broker.

If you want to know more – and there is much, much more – the best basic guide, as I said before, is *Traded Options – A Private Investor's Guide* by Peter Temple.

CHAPTER FIFTEEN

Thank You

Thank you for buying this book. I hope it helps, and if you do make a real killing, so much the better. Above all, it would be nice to think that *How to Make a Killing in the Share Jungle* has given you confidence to venture into the share jungle, and feel you might be able to play the stockmarket, if you choose.

The scene is changing all of the time, but though the day-to-day detail alters, the basics remain the same. It is your money, so do it your way. Above all, only use what you can afford to lose, only do what you understand, remember someone else always knows more than you, and run your profits and cut your losses quickly.

More than anything, have fun. If it starts to worry you, then you must stop. Good luck.

Index